Kathy Kirby   217-84
309-33 7777

A Pikes Peak Partnership

Spencer Penrose, *left,* and his boyhood Philadelphia chum, Charles L. Tutt, formed a Colorado Springs partnership in 1892 that would transform the region. Here, the bearded 28-year-old Tutt shows 27-year-old Penrose stock certificates for their C.O.D. (Cash on Delivery) Mine in Cripple Creek. Tutt and Penrose paid $20,000 for it and sold it for $250,000, which they invested in mining and ore-processing operations that made them both millionaires.

A Pikes Peak Partnership

THE PENROSES AND THE TUTTS

by Thomas J. Noel and Cathleen M. Norman

THE UNIVERSITY PRESS OF COLORADO

Copyright © 2000 by the University Press of Colorado
International Standard Book Number 0-87081-609-8

Published by the University Press of Colorado
5589 Arapahoe Avenue, Suite 206C
Boulder, Colorado 80303

All rights reserved
First paperback edition 2002
Printed in the United States of America

The University Press of Colorado is a cooperative publishing enterprise supported, in part, by Adams State College, Colorado State University, Fort Lewis College, Mesa State College, Metropolitan State College of Denver, University of Colorado, University of Northern Colorado, University of Southern Colorado, and Western State College of Colorado.

The paper used in this publication meets the minimum requirements of the American National Standard for Information Sciences—Permanence of Paper for Printed Library Materials. ANSI Z39.48-1992

Library of Congress Cataloging-in-Publication Data

Noel, Thomas J. (Thomas Jacob)
    A Pikes Peak partnership : the Penroses and the Tutts / by Thomas J. Noel and Cathleen
  M. Norman.
       p. cm.
    Includes bibliographical references (p.) and index.
    ISBN 0-87081-609-8 (hardcover: alk. paper) — ISBN 0-87081-715-9 (pbk: alk. paper)
    1. Penrose, Spencer, b. 1865. 2. Tutt, Charles Leaming. 3. Businessmen—Colorado—
  Colorado Springs—Biography. 4. Industrialists—Colorado—Colorado Springs—
  Biography. 5. Philanthropists—Colorado—Colorado Springs—Biography. 6. Colorado
  Springs (Colo.)—Biography. I. Norman, Cathleen M. II. Title.

CT275.P5643 N64 2000
338.092'278856—dc21
[B]
                                                                                    00-051232

Design by Laura Furney
Typesetting by Daniel Pratt

11 10 09 08 07 06 05 04 03 02   10 9 8 7 6 5 4 3 2 1

Contents

Acknowledgments

R. THAYER TUTT PROPOSED THIS BOOK and arranged El Pomar funding for the research, writing, illustrating, and publishing. We jumped at the opportunity to explore some of Colorado's most colorful characters and the largest and most influential philanthropic foundation in the Rocky Mountain West (El Pomar Foundation). Thayer also shared his remarkable knowledge, records, photographs, and artifacts, greatly enriching this project. Most important, he opened to us the El Pomar Archives, with its priceless Julie and Spencer Penrose Papers.

El Pomar Foundation Chief Executive Officer (CEO) William J. Hybl was most helpful, arranging, among other things, a tour of El Pomar projects by foundation interns. Beverly Mason, senior investment officer for El Pomar, helped coordinate the project from beginning to end. We appreciate the assistance of Carol Drewry and several El Pomar fellows as well. We are also indebted to Nancy Lyons, who generously shared the fine research she conducted for the 1995 nomination of the Penrose House to the National Register of Historic Places.

Many people helped us retrace the steps of the Penroses and Tutts through the Pikes Peak region. Betty Kane, curator of Pauline Chapel, gave us a tour of that exquisite monument to Julie Penrose's faith and fine taste and also granted us an interview. Thanks go to Patty Cameron of the Cheyenne Mountain Zoo, Will Rogers Shrine curator George Guerrero, Elaine Freed at Colorado College, Nancy Steward of the Broadmoor Hotel, and Bea Vradenberg at the Pikes Peak Center. We also extend our appreciation to Monica Ray, public relations specialist, for providing guided tours, photographs, and information at Rio Tinto Zinc Corporation in Salt Lake City. Pat Chenoworth and Robert L. Fuchs of the Geological Society of America generously shared the biography, photographs of, and other information on

R.A.F. Penrose Jr., whose philanthropy created that society and gave it an impressive national headquarters on Penrose Place in Boulder.

Spencer Penrose's grandniece Frances Penrose Haythe shared family letters, photographs, and stories. The staff of the Philosophical Society of America in Philadelphia greatly aided our research, as did staff at the Philadelphia Free Library, Temple University Library, and the Historical Society of Pennsylvania. The Colorado Historical Society Library, Denver Public Library's Western History Department, Detroit Public Library, Grosse Point Historical Society, Utah State Historical Society, and Library of Congress also graciously provided photographs.

Steve Leonard, Elaine Freed, Duane Smith, and Silvia Pettem reviewed the manuscript along with CU-Denver graduate history students John Stewart and Don Walker. Rosemary Fetter and Cheryl Carnahan served as our primary editors. Thanks also to Bill Bessessen, Jamie Field, Brandon Huffman, Jolene Huffman, Vi Noel, Ronald Norman, and Marne Tutt.

At Penrose Public Library in downtown Colorado Springs and the Local History Collection in the Old Carnegie Library, Mary Davis, Ree Mobley, and the Local History Collection staff provided knowledgeable, cordial, and expeditious assistance.

Ed and Nancy Bathke shared their tremendous knowledge, as well as their photos of the Pikes Peak region. Paul Idleman copied old photographs and shared his rich knowledge of Old Colorado City and its smelters and mills. Jackson Thode, biographer of William J. Palmer and historian of the Denver & Rio Grande Railroad, generously provided information and previously unpublished photographs of the Palmer family.

Thanks also to Jean Doddenhoff, curator at the Grosse Pointe Historical Society; Ginny Kiefer, curator and archivist for Special Collections at Tutt Library at Colorado College; Dale Reed and the Stanford University Archives crew; and the Colorado School of Mines Library.

We especially express our gratitude to the many people who provided memories and insight through interviews for this book: Paul Baschleben, Dr. J. Whitfield Bell Jr., Nancy Brittian, Peter A.G. Brown, Sherry Clark, Patricia Bates Croke, Beth Davis, Karl E. Eitel, Kathy Fleming, Elaine Freed, Russell G. Freymuth, Dr. Timothy Fuller, William J. Hybl, Steve Knowlton, Caroline Kruse, Harold U. Littrell, John A. Love, Ellie McColl, Dougald McGregor, Robert McIntyre, Eugene McCleary, David Miller, Quigg Newton, Kent Olin, Dorothy Palmer, Charles Penrose, Dr. E. R. Peterson, William Roub, Peter Susemihl, Robert F. Sweeny, Charles Tutt IV, John Wood Tutt, Russell Thayer Tutt Jr., William B. Tutt, Richard Vanderhoof, Bea Vradenberg, and William R. Ward.

Unless otherwise credited, all illustrations are from the El Pomar Foundation Collections.

Foreword

My GREAT-GRANDFATHER, Charles Leaming Tutt, came to the Pikes Peak region in 1884. He tried ranching in the Black Forest and real estate in Colorado Springs before striking pay dirt in Cripple Creek with his C.O.D. Mine.

In 1891, great-grandfather invited an old Philadelphia family friend, Spencer Penrose, to come west and help with his booming mining and real estate business. Family legend has it that he never pressed Penrose to pay for his partnership in the C.O.D.

These two ambitious—and lucky—Philadelphians sold the C.O.D. for around $250,000, the highest price paid up to that time for a Cripple Creek mine. With the proceeds they built up Cripple Creek's greatest ore-transporting and processing network. My grandfather Tutt invested in Spencer's Broadmoor Hotel, Pikes Peak Auto Highway, and Manitou and Pikes Peak cog and incline railways. He was involved in myriad other Penrose enterprises, from bottling Manitou springwater to creating the Cheyenne Mountain Zoo.

My great-grandfather died young—at the age of 45 in 1909. Spencer lived another 30 years, making millions in his Utah (later Kennecott) Copper (now Rio Tinto Zinc) Company. Spencer and Julie Penrose were childless but relied on Charles Tutt's son, Charley, who came to manage much of the Penrose empire. As Charley grew older he relied on his sons, Thayer and Russell, my father, to manage this empire.

I, too, have been fortunate to work in this remarkable Pikes Peak partnership, continuing my family's involvement with El Pomar Foundation, the Broadmoor Hotel, Colorado College, and other Penrose and Tutt interests. A rich history and tantalizing folklore still swirl around Penrose and the Tutts. During their early years, millions in gold and copper were ripped out of the earth. That wealth has been returned to Coloradans through the philanthropic El Pomar Foundation, established by Spencer and Julie and my grandfather in 1939. The vision of the Penroses continues to make a difference today under the strong leadership of William J. Hybl, El Pomar's chairman and CEO.

To tell this full, incredible history for the first time, El Pomar Foundation and I have worked with Tom Noel, an author and history professor at the University of Colorado at Denver, and his graduate student Cathleen Norman. We hope you enjoy this look at some remarkable characters whose passion for the Pikes Peak region and for Colorado still inspires us.

—R. THAYER TUTT JR.

Introduction

ON A SUNNY DECEMBER DAY in 1892, two tall Philadelphians stood out in the crowd at the Colorado Springs railway station. Spencer Penrose stepped out of a Denver & Rio Grande coach sporting a dapper moustache and brown curly hair that set off a square ruddy face with large, piercing brown eyes. He was welcomed by an old family friend, Charles Leaming Tutt, a young entrepreneur whose Colorado real estate ventures were just beginning to pay off. Tutt drove Penrose around town in his surrey and told him the story of another Philadelphian, William J. Palmer, who had founded Colorado Springs. The two Philadelphia blue bloods reveled in the promise of the young town, with expectations as great as those their forebears had brought to Philadelphia two centuries earlier. Looking up, they marveled at the snowy bosom of Pikes Peak, within whose orb they would spend the rest of their lives.

That winter Penrose and Tutt formed a partnership that would transform the Pikes Peak region. As business partners in Cripple Creek, they promoted the mining district and profited from its mining, milling, and real estate. Sales proceeds from their C.O.D. mine in Cripple Creek financed milling interests in Colorado City. When a promising copper mine at Bingham Canyon, Utah, caught their attention, they launched the highly profitable Utah Copper Company.

Both in Cripple Creek and in Utah, Penrose staunchly opposed union organizers who complained of poor pay, dangerous work, and wretched living conditions. Indeed, Penrose and his fellow mine owners not only crushed strikes but also helped to suppress the two major unions involved with hard-rock miners, the Western Federation of Miners and the Industrial Workers of the World. Not until the 1930s did the labor-friendly New Deal help unions make a comeback among miners, smelter workers, and other Rocky Mountain blue-collar workers. Although our heroes are widely praised for their numerous contributions to Colorado, one old-timer asked us, "Spencer Penrose, wasn't he the son of a bitch who said, 'Any man who wears overalls doesn't deserve more than $2 a day?' "

We never found the answer to that question from a crusty old workingman in Colorado City. Such a statement, however, would not have been out of character for Penrose and most of his generation of mining and ore-processing tycoons.

The early partnership of Tutt and Penrose had dissolved by the time Penrose sank his copper millions into building the Broadmoor Hotel and a dozen other Colorado Springs landmarks. However, Tutt's son, Charles L. Tutt Jr., assisted Penrose in his business endeavors, becoming his right-hand man and business manager.

Penrose, one of Colorado's most notorious carousers, evolved into a philanthropist after his marriage to a beautiful, persuasive woman, Julie Villiers Lewis McMillan. Following Spencer's death in 1939, Julie honored his will and funneled Penrose's millions into good works through their El Pomar Foundation.

The Tutt family has been pivotal to the Penrose story. As the Penroses had no children and the Tutts were rather productive, Charles L. Tutt's sons, grandsons, and great-grandsons have managed the multifaceted empire. They have enhanced the Penrose legacy of hospitality, enterprise, athletics, and philanthropy. They have helped sustain the Broadmoor Hotel, Will Rogers Shrine, Pikes Peak Cog Railway, and Cheyenne Mountain Zoo. They have perpetuated the Penrose vision of Colorado Springs as a cultural, educational, health, and sports center. Penrose Public Library, Penrose Hospital, Colorado College, El Pomar Great Hall in the Pikes Peak Center, and the Colorado Springs World Arena epitomize the contributions of this Pikes Peak partnership.

Today, two giant remnants of Penrose's mining ventures survive: the huge slag heap at Old Colorado City and the Bingham Canyon copper mine (the world's largest hole in the ground). These unnatural wonders commemorate the fortune these Pikes Peakers made in gold and copper. Those millions are being returned to the community by one of the oldest, largest, and most innovative foundations in the Rocky Mountain West—El Pomar.

El Pomar, Spanish for "apple orchard," was the name Julie and Spencer Penrose gave their hacienda behind the Broadmoor, as well as the name of the foundation the Penroses formed in 1937. Whereas the Penroses extracted fortunes and built a great tourist infrastructure, the foundation has been involved in sustaining and improving the community they helped build. This fantastic and never fully told story starts in Philadelphia.

A Pikes Peak Partnership

William Henry Penrose, Spencer's cousin, was the first member of that prominent Philadelphia clan to make a name for himself in the Pikes Peak region. As Captain Penrose he commanded Fort Lyons in southeastern Colorado. His ferocious temper was aggravated by a July 1869 incident at this fort on the Arkansas River. Satanta (White Bear), a clever and embittered Indian leader, showed up at the fort with 108 Kiowas and asked Penrose for food. Penrose sent Satanta away empty-handed. Angered, Satanta and his men killed cattle and hogs just outside the fort and carried them away. The Kiowas rode their horses through the vegetable gardens supplying the fort, deliberately trampling corn and other crops. Satanta was later imprisoned and committed suicide by leaping headfirst from a second-story window. Courtesy Library of Congress.

1

Philadelphia

THE PIKES PEAK PARTNERSHIP of Spencer Penrose and Charles L. Tutt Sr. had its roots in Philadelphia. Both were sons of Philadelphia physicians, and both were born at the close of the Civil War. The men were blue bloods, but they had different family and financial circumstances. Penrose was the fourth-eldest of six sons. His older brothers, Boies, Charles, and Richard, earned Harvard degrees and distinction in the fields of politics, medicine, and geology. Spencer also graduated from Harvard, where he distinguished himself for drinking beer.

Charles L. Tutt enjoyed a less privileged upbringing. His father, Dr. Charles P. Tutt Jr., died, leaving his two-year-old son to be raised by his mother and grandfather. He went to work at age 17. His poor health led him to seek a cure in the Colorado climate as a young man. Renewed by the high, dry, sunny Colorado atmosphere, he used his connections with the Penrose brothers to unearth an unforeseen bonanza.

The Penroses traced their American origins to Bartholomew Penrose, who arrived in Philadelphia in 1698. The City of Brotherly Love had been founded 16 years earlier by William Penn. Penn invited Penrose, a Bristol shipbuilder of Cornish lineage, to establish a shipyard on the Schuylkill River. The family ran the shipyard for nearly 150 years. Their pioneering role is commemorated by Philadelphia's Penrose Boulevard and Penrose Bridge.

The Penrose family produced many influential Philadelphians. Spencer's grandfather, Charles Bingham Penrose, was state senator from 1833 to 1841 and a solicitor for the U.S. Treasury Department. Spencer's uncle, Judge Clement Biddle Penrose, presided over the Orphan's Court of Philadelphia County for more than 30 years.[1] A cousin, Gen. William Henry Penrose, had a long military career that took him out west. He enthralled the Penrose lads with tales of fighting Indians on the Kansas and Colorado

Dr. Richard Alexander Fullerton Penrose Sr., a prominent Philadelphia physician, professor of obstetrics, and a founder of Philadelphia's Children's Hospital, pushed his six sons hard. They became notable physicians, politicians, and geologists, except for Spencer. Striving to escape and yet impress his doubtful dad, Spencer headed west to Pikes Peak and ultimately made more money than any of his siblings. John Frederick Lewis Portrait Collection, Print and Picture Collection, the Free Library of Philadelphia.

frontier. He also told how he had rubbed shoulders with legendary westerners. Kit Carson died at the general's residence at Fort Lyon, Colorado, and William F. "Buffalo Bill" Cody was the general's guide during the winter of 1867–1868.[2]

Spencer's father, Richard Alexander Fullerton Penrose, was Philadelphia's leading obstetrician and gynecologist. An 1849 graduate of the University of Pennsylvania, he practiced at various Philadelphia hospitals. He was a founder of the city's Children's Hospital in 1854.[3] For 25 years he taught obstetrics and gynecology at the University of Pennsylvania. His wit and humor made him a favorite with students.

On September 28, 1858, he married Sarah Hannah Boies Penrose. The Penroses had seven sons. The first, Boies, died in infancy. Then followed Boies, November 1, 1860; Charles Bingham, February 1, 1862; Richard Alexander Fullerton Jr., December 17, 1863; Spencer, November 2, 1865; Francis Boies, August 2, 1867; and Philip Thomas, March 10, 1869.[4] The Penrose brothers grew up in a tall, narrow townhouse at 1331 Spruce Street. The three-story brick dwelling was a "comfortable house of small dimensions, few ornaments and no pretensions,"[5] reflecting the Spartan

Sarah Hannah Boies Penrose doted on her sons, personally escorting them to Harvard and writing them long, loving letters until her early death from tuberculosis in 1881. Sixteen-year-old Spencer took her death particularly hard. For years, the mention of her name brought tears to his eyes. John Frederick Lewis Portrait Collection, Print and Picture Collection, the Free Library of Philadelphia.

Dr. Richard A.F. Penrose Sr. and sons, *left to right,* Boies, Spencer, Philip, R.A.F. Jr., and Charles, posed without a single smile for this 1882 photo. Courtesy, Denver Public Library, Western History Department.

In later years, Spencer Penrose continued to return to the family home at 1331 Spruce Street in Philadelphia. In some ways the great promoter-developer of the Pikes Peak region never left Philadelphia. His papers are filled with homesick requests such as this 1937 letter to the Philadelphia Club: "Gentlemen: Will you kindly send me by express one pound of the finest, fresh Beluga Caviar, also your bill. Simply send it to 'Spencer Penrose, Colorado Springs, Colorado.' When do you commence in the Fall to have Diamond Back Terrapin?"

tastes of Doctor and Sarah Penrose.[6,7] The doctor advocated a healthy diet, temperance, and exercise. Mrs. Penrose turned her back on Philadelphia high society and devoted herself instead to the education of her children.[8] She belonged only to the Saturday Evening Club, which promoted simple living and discouraged members from wearing jewels. This austerity backfired, as few of the Penrose sons adhered to their parents' abstemious lifestyle. Like many upper-class Philadelphia families, the bustling Penrose household included several Irish maids.[9] Supposedly, the lusty Penrose lads threw money on the dining room table, betting who could bed the new maid first.[10]

The Penrose children were tutored at home. They enjoyed socializing with cousins and other relatives of the sizable Penrose clan. The brothers fished off bridges and piers and swam across the Delaware River. They rowed on the Schuylkill and in winter ice-skated on the rivers. They went to Fairmont Park for the Centennial Exposition in May 1876, where the first great American fair attracted around 230,000 people.[11] The Penroses probably viewed Rocky Mountain gold, silver, and copper specimens and Martha Maxwell's taxidermy collection of Colorado wildlife. Eleven-year-old Spencer presumably first saw the gold, copper, and Colorado animals and minerals that would become lifelong obsessions.

Both the doctor and his wife valued education. Sarah Penrose, known as a woman of culture, refinement, and unusual intelligence, proudly traced her roots to two members of Harvard's first graduating class in 1642, Benjamin Woodbridge and William Hubbard. She was determined that her sons would attend Harvard and distinguish themselves academically. After their private tutoring at home, the Penroses sent their sons to Philadelphia's Episcopal Academy college preparatory school. When the boys entered Harvard, Sarah escorted them to Boston and set them up in a house on Gerry Street, chaperoned by their maiden aunt, Sarah Beck.

Both parents encouraged their sons' academic success. The doctor hired a private tutor for them at Harvard. He also edited their term papers and monitored their schoolwork, athletics, study habits, hygiene, and poise, as one of his letters reveals:

> I am glad your work is so interesting and so easy for you. I highly approve of your French memorizing and your German studies. . . . Read up for your theme, if you can, before writing it and if possible let me have it at least a week before you have to hand it in. *Cultivate* all your instructors and professors. It certainly will secure for you better marks, as well as present and future good will. . . . Go on with your gymnastics, but never forget my direction "Nose at angle 45 degrees, head up, shoulder back, chest out, stomach in, and look right down to the bottom of a fellow's eyes." Even though you never intend to be a soldier you may possess a military bearing.[12]

The doctor also provided his sons with a list of rules: "When invited out to dinner or tea be careful about dress, etc. If offered wine or cigars, quietly decline by saying you never smoke or use wine, and, at all times, give the same answer, no matter where or by whom offered. . . . Form at first no intimacies—afterwards, only with quiet, hard-working students. Avoid all 'swell' fellows. And, by all means, join no secret society or club until the sophomore or junior year."[13]

Mrs. Penrose counseled them, too. She wrote Richard:

> You ought to take some pains to get your marks in geometry changed. Go yourself to Briggs and ask him politely to look over your paper again; tell him that you feel sure you did all that was given you. I want you to get a good grade. . . . Be sure to change your pantaloons when

you get wet. I think it is cold enough now for you to put on your winter flannels. . . . I am glad to find you go regularly to Church with Cousin Sarah and I feel sure that you will pass through your college course without one censure mark. Good night to you all my darling boys. SHBP[14]

Sarah Penrose died of pneumonia on March 30, 1881, two months before Boies and Charles graduated. Her concern for her three older sons' education paid off. Boies and Charles graduated second and first in their class, respectively. In 1884 Charles earned both a Ph.D. in physics from Harvard and an M.D. from the University of Pennsylvania. The third brother, Richard, studied chemistry and graduated summa cum laude from Harvard in 1884. He returned to receive a Ph.D. in natural history in 1886, the same year younger brother Spencer completed his undergraduate degree.

Although his brothers excelled at Harvard, Spencer did not. His major accomplishment was drinking a gallon of beer in 37 seconds. His essay on "Ruskin and His Place Among English Writers" earned the Bedouin Prize, but his chief interests were boxing, rowing, and drinking. His 1886 paper, "Do Great Men, Climate, or National Stock Most Influence National Development," hinted at the tremendous personal impact Penrose would have on the Pikes Peak region. He concluded the twenty-two-page paper: "The fact is one great man opens and prepares the way for many others. Thus, the influence of great men is continually multiplied and increased."[15]

The handsome Penrose men inherited the raven hair, dark eyes, and expressive eyebrows of their mother, regarded as "a phenomenal and magnificent beauty." All were at least six feet tall and muscular. They relished rowing and belonged to Philadelphia's prestigious University Barge Club. They learned boxing from a black prizefighter who "will teach you how to slug a fellow, including tripping up, smashing in a man's head, etc. etc."[16] Spencer used these tricks later in the Cripple Creek barroom brawls that earned him a fearsome reputation.

Their brotherly bond included a passion for hunting. Their first western hunting trip took them to Wyoming and Montana in 1884, where they built a log cabin to live in for several weeks. They hunted game and panned for gold. Richard collected mineral specimens, heaping them in a huge pile they christened "Mount Penrose." Photographs show the brothers squatting by the campfire, posing beside mounds of antlers and animal skins, and plunging naked into a river. "These trips were designed and carried out for the pure delight of the chase," Richard later reminisced. "In these early days we never took guides, cooks, packers, or any other employees. We acted as our own guides, because we knew the country as well as anyone else. . . . There was no tenderfoot element in these expeditions."[17] This was their first taste of the West, and the fraternal outings

Spencer Penrose, *left*, and his brother Boies, atop Mount Penrose overlooking the Fraser River in British Columbia. This August 17, 1903, photo may have been taken by R.A.F. "Dick" Penrose Jr., a prominent mining engineer who joined his brothers on western camping trips and guided Spencer's lucrative mining investments.

SPENCER PENROSE with wounded Rocky Mountain Goat - at head waters of Fraser River, British Columbia - Aug - 25 - 1903.

Spencer Penrose, shown here with a Rocky Mountain goat, joined his brothers for hunting and animal-gathering expeditions, such as this 1903 foray into Canada. Courtesy, Denver Public Library, Western History Department.

continued for years. But Speck, as his family and friends called Spencer, chose to remain out west, escaping the narrow colonial streets and smothering social expectations of Old Philadelphia.

The West appealed to Charles L. Tutt, too. A Philadelphia native, he was descended from Richard Tutt, an Englishman who had become a large landholder in the Virginia tidewater region around 1700. C. L. Tutt's grandfather, Charles Pendleton Tutt, a navy agent and friend of President Andrew Jackson, died in 1832. One month later his only son, Charles Pendleton Tutt Jr., was born on Santa Rosa Island in Pensacola, Florida. Charles P. Tutt Jr. graduated from the University of Pennsylvania in 1856, seven years after Dr. R.A.F. Penrose.[18] Doctor Tutt practiced at Blackley Hospital in Philadelphia. He married the only daughter of Jeremiah Fisher Leaming, a Philadelphia financier, and they lived at 906 Walnut Street.[19] The doctor contracted typhoid while treating a patient at Saterlee Hospital, one of Philadelphia's largest Civil War facilities. He died on May 11, 1866, leaving his wife Josephine, daughter Rebeccah, and two-year-old son Charles.[20]

Charles grew up with his mother and sister at his grandfather's home at 922 Spruce, four blocks from the Penrose family. He was sent to Ury Boarding School, then studied briefly at Ferris Institute. At age 17 he went to work as a clerk for Peter Wright Company in Philadelphia for $2.30 a week. Two years later Tutt accepted an office position at the Pennsylvania Railroad Company. He moved to Colorado in 1884 to improve his health, weakened by a childhood bout with rheumatic fever. With fellow Philadelphian Dr. Jesse Williamson, he started Thayden, a Black Forest cattle operation 18 miles northeast of Colorado Springs.[21] The bachelor ranchers were courting the daughters of Judge Martin Russell Thayer, a Philadelphia jurist and former U.S. congressman. Williamson married Sophia Thayer and set up a medical practice in Delaware. Tutt married Josephine Thayer on December 29, 1885, after a two-year engagement. Legend has it that Tutt sold two cows to buy his train ticket home for the wedding.[22] Charles stayed out west, and Josephine joined him in Colorado Springs, where he started the real estate firm of Tutt, McDaniel, and Company.

Tutt's business thrived. He opened a second office in Pueblo and even branched out into gold mining. In late 1891 he staked a mining claim in Cripple Creek, a new gold camp southwest of Colorado Springs. Early the next year he opened a branch office there, too. He asked his Philadelphia friend Spencer Penrose, who had just arrived in the Pikes Peak region, to manage it. This proved to be a turning point for both men.

After finishing at Harvard, Spencer rejected a clerk job at a Boston bank. Instead he went west with $2,000, a graduation gift from his father. He visited his brother Richard in Texas, where Dick was conducting a survey of mineral deposits. Spencer continued on to Las Cruces, New Mexico, where he tried a series of unsuccessful business ventures. His

Mesilla Valley Fruit and Produce Company sold produce, hay, grain, coal, lime, agricultural implements, and stoves.[23] He also dabbled in fruit cultivation, cattle ranching, real estate sales, and silver mining. He failed at each.

Richard, who considered Las Cruces "a wretched hole," told Dr. Penrose: "Speck has got a commission business, which will grow in time. I do not see how it can ever be a very big thing. . . . I cannot see how Las Cruces would ever be a great center for anything but fruit and produce of the surrounding farms. . . . I should advise Speck to hold his lands at Cruces until he can get a good price for them, as they will undoubtedly sometime be far more valuable than now, and I should also advise him *not* to stay there himself but to start up in a better place."[24] In 1890 Speck sold his New Mexico interests for $2,000 and spent the money touring the Rocky Mountains in search of other opportunities. He speculated in gold mining claims in Utah, which Richard thought promising.

"I think he is on the track of a big thing," Richard informed the doctor. "He deserves to succeed as he is working hard and is a man of nerve. I wish I could be in Utah with him."[25] This investment failed when President Benjamin Harrison vetoed a federal bill that would have allowed mining on the Ute Reservation. Supposedly, the doctor sent Boies and Charles to check up on Spencer, whom they found peddling apples near Denver's Union Station.[26] After two years Spencer's luck changed. He arrived in Colorado Springs in 1892, nearly broke. Richard and their friend Charles Tutt had written to him about a gold rush in nearby Cripple Creek.

As Penrose and Tutt's mining partnership became a golden success, their birthplace exerted its influence in several ways. During the late 1700s and early 1800s, Philadelphia was America's largest city, vying with Boston and New York City as the East Coast center of culture, shipping, and commerce. It was also a city of firsts. Benjamin Franklin had established the country's first fire volunteer department, first subscription library, first hospital, and first medical school.[27] Philadelphia served as the nation's first capital from 1790 until 1800, when the government moved to Washington, D.C. Philadelphia also boasted the country's first museum and first zoological gardens.

Along with an assumption of Philadelphia's supremacy, Penrose brought the city's tradition of good food, drink, and fellowship. "I have never observed such a wealth of taverns and drinking establishments as are in Philadelphia," Thomas Jefferson had commented in 1790. "There is hardly a street without several, and hardly a man here who does not fancy one his second home."[28] The Philadelphia Fishing Company, formed in 1732 and famed for its Fish House Punch, was the country's first gentlemen's association.[29] The city was also the birthplace of the soft pretzel, ice cream cone, cinnamon bun, and scrapple.[30] When Spencer relocated to Colorado, he never lost his taste for his hometown's food and had oysters and scrapple shipped west by the barrel. Spencer's tastes also remained those of a Philadelphia aristocrat—clothes fitted by a Chestnut Hill tailor, boots from New York City, and memberships in elite East Coast clubs.

Most significant, however, were Penrose's Philadelphia family connections. Relatives and friends back East invested in various Penrose and Tutt enterprises. Speck sold gold-mining stocks to his father, brothers, Aunt Lydia, and cousin Christine Biddle. Spruce Street neighbors, Philadelphia Hospital doctors, and University of Pennsylvania professors also invested in Speck's mining, milling, and transportation businesses.

Each Penrose brother excelled in his own arena—politics, medicine, geology, and business. The eldest, Boies, became the undisputed boss of Philadelphia politics and for a quarter century was a powerful U.S. senator. A Republican Party stalwart, he was a key player in the legendary smoke-filled backroom deals at Chicago's Blackstone Hotel, where Warren G. Harding was nominated for the presidency. Although weak and scandal-plagued, the handsome Harding proved popular with voters, especially capitalists like the Penroses. Forsaking the reforms and idealism of his predecessor, Woodrow Wilson, Harding championed a "return to normalcy" and agreed with his vice president, Calvin Coolidge, that "the business of America is business." Senator Boies Penrose could not have agreed more.

Boies practiced law for three years following his graduation from Harvard, then was elected state senator in 1884. At that time he was the youngest man ever chosen for the Pennsylvania senate. Twelve years later he was elected to the U.S. Senate, where he quickly became known as a backer of liquor interests, steel, oil, and railroads.[31] Boies's critics accused him of manipulating votes, granting political favors, bribing officials, and fixing juries. "Uncle Boies had a bouncer at the polls," admitted his great-niece Frances Penrose Haythe. "If you didn't vote Republican, they'd throw you out."[32]

The senator liked to say that he was born, lived his whole life, and would die in the family home on Spruce Street. During legislative sessions he rented hotel rooms, first near the Harrisburg, Pennsylvania, Statehouse, then at the Wardman Park in Washington, D.C. He was a voracious reader and collected first-edition travel books and manuscripts.[33] His idiosyncrasies ranged from paranoia about germs to a phobia about being touched. He never owned an alarm clock. He awoke when he pleased and rode to his office, chauffeured in his fire-engine red motorcar.

Boies's laziness and vices were legendary. His motto was "I do as I please," and he openly drank, swore, and chased women. Parties aboard his yacht *Betty*, folks whispered, were Bacchanalian brawls. These soirees were more likely congregations of the political power brokers of the day. His sentiments toward women remain a mystery. The senator never took a wife, claiming he was married to politics. However, lascivious living lost

Boies Penrose, oldest of the Penrose brothers, became a lawyer, state legislator, and coauthor of *The City Government of Philadelphia* (1887). Using his flair for political organization, he emerged as the Republican boss of Philadelphia and in 1896 joined the U.S. Senate. He rose to the top of the Republican Senate leadership and was among the handful of politicos who championed the successful presidential campaign of Warren G. Harding. Senator Penrose died in 1921 at age 61. Courtesy, Library of Congress.

him his 1892 bid for mayor of Philadelphia. He withdrew from the race when the *Philadelphia Inquirer* threatened to publish photographs of him leaving a well-known brothel at daybreak.[34]

At 6'4" and 200 pounds, Boies was the largest of the Penrose men. He declined an invitation to play football at Harvard, shuddering at the thought of coming into physical contact with other sweaty youths. His enormous appetite was legendary. He once won a $1,000 bet by eating fifty iced oysters, washed down with a quart of bourbon. His rival was rushed to the hospital. "I've probably made a damned hog of myself," he explained to astonished onlookers. Boies's weight eventually reached 300 pounds, earning him the nickname "Big Grizzly." He required custom-made furniture to accommodate his girth. He had wasted away when he died in Washington in 1921. Boies had held public office for nearly four decades. Rumors of "mythical millions" turned out to be false. His estate amounted to $610,341, most of it stock in Spencer's Utah Copper Company.[35]

The second Penrose brother, Charles Bingham, was a brilliant scholar and dedicated physician whose love of surgery "bordered on mania." After graduating from Harvard and the University of Pennsylvania, "Tal" entered private practice in Philadelphia. In 1888 he and his father helped found the Gynecean Hospital for women. On November 17, 1892, at age 30, he married Katherine Drexel, a New York millionairess attracted by the "good-hearted, good-natured manly man who hunted big game." Charles's rugged masculinity and exploits out west appealed to his fiancée but raised the eyebrows of Philadelphia socialites. He had been jailed in Cheyenne during Wyoming's Johnson County cattle wars. He had stitched up bullet wounds for the gun-toting cattle ranchers and narrowly escaped trial for aiding and abetting murderers.

While engaged to Katherine, he went to Wyoming for a three-month rest to recuperate from a lung infection sustained while swimming a 15-mile race. After they married, the newlyweds returned west, spending their honeymoon camping in Montana and Wyoming. Four years later a western hunting trip ended Charles's career as a surgeon. He was attacked by a female bear whose cub he had just killed. The beast mauled his wrist and forearm, and Charles never performed surgery again. He would have died if not for Boies, who carried him on his back to the nearest railhead, then rushed him to the Mayo Clinic.[36]

After his accident Charles turned to teaching, writing, and philanthropy, beginning his professorship in gynecology and obstetrics at the University of Pennsylvania. He published *A Text-Book of Diseases of Women* in 1897. Charles, who was interested in animals, science, and nature, became president of the Philadelphia Zoo from 1910 to 1925 where he pioneered medical care for sick creatures and built the Penrose Laboratory for animals. Their grandniece claims Spencer started his zoo near the Broadmoor to one-up his older brother.[37] Charles was a Philadelphia Fairmont Park commissioner and sat on the board of the Philadelphia Academy of Natural Sciences. He helped organize the state health department, the first in the nation, and presided over the Pennsylvania Board of Game.[38] He maintained a small private practice in the family home on Spruce Street. He and Katherine lived with their two children—Boies Penrose IV and Sarah—at 1722 Spruce Street on fashionable Rittenhouse Square. Charles was widowed in 1918 and died of a heart condition in 1925.

Richard Alexander Fullerton Penrose Jr. graduated from Harvard at 23, summa cum laude and Phi Beta Kappa with a Ph.D. in geology. Penrose's pioneer explorations of western mineral regions led to several scholarly books, including the first scientific report on the Cripple Creek goldfields. Penrose successfully invested in mining, most notably the Utah Copper Company. When he died in 1931 he left $5 million to establish the Geological Society of America Headquarters in Boulder, Colorado, at 3300 Penrose Place. Courtesy, Geological Society of America.

The third Penrose brother, Richard Alexander Fullerton Jr., distinguished himself as a geologist and university professor. His Cornish blood perhaps accounted for a fascination with mining and proved the adage "Wherever there is a hole in the earth, you will find a Cornishman at the bottom of it."[39] After receiving his Ph.D. from Harvard, Dick conducted geological surveys in the West, first for the U.S. government, then for private firms. His geological advice helped his brother Speck develop the Midas touch. Dick evaluated his brother's mining properties, bought Speck's stock, and sat on the boards of his mining and milling companies.

Richard had a gold mine of his own, the Commonwealth Mining and Milling Company in Pearce, Arizona. He founded the company in 1895 and served as president for seven years. Richard's professional prominence prompted Arizona businessmen and local politicians to promote him as territorial governor. When someone else received that political plum, Richard turned to mineral exploration and teaching. He lectured regularly at Stanford University in the 1890s and taught at the University of Chicago from 1893 to 1911. For 20 years he conducted geological surveys worldwide and served on several corporate boards.

Like his brother Charles, Richard became involved in philanthropic and educational causes. He founded the Society of Economic Geologists and for sixteen years served as trustee of the University of Pennsylvania. He was president of the Philadelphia Academy of Natural Sciences, a Fairmont Park commissioner, and a Philadelphia Free Public Library trustee.[40] Richard died on July 31, 1931, of chronic nephritis and arteriosclerosis at age 67. He left his $9 million estate to be divided between the Geological Society of America (GSA) and the Philosophical Society of America in Philadelphia. The GSA, now headquartered in Boulder, Colorado, compiled and published Richard's voluminous correspondence in 1952 as the *Life and Letters of R.A.F. Penrose, Jr.* The Philosophical Society was founded by Benjamin Franklin in 1743 to promote learning and knowledge. Its members included University of Pennsylvania faculty and doctors, bankers, railroad presidents, and thirteen U.S. presidents.[41]

Boies's political influence and Richard's geological genius helped Spencer further his endeavors. But it was his partnership with Charles L. Tutt that launched Spencer's business empire. Tutt and Penrose combined business savvy, a promotional flair, and good timing to reap huge profits in real estate, mining, milling, and railroading. As one of Colorado's most affluent men, Penrose became a near-legendary figure. His flamboyant personality, extravagant lifestyle, and business triumphs shaped Colorado history. He still shapes that history, for his El Pomar Foundation is making a lasting contribution to Colorado Springs, the Pikes Peak region, and the state of Colorado.

NOTES

1. Dumas Malone, ed., *Dictionary of American Biography,* Vol. XIV. New York: Charles Scribner's Sons, 1934, pp. 448–450.

2. Josiah Granville Leach, *History of the Penrose Family of Philadelphia.* Philadelphia: Wm. Fell, 1903, pp. 114–119.

3. Helen Fairbanks and Charles P. Berkey, *Life and Letters of R.A.F. Penrose, Jr.* New York: Geological Society of America, 1952, p. 35.

4. Ibid., p. 39.

5. John Luckas, "Big Grizzly," *American Heritage Magazine.* New York: American Heritage, October–November 1978, pp. 72–81.

6. The Penrose family home was replaced by a parking lot in 1934.

7. Leach, *History of the Penrose Family,* p. 106.

8. Robert Douglas Bowden, *Boies Penrose: Symbol of an Era.* Freeport, N.Y.: Books of Liberties Press, 1937, p. 73.

9. National Archives, Mid-Atlantic Office, Philadelphia. The 1860 census reported three Irish-born domestic servants living at the Penrose household. The 1870 census reported four Irish women, two of whom were illiterate. It also placed the value of the Penrose home at $25,000 and its contents at $30,000.

10. Frances Penrose Haythe interviewed by Cathleen Norman, May 16, 1997.

11. George Wilson, *Yesterday's Philadelphia.* Miami: E. A. Seemann, 1975, p. 33.

12. Fairbanks and Berkey, *Life and Letters,* pp. 55–56, letter dated November 11, 1881.

13. Ibid., "Rules" dated October 1, 1877.

14. Ibid., letter dated November 18, 1880.

15. Penrose papers, El Pomar, Box 32, File 87, Harvard University and Life of Penrose.

16. Fairbanks and Berkey, *Life and Letters,* p. 71, letter dated November 30, 1882.

17. Ibid., p. 75.

18. *The Tutt Family of Virginia, Philadelphia, and Colorado Springs.* Colorado Springs: Russell T. Tutt, 1975, pp. 1, 3, 6.

19. *Philadelphia City Directory.* Philadelphia, 1870.

20. *The Tutt Family of Virginia, Philadelphia, and Colorado Springs,* pp. 10–11.

21. Leach, *History of the Penrose Family,* p. 99.

22. Wilbur F. Stone, *History of Colorado.* Chicago: S. J. Clarke, 1918, pp. 528–530.

23. *Harvard College Class of 1886, Secretary's Report No. II.* June 1889, pp. 44, 74.

24. Fairbanks and Berkey, *Life and Letters,* pp. 112–114, letter dated January 13, 1889.

25. Ibid., pp. 152–153, letter dated July 9, 1890.

26. Frances Penrose Haythe interviewed by Cathleen Norman, May 18 and 20, 1997.

27. Robert H. Wilson, *Philadelphia USA.* Radnor, Pa: Chilton Books, 1976; George Wilson, *Yesterday's Philadelphia.* Miami: E. A. Seeman, 1975, pp. 18–19.

28. Jay Goln, *Comprehensive Travel Guide—Philadelphia '93–94.* New York City: Prentice Hall, 1994, p. 13.

29. E. Digby Baltzell, *Philadelphian Gentleman—The Making of a National Upper Class.* Glencoe, Ill.: Free Press, 1958, p. 54.

30. Wilson, *Yesterday's Philadelphia,* p. 64.

31. Bowden, *Boies Penrose,* p. 109.

32. Frances Penrose Haythe interviewed by Cathleen Norman, August 18, 1997.

33. His namesake and nephew, Boies Penrose IV, collected travel manuscripts and wrote a book on Renaissance travel, published by Harvard University from where he graduated summa cum laude in history.

34. "Penrose Estate Totaled $610,341, Audit Reveals," *Philadelphia Bulletin,* June 18, 1923.

35. "Men and Things: Talented Sons of an Ancestry That Runs in Form to Days of Penn," *Philadelphia Bulletin,* March 2, 1925.

36. "Dr. Penrose, Clawed and Bitten by Bear, May Lose His Arm," unidentified article, Rochester, Minn., September 19, 1896.

37. Frances Penrose Haythe interviewed by Cathleen Norman, August 22, 1997.

38. John W. Jordan, *Encyclopedia of Pennsylvania Biography.* New York: Lewis Historical Publishing, 1917, p. 83.

39. A. L. Rouse, *The Cousin Jacks: The Cornish in America.* New York: Charles Scribner's Sons, 1969, p. 6.

40. Malone, ed., *Dictionary of American Biography,* pp. 146–147.

41. The society today owns two buildings, Philosophical Hall next to the State House (1879) and the new Philosophical Library, built in 1959 as a replica of the 1879 Library Company building that stood on this site. Nathaniel Burt, *The Perennial Philadelphians.* Boston: Little, Brown, 1963, p. 238.

2

Pikes Peak

SPENCER PENROSE AND CHARLES TUTT, like innumerable other pilgrims, found Pikes Peak enchanting. Rising abruptly from the Great Plains, the 14,110-foot landmark is America's best-known mountain. Its gray granite pinnacle beckoned Colorado's earliest inhabitants—the Native Americans—as well as latter-day explorers, pioneers, and tourists.

Prehistoric Indians occupied the Pikes Peak region for thousands of years before European settlers arrived. Later, the Ute tribe inhabited its forested slopes while plains-dwelling Cheyenne and Arapaho camped on the prairies below. Various tribes bathed in the mineral springs at the mountain's foot and wondered at the spectacular red rocks Anglo-American settlers would name "Garden of the Gods." The tribes followed an ancient trail that preceded present-day Ute Pass to South Park, where they hunted high-country buffalo.

As the first Europeans to explore Colorado extensively, the Spanish christened the 14,110-foot peak El Capitan. The Spanish claimed the entire Arkansas River Basin after Don Francisco Vasquez del Coronado ventured north from present-day New Mexico in 1540, searching for the rumored Seven Cities of Gold. Coronado's party of nearly 1,300 entered western Kansas, but no record indicates they sighted the Rocky Mountains. Juan Bautista de Anza saw the Pikes Peak region in 1779 while chasing a band of Comanche Indians. De Anza and his troops battled the Comanche near Wetmore in what is now Fremont County. Greenhorn, the prominent peak south of Pikes Peak, commemorates the Spanish defeat of Chief Green Horn (Cuerno Verde) and his Comanche raiders.

French explorers and trappers also penetrated Colorado, giving France a claim to the land. Eastern Colorado north of the Arkansas River was once part of Louisiana Territory. In this remote outpost of the French

The Utes had occupied the Pikes Peak region for hundreds of years—long before the Plains Indians such as the Arapaho and Cheyenne arrived in the early 1800s. Even before the Spanish began exploring and naming Colorado's mountains in the 1700s, the Utes cherished the homeland they fought fiercely to keep. Many were later pushed into present-day Utah. This 1874 photo by John K. Hilliers of the Powell Survey captured a Ute family in their wickiup. Courtesy Denver Public Library, Western History Department.

Spanish explorers, the first Europeans to see and describe Pikes Peak, called it "El Capitan." Spanish names, like Spanish claims, were ignored by English-speaking settlers. Yankees stereotyped Spaniards as inept, archaic, and laughable, as this Frederic Remington sketch of a quixotic conquistador suggests. Courtesy Denver Public Library, Western History Department.

empire, trappers and traders roamed the mountains and followed the waterways in search of beaver. These rugged mountain men also established a series of fur-trading posts along the Arkansas and South Platte Rivers. French trappers christened Fountain Creek as "Fontaine qui Bouille," or boiling springs, the stream that flows down Ute Pass through what is now Manitou Springs and Colorado Springs.

With the 1803 Louisiana Purchase, President Thomas Jefferson acquired from Napoleon modern-day Colorado north of the Arkansas River and east of the Continental Divide. This $15 million bargain inspired Jefferson to send Lewis and Clark to explore the northern part of the purchase. Lt. Zebulon Montgomery Pike explored the southern section of the vast new territory. Pike followed the Arkansas River west in 1806, seeking the headwaters of the Arkansas and Red Rivers, which defined the new Spanish-American border. In November he entered Colorado and spied the mountain that would later bear his name.

At first sight Pike described the peak as a "small blue cloud" on the western horizon. Drawing nearer, he set out with a small party to investigate.

French mountain men such as Ceran St. Vrain were among the first Europeans to explore, trap, trade, and live along waterways such as the Platte (French for flat or shallow) River and Fountain (from the French *fontaine,* "spring") Creek. Courtesy Colorado Historical Society.

Lieutenant Zebulon Montgomery Pike has gone down in history as "the lost pathfinder." Sent west in 1805 to find the southern boundary of the Louisiana Purchase, Pike lost his way in the Royal Gorge, in South Park, and in the San Luis Valley and confused the Red and Arkansas Rivers. Arrested by Spanish authorities for trespassing, he was released in time to be accidentally blown up by his own men in the War of 1812. Pike is saved from oblivion by the glorious peak named for him—although he never climbed it. Courtesy Denver Public Library, Western History Department.

Many readers learned of the wonders of the Pikes Peak region from the English adventurer George F.A. Ruxton. His often reprinted 1848 book, *Adventures in Mexico and the Rocky Mountains,* described encounters between trappers and Indians, as shown in this drawing for Ruxton's work. Ruxton provided vivid, detailed accounts, such as this of a Ute camp: "The lodges of the village, numbering some two hundred or more, were erected in parallel lines, and covered a large space of the level prairie in shape of a parallelogram. In the centre, however, the space which half a dozen lodges in length would have take up was left unoccupied, save by one large one, of red-painted buffalo skins, tattooed with the mystic totems of the 'medicine' peculiar to the nation. In front of this stood the grim scalp-pole, like a decayed tree trunk, its bloody fruit tossing in the wind; and on another, at a few feet distance, hung the 'bag' with its mysterious contents. Before each lodge a tripod of spears supported the arms and shields of the Yuta [Ute] chivalry, and on many of them, smoke-dried scalps rattled in the wind." Ruxton Creek, which joins Fountain Creek in Manitou Springs, commemorates this writer, who died in St. Louis in 1848 at age 27. Courtesy Denver Public Library, Western History Department.

They struggled through a blizzard to the top of Cheyenne Mountain. Subzero weather and stockingless soldiers outfitted only in light overalls kept Pike from scaling the peak's summit. "The summit of the Grand Peak, which was entirely bare of vegetation and covered with snow, now appeared at the distance of 15 or 16 miles from us, and as high again as what we had ascended," Pike wrote in his journal on November 27, 1806. "[It] would have taken a whole day's march to arrive at its base, when I believe no human being could have ascended its pinnacle."[1] The lieutenant's claim that humans would never conquer it was later refuted by millions of motorists, cog railway passengers, and hikers.

Other explorers surveyed and mapped America's vast new Louisiana Purchase. Expeditions led by Stephen H. Long in 1820 and by John C. Fremont in 1844 camped at the mountain's base. Traveling with the Long party was Dr. Edwin James, a botanist, geologist, and surgeon who scaled the summit with a few companions and collected specimens of alpine flora. James was probably the first Anglo-American to climb to the top of what was briefly called James Peak before being renamed for Pike.

One of Colorado's first tourists, George Ruxton, vividly described the Pikes Peak region in hair-raising stories. This English author-adventurer camped at present-day Manitou Springs in 1846 and described a primitive wilderness inhabited by a few shaggy fur trappers and warring Ute and Arapaho tribes.

During the California gold rush, easterners heading for the Sierra Nevada goldfields regarded Pikes Peak and the entire Rocky Mountain

The Pikes Peak gold rush of 1859 drew an estimated 100,000 argonauts to what became Colorado Territory in 1861. One of the great mass migrations in U.S. history, it rivaled the California gold rush of 1848–1849 and put Pikes Peak on the map as America's magic mountain. Courtesy Tom Noel Collection.

range as an impediment. Gold rush trails headed north through Wyoming or south through New Mexico. Not until a decade later would the Colorado Rockies become a destination rather than an obstacle.

An 1858 gold discovery near the confluence of Cherry Creek and the South Platte River in present-day metropolitan Denver unleashed the Pikes Peak gold rush. Wild exaggerations of gold came on the heels of a national depression. Thousands of hopeful prospectors crossed the plains. Although the gold strike was 70 miles north of the famous mountain, it became synonymous with the gold rush. All across America the words "Pikes Peak" were on the tip of people's tongues. Westbound prospectors painted "Pikes Peak or Bust" on their wagons. Publishers printed around thirty guidebooks to the so-called Pikes Peak Gold Region. These goldfield guides were eagerly sought at Missouri River jumping-off points such as Independence, St. Charles, Council Bluffs, Leavenworth, and Kansas City. Booklets such as "New Gold Mines of West Kansas" told readers what provisions and equipment they would need, how to stake a claim, and how to harvest a fortune. The guidebooks spurred commerce, urging prospectors to buy Pikes Peak hats, Pikes Peak guns, Pikes Peak boots, Pikes Peak shovels, and other gear.[2]

Argonauts streamed into the frontier towns of Auraria and Denver City on Cherry Creek. Farther south, a small settlement called Colorado City sprang up near the base of Pikes Peak. Townsfolk built a wagon road up Ute Pass to reach the mountain mining camps of Fairplay, Breckenridge, and Oro City. The infant city's hopes of becoming the main supply center and the territorial capital were thwarted when a road built from Denver provided easier access to the high-country mining. The Civil War slowed the influx of gold seekers and pioneers, but immigration to the Pikes Peak region increased after 1865. Among the newcomers was Gen. William Jackson Palmer, who came to build railroads but stayed to build a town. After surveying the Front Range, he laid out a model city at the base of Pikes Peak.

Unable to scale the peak named for him, Lt. Zebulon Pike pronounced it unclimbable. Fifty-two years later, in 1858, Julia Archibald Holmes, a spirited 24-year-old, climbed to the top in her bloomers. She wrote home to her parents: "Nearly every one tried to discourage me from attempting it, but I believed that I should succeed; and now, in all probability I am the first woman who has ever stood upon the summit of this mountain and gazed upon this wondrous scene." Courtesy Denver Public Library, Western History Department.

Palmer recognized that health as well as wealth would attract folks to Colorado's mild sunny climate and mineral water spas. He founded Colorado Springs in 1871, naming it for the mineral springs at nearby Manitou Springs. The arrival of Palmer's Denver & Rio Grande Railroad later that year helped make the city a tourist destination. Disembarking passengers, however, found the town cemetery next to the depot. To squelch any doubts

Spencer Penrose, the great visionary who transformed the Pikes Peak region into a tourist haven, had only one good eye after a rowing accident at Harvard. His self-consciousness about matching his glass eye to his good eye led to a lifelong search. In a 1933 letter to Kohler and Danz in New York City, he grumbled: "The new eye, which you have made for me, [is] entirely unsatisfactory. The rim was of a new shape and different from the one I bought from you several days ago. The color on the side of the eye was too bloody and did not show the natural vein system. The pupil of the eye was not in the center." Three years later Penrose ordered a special glass eye to be reddened to match his other eye when he was hung over. When that eyeball with red veins arrived from Dr. Bruneau, Spencer sent a check for 400 francs and a note saying, "The eye you sent me is quite satisfactory but sometimes it seems a little small."

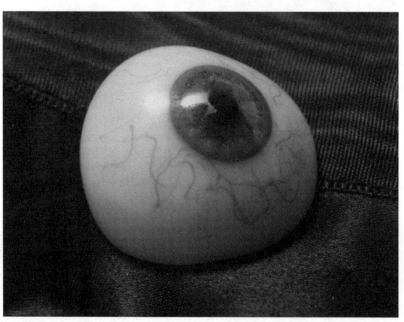

To process Cripple Creek's gold ores, Charles M. MacNeill, Penrose, Tutt, and Bert Carlton opened the Colorado-Philadelphia Reduction Company on a mesa overlooking Colorado City. The state-of-the-art 1896 plant opened as one of the largest chlorination plants in the United States. This lithograph by D. D. Robertson was produced to impress stockholders. Millions of dollars in gold refined here left behind a huge dump that still dominates the Colorado City landscape.

Penrose family members invested heavily in the U.S. Reduction and Refining Company (USR&R), created in 1900 by Penrose, Tutt, and associates. Capitalized at $134 million, the USR&R consolidated many Cripple Creek ore-processing plants, including the Colorado-Philadelphia and National plants of Colorado City; the Union, Metallic, and National Gold Extraction Company mills of Florence; and the Cripple Creek Sampling and Ore Company. Courtesy Tom Noel Collection.

Half Way House, Cog Road, Manitou, Colo.

7248. After a Snowstorm, on Summit of Pike's Peak, Colo. Altitude 14, 147 feet.

Postcards such as these helped lure millions of visitors to Pikes Peak.

5336. Sunrise from Pikes Peak, Altitude 14,110 Feet

about the town's salubriousness, Palmer had the boneyard moved to its eastern outskirts, where Evergreen Cemetery lies to this day.[3] The newly minted city's majestic setting and crisp mountain air attracted wealthy travelers and genteel invalids who brought more culture than had the gold-grubbing prospectors.

Colorado Springs quietly took root in the shadow of Pikes Peak. Cattle ranches and farms sprang up on the prairie outskirts to feed miners and health seekers. In the mid-1880s the Colorado Midland Railroad linked Colorado Springs with the mining towns of Leadville and Aspen. During the city's first twenty years, nobody suspected that gold would be discovered in an extinct volcano crater on the west side of Pikes Peak. This treasure, found three decades after gold strikes at Central City, Idaho Springs, and Breckenridge had flared and faded, sparked the state's greatest gold rush.

NOTES

1. Quoted in Henry L. Carter, ed., *The Pikes Peak Region—A Sesquicentennial History.* Colorado Springs: Historical Society of the Pikes Peak Region, 1956, p. 63.

2. Carl Abbott, Stephen J. Leonard, and David McComb, *Colorado: A History of the Centennial State.* Niwot: University Press of Colorado, 1982, pp. 54–56.

3. Evergreen Cemetery is now a large necropolis bounded by Hancock Expressway, Fountain Boulevard, and Union Boulevard, the site Palmer chose. He is among the many pioneers buried in the elegant cemetery with many notable tombstones and mausoleums. Denise R.W. Oldach, ed., *Here Lies Colorado Springs: Historical Figures Buried in Evergreen and Fairview Cemeteries.* Colorado Springs: City of Colorado Springs, 1995.

3

Cripple Creek

SPENCER PENROSE AND CHARLES L. TUTT were among the first to cash in on Cripple Creek. Tutt came to Colorado Springs in 1884 and tried his hand at cattle ranching before going into real estate sales. Penrose, whose father had given him $2,000 when he graduated from Harvard, had exhausted the capital on unsuccessful business dealings in New Mexico and Utah before arriving in Colorado Springs in 1892. Tutt offered Penrose a half interest in his Cripple Creek real estate office, forging a partnership that would make them both millionaires.

By 1890 many thought Colorado's richest gold deposits had already been found. The Cripple Creek boom, the state's last and greatest gold rush, proved them wrong. Cripple Creek's deposits—embedded in volcanic rock formations—form a "bowl of gold" covering about 6 square miles in the crater of a huge extinct volcano. Volcanic eruptions in the Miocene Era forced gold-bearing magma upward through fissures in the earth's surface. As this volcanic cone eroded over the millennia, it left gold veins embedded in the rock.

Gold did not cause an uproar before palefaces arrived. The Utes supposedly regarded the yellow metal as excrement of the gods, a curse that would drive them from their mountain home. Cripple Creek gold eluded early prospectors and geologists. Whites first poked into the area in 1844 when the John C. Fremont expedition passed nearby. The Ferdinand V. Hayden survey party came through thirty years later, producing the first detailed map of the Pikes Peak region. Not until prospectors sunk a shaft in 1874 and bored a tunnel in 1879 did gold rumors begin drifting out of Cripple Creek. The "Mount Pisgah Hoax" brought prospectors to the area in 1884, after a railroad agent salted a "gold" mine 13 miles west of Cripple Creek. Several thousand argonauts flocked to the site but failed to discover

Robert M. Womack did not have his heart in cowboying. While herding cattle for Cripple Creek ranchers Horace Bennett and Julius Myers, he frequently stopped to examine rocks and poke around in the gritty soil. Bob had a bad case of gold fever. Bennett and Myers, two Denver real estate tycoons, let "Crazy Bob" chase his golden fantasies as long as he covered up his prospect holes.

"Crazy Bob" found the gold that had eluded experienced prospectors and knowledgeable mining engineers. He staked out Cripple Creek's first mine, the Gold King, on Tenderfoot Hill in 1890. Womack's strike gave birth to the world's richest gold camp and created at least twenty-eight new millionaires, but Bob wasn't one of them. "Father of Cripple Creek dies in abject poverty," lamented the *Cripple Creek Times,* August 11, 1909. "Bob Womack paved the way for other men's fortunes [while] fickle fortune played with him. Time and time again the capricious dame flirted with him, dangling the prize within his grasp." Courtesy Colorado Historical Society.

After Womack found gold at Cripple Creek, the town sprang up from a cow pasture with a few log and tent structures, as this November 1, 1891, photo by Andrew James Harlan shows. By 1893 frame buildings were replacing tents along Bennett Avenue. Seven years later Cripple Creek sprawled around the base of Mount Pisgah. For a few years after 1900, "the World's Greatest Gold Camp" outproduced all rivals in Canada, Russia, South Africa, and the United States. Harlan photo courtesy El Pomar; © 1893 William Henry Jackson photo courtesy Colorado Springs Pioneer Museum; © 1900 Louis McClure photo courtesy Denver Public Library.

the golden treasure in the nearby Cripple Creek volcanic caldera. Instead, the Mount Pisgah humbug raised skepticism about mineral deposits on the west side of Pikes Peak.

In 1890 a persistent cowboy-prospector, Robert M. Womack, found evidence of the gold deposits that underlay the high-country cow pasture. Womack took gold specimens into Colorado Springs but failed to convince skeptical investors. Finally, Womack convinced Edward De LaVergne, Count James Pourtales, and other investors of the area's potential. By late 1892, 2,000 people had poured into the district like "a pack of hounds

Cripple Creek arose in 1891 as an instant city of canvas and logs. The pioneer newspaper the *Cripple Creek Crusher,* the first church, the attorney's office (which also served as the first court), and cafés such as Matt's American Kitchen all opened in tents. Later businesses graduated to frame and—after two disastrous fires in 1896—masonry edifices. Courtesy, three Colorado Historical Society photos by William Henry Jackson; "Whosoever Will" tent chapel photo by W. E. Hook.

hunting a fox," according to Colorado School of Mines geologist Arthur Lakes.[1]

The Cripple Creek Mining District became a brawling, sprawling free-for-all, spreading from smooth grassy hills into the forested ridges and peaks. The gold strike grabbed national headlines, luring risk takers of all kinds. Thousands swarmed in, camping in canvas tents or bunking in log cabins and frame shacks. Food was expensive yet of poor quality. Water was scarce, whiskey plentiful. There was no shortage of saloons, lawyers, stockbrokers, and land offices.

Charles L. Tutt was one of the first men to enter the district. On December 29, 1891, he staked claim to the C.O.D. (Cash on Delivery) Mine about a half-mile north of Bob Womack's original El Paso Mine Claim in Poverty Gulch. An article depicting Tutt's discovery appeared on the front page of the *Philadelphia Inquirer* three years later:

The story of the C.O.D., a private mine owned by five men, and one of
the richest strikes in camp, is hard to credit. In December 1891 Mr.
Charles Tutt teamed it over the dangerous Cheyenne route to make a
review of the young mining town. At Cripple Creek he met a friend,
and with him started over the mountains—called "hills." At noon they
had reached the Poverty Gulch district and just opposite the Gold King
claim. They brushed away the several inches of snow, and hauling up a
log, sat down to regale the inner man. Tutt suggested they put up a
stake at this point, and inscribe their location upon it, so it was done.
Then after their pipes were lighted, Tutt, half in jest, half as "bluff,"
said to his friend "Old man, I'll give or take $50 for my interest in this
C.O.D. location." The bluff didn't work, for Tutt's friend was hard up;
accordingly he said, "I'll go you, and sell my interest for $50."[2]

Suspiciously clean-looking miners and well-dressed boys and a girl posed for this 1893 Cripple Creek "placer mining" promotion. Very little placer (surface) gold lay in Cripple Creek. Most of the pay dirt was underground in veins encased by rock, also called lodes, which yielded fortunes only after heavy capital investment. Courtesy Colorado Historical Society.

Within five years the boom produced the thriving cities of Cripple Creek, Victor, and Goldfield. Ten smaller nearby camps were large enough to merit post offices: Altman, Anaconda, Arequa, Berry, Cameron, Elkton, Gillett, Independence, Lawrence, and Mound City. Thousands of miners thrown out of work by the Silver Panic of 1893 poured into the district, feeding its fantastic growth. "The silver miner has turned his back on the scene where . . . his darling industry lies cold in death," declared the *Cripple Creek Sunday Herald*.[3] Skilled miners and major financial investment transformed Cripple Creek into Colorado's greatest mining district. By 1900 Cripple Creekers enjoyed many of the urban amenities of Denver, Chicago, or even New York City: electricity, indoor plumbing, telephones, and streetcar lines. Three railroads served the district—the Midland Terminal, the Florence & Cripple Creek, and the Colorado Springs & Cripple Creek District.

Gold extraction in Cripple Creek required intensive capital investment to acquire mineral claims, sink shafts, buy mining equipment, pay workers, and finance ore transportation and milling. Much of this capitalization came from selling gold-mining stock in the East and in Europe. By 1896 the district had nearly 100 brokers and four stock exchanges—the Metropolitan, Gold Mining, Cripple Creek, and Victor Exchanges. In the first year of trading on the Cripple Creek Stock Exchange, more than 60 million shares worth $4 million were sold.[4] The Colorado Springs Gold Mining Stock Exchange traded $7,573,629 in 1897, $10,253,146 in 1898, and $34,446,956 in 1899. By 1899, $11,570,077 in dividends had been paid on Cripple Creek stock.[5] Buying and selling mining stock soon became as profitable as mining itself.

Little of the golden millions extracted from the Cripple Creek mines stayed in the camp; instead, those millions built large and beautiful homes in Colorado Springs and Denver. The Pikes Peak region's economy soared with the fortunes dug out of Cripple Creek. By 1897 Colorado Springs

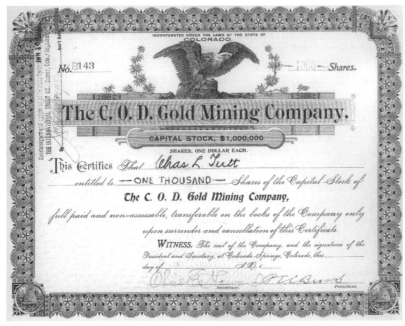

Charlie Tutt (*left*) and Spencer Penrose (*right*) at their C.O.D. (Cash on Delivery) Mine, 3 miles northeast of Cripple Creek on July 22, 1893. Tutt staked the claim on December 30, 1891, across Poverty Gulch from Bob Womack's original discovery claim. He offered Penrose half interest if he would run the Cripple Creek office and keep an eye on the C.O.D. Penrose spent the next three years in Cripple Creek, where the firm flourished. The C.O.D. became the first Cripple Creek mine to pay off big time. Incorporated in 1892 and capitalized at $1 million, the C.O.D. was sold in 1895 to a French syndicate for $250,000. Courtesy Colorado Historical Society (*top*), Tom Noel Collection (*left*).

In January 1893 Penrose moved to Cripple Creek to manage Tutt and Penrose properties. He shared this log cabin at 113 Prospect Street with William H. "Harry" Leonard, *left,* a fellow Ivy Leaguer, investor, and bachelor friend. This February 1894 photo by William J. Gillen captured the two posing at their sod-roofed cabin. Rabbit, Penrose's white horse, was named after the Rabbit Club in Philadelphia.

boasted 420 mining companies. Nearly fifty millionaires lived in the city's "North End" neighborhood.[6] Wood Avenue, supposedly named for the Wood brothers who founded Victor and operated top-producing mines, was nicknamed "Millionaire's Row."

"The real secret of success," as Mark Twain declared in his classic account of the mining frontier, *Roughing It,* "was not to mine ourselves by the sweat of our brows and the labor of our hands, but to sell the ledges to the dull slaves of toil and let them do the mining."[7] This was a lesson well learned by Penrose, Tutt, and other mining magnates. They quickly moved from mining gold to selling gold mines, mining stocks, and real estate. Their partnership began in a crude Bennett Avenue shack with a desk in front, a bed in back, and a curtain across the middle. In this shack Tutt & Penrose became one of the first Cripple Creek real estate firms. Expanding on Tutt's successful land business, they promoted lots in the Hayden Placer, later incorporated as part of Cripple Creek. During the 1890s they built speculative homes such as those that can still be seen at 400 East Eaton and 208 North Fourth. They also constructed brick commercial buildings such as the extant Tutt Block at 335 Bennett, as well as other buildings now demolished. The partners also owned several buildings in the Myers Avenue red light district. Their Topic Theater was denounced as a "variety den and skin game dive" by a local newspaper editor, who demanded that it "be removed with the rest of the filth."[8]

The partners soon branched out into mining stock, and real estate sales became merely a sideline. Marketing was one key to their success. Tutt & Penrose advertised widely, currying favor with the press both locally and back east. The *Cripple Creek Sunday Herald* in 1895 praised "the representative and reliable firm [that] have established for themselves a reputation for reliable, conservative yet aggressive business dealings. . . .

Penrose moved from the Prospect Street log cabin into this shingled cottage on Mineral Street where he, Charles Tutt, Harry Leonard, and other "socialites" entertained these guests on March 29, 1894. The woman on Penrose's white horse may be Sally Halthusen, who aimed to end Spencer's bachelor days. Spencer's family reacted adamantly: no Colorado cowgirl would do for a Philadelphia blue blood.

In 1891 Tutt and Penrose opened their first office in Cripple Creek, a shack at 306 Bennett Avenue with a huge wooden sign hawking "town lots, real estate, mines, and mining stock." With profits from the sale of the C.O.D. Mine, the partners built this two-story brick and stone building in 1894 at 113 Third Street and Bennett Avenue. Speck, as in "speculator" Penrose, wrote catchy ads such as "Buy a Block of Lots from Tutt & Penrose and net enough to go to the World's Fair" and "Tutt & Penrose are record breakers in selling Real Estate. List with them and they will sell it before you leave the office!" Photo c. 1894 by William Henry Jackson.

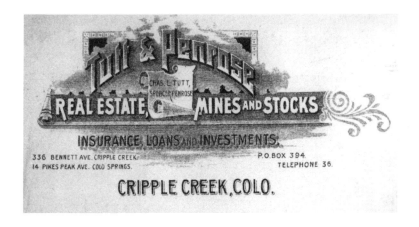

Tutt and Penrose quickly progressed from the hard, risky work of mining to the easier, more lucrative business of buying and selling mines. As their letterhead reveals, they boasted offices in both Cripple Creek and Colorado Springs, along with one of the first telephones in the Pikes Peak region. Courtesy Tom Noel Collection.

Tutt and Penrose's extensive Cripple Creek properties included two notorious Myers Avenue establishments, the Tropic Dance Hall and Lola Livingston's Parlor House. As this photo clearly indicates, Myers Avenue was a red light district. Courtesy Colorado Historical Society.

Messrs. Tutt & Penrose are an example of what a firm of sagacious and persevering men can do in this great gold camp of the state of Colorado."[9] To lure buyers Tutt & Penrose also hired a professional, Andrew J. Harlan, to photograph their C.O.D mine, Cripple Creek real estate office, and newly opened Cripple Creek Sampling & Ore Company. These photographs illustrated a series of front-page articles that appeared in Philadelphia newspapers in 1894 and 1895.

A front-page article in the *Philadelphia Morning Times* proclaimed: "Philadelphians Start a Boom—The Town of Gillett, In Colorado, a Wonder. Spencer Penrose and Charles Tutt Promote a New Town, Which in Two Months Gains One Thousand Inhabitants and a Railroad." Philadelphians read how "Presto! A town appeared, with stamp and sawmills, gambling houses, hotels, stables, and its suburbs pitted like smallpox with the prospector's pick and shovel. . . . In the present stage of Gillett's existence 'everything goes,' and so far, although only two months old, about a dozen shooting affairs have happened and about six murders."[10] Penrose and Tutt, in cowboy hats, were shown next to their Gillett real estate office tent. Nearly a half-dozen such articles stirred interest and helped open pocketbooks when the partners marketed stock for their mining and milling enterprises.

The article also perpetuated the rough and rowdy image of the western mining frontier, an enticement Tutt and Penrose used to woo investors. With several gambling halls and a hilltop casino, Gillett earned the nickname "Bachelortown." Tutt and Penrose furthered the town's role as the district's sporting center by building a racetrack there. They helped organize the famous August 1895 Gillett bullfight, the first (and last) ever seen in the United States. This spectacle attracted thousands of people, as well as the ire of the Colorado Springs Humane Society.

Although promotion was important, Tutt and Penrose's Cripple Creek success also resulted from their knowledge of mining and geology. This expertise came from Spencer's geologist brother, Richard Penrose, who evaluated their C.O.D. Mine and advised them on its operation. Fortuitously, the U.S. Geological Survey (USGS) had hired Richard to survey the entire district. Whitman Cross and Penrose evaluated each mine and published their findings in 1895. The local press hailed their *Geology and the Mining Industries of the Cripple Creek District, Colorado,* as a way to "shed light into the darksome nooks, dispel that baleful gloom and take away reproach of the Cripple Creek mine owners who possess treasure without being able to give a scientific account of the rock and earth."[11] Local mine owners and promoters used this report to raise outside capital and expand Cripple Creek mines.

The Cross and Penrose report boosted the Tutt & Penrose endeavors. It referred to their C.O.D. Mine as "remarkable in many respects" and provided a three-page, well-illustrated narrative that outshone the paragraph or two given most other district mines.[12] The report also lauded Tutt & Penrose, mining brokers, for "a great deal of assistance, which was made possible by their extensive knowledge of the district and their willingness to give all aid possible, often at the expense of much time and labor."[13] Although Richard Penrose's involvement in Tutt & Penrose enterprises may have influenced the C.O.D.'s rosy report, Cross described Richard Penrose as "one of most thoroughly trustworthy men I have ever met. . . . Penrose had high ideals of conduct and never violated them for personal gain, I am sure."[14] Nevertheless, the Cross and Penrose report likely facilitated the highly profitable sale of the C.O.D.

Tutt & Penrose prospered in mining stock and real estate sales but realized that processing gold ore was far more profitable than mining it. They opened their Cripple Creek Sampling & Ore Company in June 1895 on East Bennett Avenue, an operation the local press called "first-class in every particular" and "one of the very best samplers in the district."[15] The Cripple Creek Sampler bought ore from small mine owners and paid according to the gold content of the ore. This was the first of a series of increasingly profitable ore-processing ventures developed by Tutt & Penrose.

The Philadelphians sold the C.O.D. in 1895 to a French syndicate for $250,000, apparently the largest sales transaction in the district to that date.[16] They invested proceeds into their next venture, building the Colorado-Philadelphia Reduction Company plant at Colorado City. Meanwhile, the disappointed Frenchmen mined more water than gold from the C.O.D. Like many mines in the district, the rich deposit suffered underground flooding.

Constructing the Colorado-Philadelphia facility, touted as the largest reduction mill in the world, was possible only with extensive capital investment. Selling the C.O.D. provided start-up capital, but Tutt & Penrose also raised hundreds of thousands in funds by issuing stock. Penrose's connection to old Philadelphia money became one of the partners' greatest assets. As Tutt & Penrose incorporated successively larger companies, money flowed from bank accounts, inheritances, and trust funds back east. Spencer's brothers, aunts, uncles, cousins, and neighbors bought his fancy, glittering mining stock certificates, hoping to cash in on "the World's Greatest Gold Camp."

To expand into the ore-processing industry, Tutt and Penrose also partnered with an experienced mill man, Charles Mather MacNeill. The son of a doctor, MacNeill was born near Chicago on November 25, 1871, and moved to Colorado at age 14. As a young man he worked at smelting companies in Aspen and Leadville.[17] He went to Cripple Creek to manage the Lawrence Gold Extraction plant southwest of Victor. When that plant burned down in December 1895, MacNeill became a partner with Tutt and Penrose. Together they built the Colorado-Philadelphia Reduction Company plant in Colorado City. Within five years the Tutt-Penrose-MacNeill partnership would control most ore processing in the Cripple Creek District. The Colorado-Philadelphia plant opened in the fall of 1896, processing 200 tons of ore per day with a chlorination method introduced by MacNeill. Tutt & Penrose claimed it was the largest such plant in the world, constructed of 1 million feet of lumber and 100,000 bricks.[18] By 1899 it was treating over $3 million a year in ore.[19]

By 1900 Tutt, Penrose, and MacNeill had expanded the plant into a milling conglomerate. The "Big Three" had acquired nearly every mill and smelter that processed Cripple Creek gold. Exceptions included Albert E. Carlton's Golden Cycle Mill and the Portland Mill owned by James Burns and James Doyle. Tutt, Penrose, and MacNeill consolidated their ore-processing operations as the United States Reduction and Refining Company (USR&R), incorporated in New Jersey in 1901 and capitalized at $13 million. The "mill trust" owned the Colorado-Philadelphia and Standard Mills at Colorado City; the National Gold Extraction, Metallic Extraction, and Union Gold Extraction Companies at Florence; the National Sample in Goldfield; and the U.S. Smelting Company at Cañon City. Investors

To avoid the "mill trust" and its Midland Terminal Railroad, Winfield Scott Stratton and other gold kings built the Colorado Springs & Cripple Creek District Railway (CS&CCD), popularly known as the "Short Line." Independent mine owners celebrated the CS&CCD completion in 1901, along with the exuberant young lady in the photo. The Cripple Creek Central, a holding company under the control of A. E. Carlton, MacNeill, Penrose, Tutt, and the "mill trust," acquired the line in 1905. Courtesy H. H. Buchwalter photo, Colorado Historical Society.

included not only Tutt, Penrose, and MacNeill but also Winfield Scott Stratton, Irving Howbert, Penrose relatives, and various Philadelphians.[20]

The Tutt-Penrose-MacNeill group opened an office at 54 Wall Street in New York City. Charles MacNeill manned the office, traveling between Colorado and New York in his private railcar, the *Mather*. Tutt served as USR&R president, MacNeill as vice president, and Penrose as secretary-treasurer. The mill trust was one of many that proliferated at the turn of the century, unchecked by antimonopoly legislation. Not until 1906 would the partners sell the USR&R to the Guggenheims, operators of the Pueblo-based American Smelting and Refining Company.

The USR&R mill trust dominated not only Cripple Creek ore processing but also transportation. Penrose, Tutt, and MacNeill, in partnership with Clarence C. Hamlin and Albert E. Carlton, strove to control the district's railroads. They held a majority share of stock in the Midland Terminal and Florence & Cripple Creek lines. Winfield Scott Stratton and other large mine owners circumvented this monopoly by building the Colorado Springs & Cripple Creek District Railway, known as the "Short Line," in 1901. By 1905, however, Stratton was dead and the Carlton-Penrose interests gained control of the Short Line. Penrose owned $200,000 in Midland Terminal stock and became chairman of the board in 1917. The Florence & Cripple Creek line shut down after a Phantom Canyon flood tore out the track in 1912, and the Short Line died in 1919. The Midland Terminal monopolized district rail transportation for another thirty years.

Within a decade the Tutt & Penrose firm had grown into a mining, milling, and railroad conglomerate. In addition to the mill trust and the railroads, they owned significant interest in several district mines, including the Gold Coin (later renamed the Granite) and the Ajax. This vertical integration characterized consolidations and mergers occurring throughout U.S. industry at the time. Manufacturing plants, railroads, and mines were often owned by the same investors.

The era of corporate consolidation, mergers, and trusts was also one of great conflict between capital and labor. As with many other American capitalists, the financial success of Tutt, Penrose, and MacNeill depended on the muscle of thousands of miners and millworkers. During the 1890s many miners joined the Western Federation of Miners (WFM), a powerful union headquartered in Denver. Thanks to a sympathetic Populist governor, Davis H. Waite, the WFM had won the Cripple Creek strike in 1894. Subsequently, Cripple Creek became one of the country's most heavily unionized districts. With fifty-four local organizations, nearly everyone belonged to a union, even bakers, barbers, and bartenders.[21]

After recruiting a majority of Cripple Creek miners, the WFM strove to organize mill and smelter workers at the antiunion USR&R plants. Penrose, Tutt, and MacNeill collaborated with most other mine owners to crush this effort. They blocked WFM attempts to organize USR&R work-

ers at the Standard Mill in Colorado City by hiring Pinkerton agent A. H. Crane to infiltrate the workforce. Employees who joined the union were fired.[22] When MacNeill refused to meet with union representatives, the WFM Mill and Smeltermen's Union No. 125 walked out on February 14, 1903.[23] This episode at the Standard Mill triggered the 1903–1904 Cripple Creek Labor War.[24]

Smelter workers demanded $3 in wages for an eight-hour workday. Cripple Creek miners had already won the $3 day in the 1894 strike, but smeltermen received as little as $1.80 for ten- to twelve-hour days. The smeltermen's strike escalated when WFM president William "Big Bill" Haywood met with a committee of Cripple Creek miners on August 10, 1903, and persuaded them to join in a sympathy strike. The labor union struck every mine in the district that shipped ore to USR&R plants. The order called out 90 percent of the miners employed—3,500 miners at fifty mines.[25]

The tactic worked. Penrose, secretary of the USR&R, sent a letter to stockholders on December 10, 1903, explaining that their January 1904

Colorado miners, like this underground crew in Cripple Creek's Gold Standard Tunnel, extracted the gold that helped to build Colorado Springs and the Penrose empire. Courtesy Colorado Historical Society.

When the "mill trust" and others reneged on the 1894 agreement of $3 per eight-hour-day, William D. "Big Bill" Haywood led the Western Federation of Miners (WFM) in a statewide 1903–1904 strike. Haywood told miners they were underpaid while their labor financed Charles MacNeill's $12,000 Rochet-Schneider car, Spencer Penrose's 1899 around-the-world cruise, and C. L. Tutt's yacht *Anemone.* That trio of capitalists had little love for Haywood and the WFM. In a December 10, 1903, letter to USR&R stockholders, Penrose explained that there were no dividends because the strike had closed the firm's Colorado City and Florence plants. He assured stockholders that mines and mills would soon be open and profitably worked "with non-union workmen," as management had "resolved to wage a war against the outrageous extractions of the Western Federation of Miners." Unionists spread the rumor that Penrose had once said, "Any man in overalls isn't worth more than $3 a day." Although Penrose, Tutt, and other capitalists "won" the labor war, Cripple Creek never recovered from the lawlessness, violence, and ill will. Production went downhill, even though mines and smelters reopened in 1904. Archives, University of Colorado at Boulder Libraries, Western Historical Collections.

dividend would not be paid. The strike had forced closure of the Colorado City and Florence plants because of a lack of ore. Penrose resolved to "wage a warfare against the outrageous extractions of the Western Federation of Miners." He and other mine and mill owners persuaded Governor James H. Peabody to send in the state militia, and they provided funds to crush the Cripple Creek strike.

Penrose and Tutt's participation in the 1903–1904 strike was behind the scenes, in contrast to their 1894 involvement. During the earlier strike Tutt and Penrose had enlisted in "Company K" of the National Guard, publicizing their exploits in a front-page article in the *Philadelphia Sunday Times*.[26] The strike lasted 120 days, supposedly the "longest and bitterest of all American labor disputes up to that time." The 1903–1904 strike appears to have been something of a lark for Penrose and Tutt. "I guess by the time you get this the Cripple Creek war will be a thing of the past, the Union so badly licked that forever, and a day, they will lay low," Tutt wrote Penrose in June 1904. "It must have been some sport up there, and you and I missed seeing a little Hell for once in Cripple Creek."[27]

During the 1903–1904 strike MacNeill, Tutt, and Penrose joined fellow members of the Cripple Creek Mine Owners Association to wage war on the WFM. Adjutant General Sherman Bell, head of the strikebreaking state militia, enlisted the three men as aides-de-camp, but the nature of their duties is unknown.[28] Apparently, they never saw action. Tutt and Penrose's involvement was more likely financial: funding the payroll of the state militia and other strikebreakers. It was MacNeill and Penrose's attorney, Clarence Hamlin, who dealt publicly and ruthlessly with the strikers, according to Emma Langdon's *Mass Violence in America: The Cripple Creek Strike* (1969). However, Penrose's support for the illegal strong-arm tactics of Sherman Bell and the state militia is implied in a letter Bell sent to "Colonel" Penrose in 1910, begging for a $200 loan. "I went beyond all limits for you people and made good when everything was at stake with your interest and perhaps existence. . . . You know there was nothing that ever came up during that time or since that I didn't knock-in-the-head and grab by the throat day or night and take care of." A day later Penrose sent the requested $200 to Bell in Cripple Creek.[29]

Penrose and Tutt's antiunion attitudes reflected those of many U.S. capitalists. The period between 1890 and 1910 saw a nationwide transformation of industry. Consolidation of companies created powerful corporations and a growing gap between laborers and the few men who controlled corporate financial interests. Cripple Creek's long, bloody labor dispute was one of many strikes across the country. Labor unions and strikes proliferated in western mining districts. "At this auspicious time, when the technical difficulties have been largely subdued, an economic complication presents itself in the appearance of the destructive and unreasonable miners' union," remarked the *Mining and Scientific Press*.[30]

Thousands of workers organized to demand a "living wage" of $3 a day, an eight-hour workday, safer work conditions, and a share in workplace decisions. Not until the 1930s did the capital-labor conflict diminish, influenced by federal legislation enforcing an eight-hour day, minimum wage, and workplace safety. Also, some corporations voluntarily began providing health insurance and other worker benefits.

The 1903–1904 strike devastated the Cripple Creek district. Scores of men were killed, thousands of miners were violently denied their civil rights, and 225 workers were illegally deported from Colorado.[31] The strike was a significant factor in the district's drastic decline in gold production and population. Census figures for Teller County, of which Cripple Creek was the seat and principal city, show a population decrease from 29,002 in 1900 to 14,351 to 1910 and 6,696 in 1920. The misnamed Miners' Protective Association—composed of district mine owners—required workers to declare past or present union affiliations before being hired. Any man who had belonged to a union was refused employment.

Penrose's antiunion attitude stiffened after the 1903–1904 strike. He fought efforts of the Industrial Workers of the World (IWW) in Utah, where his Utah Copper Company was a major employer. When Utah Governor William Spry refused to grant a pardon to IWW organizer Joe Hill, who was executed in 1915, he received hearty congratulations in a telegram from Penrose.[32]

Spencer's antiunion attitude continued in the 1930s. He enforced a 10 to 20 percent wage reduction scale in the Cripple Creek district for miners, engineers, firemen, carpenters, machinists, hoistmen, and mule skinners.[33] His abhorrence of unions had not diminished when Broadmoor Hotel workers attempted to organize in 1939. "As soon as you give in to a union, you are gone," Penrose told New York City hotelier Thomas Green. "I have been fighting the unions since 1891 and at Cripple Creek we had a strike that lasted ten years, simply because the mine owners kept compromising with the unions. Finally the mine owners took a stand and beat them."[34]

Despite their profitable mill trust and their triumph in the Cripple Creek strike, by 1903 the Tutt & Penrose partnership had become strained. For over ten years their business had benefited from their complementary business roles and personalities. Tutt's pragmatic approach balanced Penrose's promotional flair and expertise in mining and ore processing. Older and more serious, Tutt had countered Penrose's dynamic, often abrasive business style. Tutt had become a responsible family man, happily rearing his family in their handsome Colorado Springs residence. Sophia Watmough was born January 2, 1887; Charles Leaming Jr. on January 9, 1889; and William Thayer on March 22, 1893. Russell Thayer Tutt, born Christmas Day, 1891, had died as an infant. Penrose, on the other hand, remained a bon vivant whose reputation for hard drinking and barroom brawls persisted. Tutt had attempted to temper his partner's vices. "I have tried to use my influence to stop your drinking to excess, and have generally succeeded," he reminded Spencer.[35]

The dominant role of Charles MacNeill in the mill trust emerged as another source of friction. "The situation is simply this," Tutt told Penrose. "Under Tutt, Penrose, and MacNeill we worked well together, but when it came to MacNeill, Penrose, and Tutt, the conditions changed. And I—finding that my ideas were always ignored and seldom listened to—just realized that all I had to do was to go down the line, as you two dictated." Penrose complained that Tutt devoted insufficient time and energy to managing the mill trust. Tutt responded by resigning as president of USR&R. He told Penrose to find as his replacement "a strong man . . . a man who Mac would fear to antagonize."[36]

Tutt, Penrose, and MacNeill were among the twenty-eight millionaires created by Cripple Creek gold.[37] The trio did not stop there but invested their energies and funds in various other mining opportunities. They investigated and invested in gold, silver, and copper mines in Alaska, Arizona, New Mexico, Nevada, and Baja California. They held stock in the Ajax and Granite Mines, and Penrose leased several small Cripple Creek claims to independent miners, often in exchange for tax payment.[38] However, Penrose's greatest fortune, which financed the Broadmoor Hotel and made him one of the wealthiest men in the state, came not from Cripple Creek gold but from Utah copper.

NOTES

1. Arthur Lakes, *Geology of Cripple Creek.* Denver: Chain and Hardy, 1895, p. 5.

2. "Gold in Cripple Creek," *Philadelphia Inquirer,* April 29, 1894, p. 1.

3. *Cripple Creek Sunday Herald—Souvenir Edition,* January 1, 1895, p. 2.

4. Brian Levine, *Cripple Creek Gold—A Centennial History of the Cripple Creek District.* Lake Grove, Ore.: Depot, 1988, p. 4.

5. Thomas A. Rickard and George Rex Buckman, *The Official Manual of the Cripple Creek District.* Colorado Springs: Fred Hills, 1900, p. 30.

6. Marshall Sprague, *Newport in the Rockies: The Life and Good Times of Colorado Springs.* Chicago: Sage/Swallow, 1980, p. 168. The North End, bounded by Nevada and Wood Avenues between Cache la Poudre and Madison, is now a National Register Historic District.

7. Mark Twain, *Roughing It.* Hartford, Conn.: American Publishing, 1872, p. 217.

8. *Cripple Creek Morning Journal,* April 13, 1895, p. 2.

9. "Tutt & Penrose," *Cripple Creek Sunday Herald,* January 1, 1895.

10. Henry Russell Wray, "Philadelphians Start a Boom—The Town of Gillett, in Colorado, a Wonder. Spencer Penrose and Charles Tutt Promote a New Town, Which in Two Months Gains One Thousand Inhabitants and a Railroad," *Philadelphia Morning Time,* September 12, 1894.

11. *Cripple Creek Sunday Herald—Souvenir Edition,* January 1, 1895, p. 2.

12. Whitman Cross and R.A.F. Penrose Jr., *Geology and the Mining Industries of the Cripple Creek District, Colorado.* Washington, D.C.: U.S. Geological Survey 17th Annual Report, 1894–1895, pp. 168–169, 183–185.

13. Ibid., p. 111.

14. Helen Fairbanks and Charles P. Berkey, *Life and Letters of R.A.F. Penrose, Jr.* New York: Geological Society of America, 1952, p. 183.

15. "Cripple Creek's New Sampling Works," *Cripple Creek Weekly Journal,* June 15, 1895, p. 5.

16. Figures for the sales of the C.O.D. vary between $250,000 and $300,000. Marshall Sprague in *Money Mountain* (Lincoln: University of Nebraska Press, 1979) specifies $250,000. A Denver newspaper reported $300,000 ("Sold to New York Men. The Famous C.O.D. Mine Brings $300,000," *Rocky Mountain News,* April 13, 1895, p. 6).

17. "Charles Mather MacNeill Dies in NY. Financier Also Noted Ore Expert," *Colorado Springs Gazette,* March 19, 1923, p. 1.

18. *Cripple Creek Mail,* August 8, 1896.

19. Penrose House, Spencer Penrose Collection, Box 10, File 32, letter from Charles MacNeill to Richard Penrose, March 13, 1900.

20. Sprague, *Money Mountain,* p. 176; Fairbanks and Berkey, *Life and Letters,* p. 218, letter from R.A.F. Penrose Sr. to R.A.F. Penrose Jr., May 6, 1901.

21. Elizabeth Jameson, *All That Glitters: Class, Conflict, and Community in Cripple Creek.* Urbana: University of Illinois Press, 1998, pp. 259–261.

22. Emma Langdon, *The Cripple Creek Strike: A History of the Industrial Wars in Colorado—1903–05.* New York: Arno Press and the New York Times, 1969 (original edition: Great Western, 1904), pp. 45–46.

23. *Miners' Magazine,* April 1903.

24. James E. Fell, *Ores to Metals.* Lincoln: University of Nebraska Press, 1979, pp. 130–131, 185–188, 198–199. Smelter workers struck at the Grant and Globe plants run by American Smelting and Refining Company in Denver in July 1903, but the smelter owners did not meet their demands.

25. Langdon, *Cripple Creek Strike,* pp. 66–67; Sprague, *Money Mountain,* p. 249.

26. "Colorado Deputies—The Inside History of the Mine Owners' Conflict With Their Anarchist Governor," *Philadelphia Sunday Times,* July 15, 1894, p. 1.

27. Tutt Family Collection, letter from Charles L. Tutt Sr. to Spencer Penrose, June 10, 1904.

28. Penrose House, Helen Geiger Collection, File 45—U.S. Reduction and Refining Company, letter dated October 29. 1904. Sherman M. Bell, brigadier general, Colorado adjutant general, requested that Penrose report for "special duty" June 13, 1904, but Penrose's duties are not known. In October 1904 he and MacNeill returned—uncashed—their checks for services rendered to Bell in Cripple Creek.

29. Penrose House, Spencer Penrose Collection, Box 1, File 1, letter dated February 8, 1910.

30. Percy A. Leonard, "Mining Problems in Colorado," *Mining and Scientific Press,* San Francisco, January 30, 1904, p. 17.

31. Sprague, *Money Mountain,* p. 259; Thomas J. Noel, "William D. Haywood: 'The Most Hated and Feared Figure in America,'" *Colorado Heritage,* issue 2, 1994,

pp. 2–12. By blaming the 1903–1904 Cripple Creek violence on the extremism of Bill Haywood and the WFM, mine owners such as Tutt and Penrose successfully portrayed unions as radical. This helped to undermine the union cause, and the WFM never recovered after the strike.

32. Penrose House, Spencer Penrose Collection, Box 50, File 231.

33. Ibid., unidentified newspaper clipping and typewritten wage scale, February 1932.

34. Ibid., Box 30, File 73, letter to Thomas D. Green dated March 20, 1939.

35. Tutt Family Collection, letter from Charles L. Tutt Sr. to Spencer Penrose, August 30, 1904, p. 6.

36. Ibid., p. 1.

37. Sprague, *Money Mountain,* p. 313. The millionaires were Sam Altman, George Bernard, Sam Bernard, Jimmie Burns, Albert E. Carlton, Judge E. A. Colburn, Frank Costello, Ed De LaVergne, Jimmie Doyle, Ed Giddings, John Harnan, A. D. Jones, William Lennox, Charles MacNeill, J. R. McKinnie, James W. Miller, John K. Miller, W. S. Montgomery, Frank G. Peck, Spencer Penrose, Verner Z. Reed, Van E. Rouse, Ed Stark, Winfield Scott Stratton, Sam Strong, Charles Tutt, Frank Woods, and Harry Woods.

38. Penrose House, Spencer Penrose Collection, Box 5, Files 8, 9, and 10—Cripple Creek Interests; Box 30, File 77—Gold Mining; Box 50, File 229—Annie Lode Mining Claim.

When Cripple Creek gold began playing out after 1904, Penrose shifted his capital to the much more lucrative Utah Copper Company's Bingham Canyon Mine.

4

Utah Copper

Enriched by Cripple Creek gold, Spencer Penrose, Charles L. Tutt Sr., and Charles MacNeill pushed on after 1904 to an even richer and longer-lived bonanza. Their Utah Copper Company not only pioneered open-pit mining technology in the West but also created a colossal hole that is one of two man-made structures visible from outer space.[1] Most important to Coloradans, Spencer's copper investments yielded stock dividends that bankrolled many Pikes Peak regional developments, ranging from the Broadmoor Hotel to El Pomar Foundation.

After the 1903–1904 strikes, Tutt, Penrose, and MacNeill realized that the World's Greatest Gold Camp was losing its luster. The richest Cripple Creek gold deposits were depleted, and shipments to their seven USR&R mills were declining.[2] With ongoing labor troubles, mines playing out, and stock earnings down, the USR&R's profitability was waning. So the three partners were happy to hear about an opportunity in Utah.

The proposal came from Daniel C. Jackling, a metallurgist at the USR&R plant in Cañon City. Jackling had investigated a large copper deposit at Bingham Canyon in 1899, a property partially owned by Cripple Creek investor Joseph DeLamar. Jackling found a huge body of low-grade copper he believed could be profitably mined. DeLamar was less optimistic, turning instead to Montana copper mining. Jackling, meanwhile, went to Colorado where he was hired at the USR&R facility. The Utah copper deposit had remained undeveloped until 1903. Jackling told MacNeill, Penrose, and Tutt that he believed the low-grade deposit could be profitably mined by processing the ore in the unheard-of volume of 2,000 tons per day.

The Bingham Canyon Mine is 30 miles southwest of Salt Lake City in the West Mountain Mining District, Utah's oldest and most productive

Daniel C. Jackling, a professor of metallurgy at the Missouri School of Mines,
dreamed up a fantastic scheme to dig
the world's largest open pit mine to ex-
tract and process low-grade copper ore
at Bingham Canyon, Utah. Jackling's
daring plan for industrial mining on a
massive scale began to pay rich dividends
in 1909. Profits increased even more
after 1923, when the Kennecott Copper Corporation bought Utah Copper.
Jackling, Utah's copper mining king, is
commemorated with a statue in the State
Capitol Building at Salt Lake City. Used
by permission of Utah State Historical
Society, all rights reserved.

mining district. After its 1863 formation, the district yielded $1.5 million
in placer gold within a decade.[3] In the 1890s Bingham Canyon gold production averaged 9,000 ounces per year.[4] After the gold and silver deposits
were exhausted, miners and investors investigated the district's copper
deposits but found only low-grade ones. In these "porphyry" deposits, specks
of copper lay scattered throughout the igneous rock like raisins in a cake
rather than being found in rich veins or lodes.

Jackling's 1899 exploration had revealed a 12-million-ton porphyry
deposit composed of 2 percent copper. Doubting that this low-grade ore
could be mined at a profit, DeLamar sold a 75 percent interest to Col.

Enos A. Wall. Jackling returned to Colorado and went to work for Tutt and Penrose's USR&R smelter, but he couldn't forget the large copper deposit. He told his new employers about the Bingham Canyon Copper Mine, insisting that the property could be profitably mined.

During the spring of 1903, MacNeill, Penrose, and Tutt considered Jackling's proposition and the financial challenges it posed. First, Jackling told them, they must obtain a majority interest in the property at a cost of $540,000. Colonel Wall owned a 75 percent interest and DeLamar 25 percent in the nineteen claims that covered 2,000 acres.[5] Second, they needed to build a 300-ton experimental mill to test Jackling's innovative ore-processing techniques. Findings from this pilot mill dictated construction of the gigantic concentrator and smelter needed to accommodate the huge volume of ore. They also needed to expand the Bingham-Garfield line—the "Copper Belt Railroad"—to haul ore in huge quantities to the concentrator at Magna and the smelter at Garfield.

Penrose again turned to his brother Richard, at that time a professor of economic geology at the University of Chicago. MacNeill, Tutt, and the two Penrose brothers went to see the Bingham Canyon property on June 1, 1903. Jackling's large-scale milling proposal, they concluded, could yield tremendous profits. Industry experts were less optimistic, however, claiming "it would be impossible to mine and treat ores carrying 3 per cent or less of copper at a profit under existing conditions in Utah."[6]

Ignoring the naysayers, Jackling and his converts incorporated the Utah Copper Company on June 4, 1903, issuing 500,000 shares of stock at $1 each.[7] MacNeill and the two Penrose brothers each purchased 79,250 shares. Tutt bought 33,243 shares. The USR&R bought 96,000 shares in exchange for equipment shipped from the Colorado City mill to Bingham Canyon. Most of the remaining stock was sold to Philadelphia investors, including Boies Penrose, Charles B. Penrose, and R.A.F. Penrose Sr.[8] With this capital the partners made a down payment on the mine to Colonel Wall and built the experimental mill. Little was left for operating expenses—payroll, supplies, services, and taxes.[9] The partners knew that once the experimental mill proved successful, they would need to raise operating capital and funds to construct the concentrator and smelter.

Not a financial partner himself, Jackling contributed his genius for metallurgy and his tenacious insistence that money could be made in Bingham Canyon copper. "Although Mr. Jackling had always believed in the property, he never became a very large stockholder, as he was not at that time very strong financially," Penrose later told renowned mining engineer and historian Thomas A. Rickard.[10] Jackling's mining expertise, Penrose's ability to raise cash, and MacNeill's managerial skills proved a crucial combination. Jackling had gained his expertise at the Missouri School of Mines and in Colorado and Utah mines. He came from humble, middle-American roots. Born at Hudson, Missouri, on August 14, 1869,

Jackling's brilliant strategy for Bingham Canyon involved massive ore extraction. Huge steam shovels dumped ore in railroad cars bound for Utah Copper's enormous mill. Although copper was a minor mineral used for little besides pennies in 1904, Jackling realized it would be important for use in automobiles, electrical systems, and other new twentieth-century devices. Used by permission of Utah State Historical Society, all rights reserved.

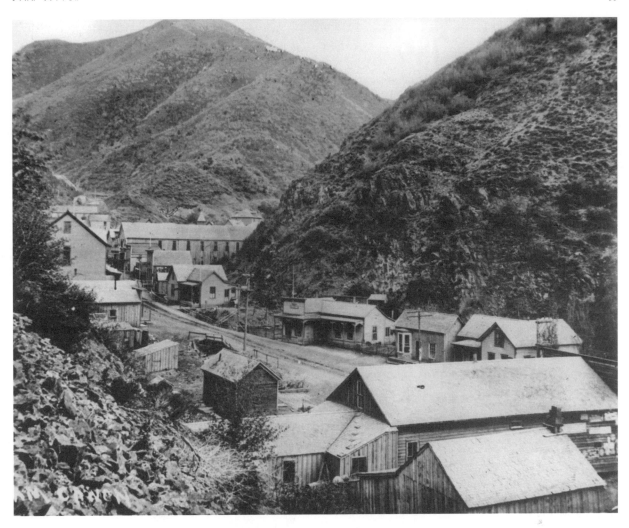

Jackling was orphaned while an infant and raised by his aunt.[11] He dropped out of eighth grade to work as a teamster, but at age 19 his interest in engineering was stirred by observing surveyors at work on his uncle's farm. He entered the Missouri School of Mines at Rolla in 1889 and graduated with a B.S. in metallurgy in 1892.[12] He taught at the Missouri School of Mines for a year and briefly worked at a Kansas City smelter before hearing about the Cripple Creek gold rush.

Jackling reached Cripple Creek in late 1893 with $3 in his pocket.[13] He had walked 20 miles from the rail station at Divide to save the $2 stagecoach fare.[14] He first worked underground as a miner, then as a fire assayer at the Lawrence Gold Extraction plant near Victor. In this company, owned by Joseph DeLamar and managed by Charles MacNeill, Jackling learned how to treat low-grade ores and came in contact with influential men in the mining district, including Penrose and Tutt. When

Processing 5,000 pounds of copper a day proved extremely profitable, but Bingham Canyon was an ugly, dangerous place to work. Management crushed striking workers who aspired to better conditions. "The Utah Copper Company," declared its vice president, Spencer Penrose, "will never recognize the union at Bingham, even if the mine is closed forever." Courtesy Tom Noel Collection.

the Lawrence plant burned in 1895, DeLamar sent Jackling to Utah to investigate the Bingham Canyon property.[15]

The pilot mill opened in Copperton, Utah, in February 1904. Production of 30 percent copper concentrates quickly rose from 15 to 1,000 tons daily.[16] To expand operations and build the mammoth concentrator and smelter, Penrose and MacNeill reorganized Utah Copper. They reincorporated in April 1904 in New Jersey, issuing 450,000 shares of stock at $10 per share and $750,000 in 7 percent bonds.[17] Captain Wall held 20 percent of both bonds and stocks. These funds also reimbursed stockholders for expenditures for developing and equipping the mines and building the Copperton mill.

Utah Copper added a 6,000-tons-per-day concentrator at Magna in 1907. An $8 million plant opened at Garfield in 1909 as the world's largest smelter.[18] These facilities were funded through a partnership with American Smelting and Refining Company (ASARCO), owned by the powerful Guggenheims.[19] This wealthy Philadelphia family had made a fortune in lace manufacturing, then pursued Western mining. Benjamin Guggenheim and his sons first struck pay dirt in Leadville, Colorado, where their mines and mills produced 9 million ounces of silver.[20] The Guggenheims expanded their Colorado operations, acquiring Denver and Pueblo smelters to dominate the smelting industry. The Guggenheims also acquired an interest in Tutt, Penrose, and MacNeill's USR&R enterprises.

The Guggenheims' milling monopoly spread west into Utah when they bought 232,000 shares of Utah Copper stock at $20 apiece and issued $3 million in 6 percent convertible bonds.[21] After funding a seven-month exploration of the Utah Copper property, they concluded that the deposit contained 40 million tons of low-grade copper ore.[22] In exchange for the capitalization of Utah Copper, Tutt, Penrose, and MacNeill awarded ASARCO a $6-per-ton 20-year smelting contract.[23]

Jackling, meanwhile, attracted much attention with his quarry-style mining and steam shovel mucking techniques. He and mining engineer Robert Gemmel traveled to the Mesabi iron mines in Minnesota to observe this new technology. They adapted the process to their Utah Copper operations. They removed a 70-foot overburden, then blasted into the exposed deposit. Finally, they "mucked" the copper ore into railroad cars with steam shovels. This "colossal scale" amazed the *Mining and Scientific Press* and the rest of the mining industry.[24]

During the financial panic of 1907, dropping copper prices jeopardized the operation, but Utah Copper paid shareholder dividends two years later. In 1909 the company doubled operations by absorbing Boston Consolidated Copper. Colonel Wall, a cantankerous old-timer whose forty-year mining career had taken him to Colorado, Montana, Idaho, and Utah, controlled this neighboring property. Ignoring Wall's condemnations of "brutal conquest," Utah Copper swallowed Boston Consolidated.

Wall demanded that his 20 percent interest in Utah Copper give him hands-on decisionmaking power in company management. Penrose and Jackling disagreed with Wall's business decisions and pressured him to quit. "Col. Wall resigned from the Board of Directors in 1908, owing to many misunderstandings with the Board of Directors," Penrose later told Rickard. "He was a very impractical man, and I doubt very much if there would have been a Utah Copper Company if he had been made Manager of the Company and had a control of its affairs from the very start, as he desired."[25] Wall remained a harsh critic of Utah Copper, lambasting the company and Jackling for years in his industry journal, *Mines and Methods.*

Utah Copper profits depended entirely on fluctuating demand. The red metal had been used in various forms through the ages for everything from coins to cooking pots to lightning rods. The malleable metal could be battered into shapes, rolled into thin sheets, or drawn into wire. It combined with tin to make bronze weapons and with zinc to form brass fixtures. Its conductive properties made it suitable for the new technologies of the twentieth century. As Richard Penrose had predicted, copper demand increased dramatically for manufacturing electrical wire, telegraph and telephone cable, batteries, and automobiles. When the huge new ASARCO smelter began operating in 1909 at Garfield, Utah Copper's future seemed secure.

The start-up years, however, had been nerve-racking for investors. Skeptical, Tutt pursued his own copper mining and smelting interests. He opened the Queen of Bronze Mine at Takilma, Oregon. Hedging his bets, Tutt had invested in the Utah Copper mining venture in 1903. "I feel sure that the Utah deal will be a winner," he admitted.[26] Within a year, however, he had sold his Utah Copper stock to prop up his faltering Takilma mine and smelting company. Penrose called the Takilma mine "the poorest business proposition I have ever seen" and blamed its failure on wretched management.[27]

These mining ventures took their toll on Tutt. His heart condition had worsened, and his physician urged him to rest. He and Josephine had bought a place on San Diego's Coronado Island. They enrolled their teenage sons, Charles Jr. and Thayer, in Thatcher, a private school near Ojai, California. Tutt also maintained an "island retreat" in Puget Sound and sailed his beloved yacht *Anemone* along the coast. He taught the boys to sail. He and his younger son, Thayer, won second place in the 1907 Pacific Yacht Race between San Francisco and Honolulu. Charles and Josephine summered in Colorado Springs at the family home at 1205 North Cascade. They traveled between Colorado Springs and the Pacific Coast, collecting Native American artifacts.

Charles L. Tutt Sr. sold his share of Utah Copper
to his partner Spencer Penrose and began enjoying life aboard his yacht *Anemone,* shown in 1906
at port in Coronado, California.

    In January 1909 Charles Tutt Sr. succumbed to the heart ailment that
had sent him west in 1884 seeking a health cure. He died at the Waldorf
Astoria Hotel in New York City at age 45. He left an estate worth $860,000
to his widow, Josephine, and children, Charles, Thayer, and Rebecca.[28]
Despite their business differences, Tutt named Penrose guardian of the
children and executor of his will. "I cannot tell you how much Thayer and
I appreciate all that you have done for us," Charles Jr. later wrote to
Penrose. "We appreciate it a lot, and hope that in some small way we will
sometime be able to return all that you have done for us."[29]

Spencer even used his political influence to Charley's advantage. In 1918 he wrote his brother, U.S. Senator Boies Penrose: "Charles L. Tutt, the son of my old partner Charley Tutt, is anxious to get some government job that will take him abroad. Mr. Tutt is in fine condition, and is 29 years

After his father's death in 1909, Charles L. Tutt Jr. became Spencer Penrose's right-hand man. Penrose, who had no children, increasingly entrusted his affairs to young Tutt.

of age. He made application for one of the Officers Training Camps late spring, but was turned down on account of his eyesight and hearing. He then made application to the Navy, but was turned down on account of his eyesight, although he is one of the best shots in the country."[30]

Charley moved into the family home on North Cascade in Colorado Springs and went to work as Penrose's business assistant.[31] Unlike his father, Charley was an employee rather than a partner. Gradually, Penrose groomed Tutt as his business administrator. Charley remained a subordinate rather than a peer, although his role as business assistant would expand into business manager and director over the next twenty-five years as Penrose expanded his financial empire. Penrose's Utah Copper stock was reaping over $1 million per year by 1910. These dividends funded a fabulous lifestyle and bankrolled scores of projects in the Pikes Peak region.

The Utah Copper operation was profitable but also problematic. The company was beset by labor problems. To keep costs low, Utah Copper and its associated ASARCO smelter hired cheap labor—primarily Euro-

pean immigrants. Many were refugees from political strife in Greece and Slavic countries who worked for less than $1.75 per eight-hour day. On May 1, 1912, at the ASARCO smelter, 800 workers walked off the job to protest the low wages.[32] This precipitated a sympathy strike among Utah Copper miners, instigated in part by the Western Federation of Miners. Strikers were antagonized by the exploitative practices of Leonidas G. Skliris. Known as "the Czar of the Greeks," Skliris supplied immigrant workers to the Bingham Canyon mines, mills, and smelters at enormous profit to himself. After five months the strike was broken. The company had hired 1,500 nonunion workers who kept the mine and mill going.[33] To break the strike and drive the WFM out of Bingham Canyon, Utah Copper President Charles MacNeill continued his heavy-handed techniques, such as firing 200 miners who failed to come to work on Miner's Union Day in June 1904.[34]

Utah Copper miners and ASARCO smelter workers endured low wages and miserable living conditions. Bingham Canyon was a string of camps and settlements, a 6-mile-long company town populated by Utah Copper miners and ASARCO smeltermen. The companies built boardinghouses and several small homes for workers, but many lived in tents and in shacks of wood and scrap metal. A journalist called the Bingham Canyon towns a "six-mile-long sewer" because many dwellings lacked indoor plumbing.

To help manage the Penrose empire, Charles L. Tutt Jr. moved back to the family home at 1205 North Cascade in Colorado Springs. There, Mrs. C. L. Tutt Jr. (Eleanor Armitt Tutt) raised Russell Thayer Tutt (in photo) and William Thayer Tutt, who would continue to work with the Penrose projects.

Another called Utah Copper a "modern inferno, a veritable slaughter pen where the workers are slaughtered and maimed wholesale" and described "dark, windowless, and floorless" miners' cabins.[35] The company did little to correct these problems. Finally, the mining company built the "modern corporate town" of Copperton in the 1940s—scores of modern houses that used copper in all ways possible.[36] The corporations demolished the old Bingham Canyon settlements and undermined them.

Utah Copper prospered despite labor disputes, and its success spurred the MacNeill-Penrose group to develop other copper properties. MacNeill, Penrose, and Jackling developed porphyry copper deposits in Arizona, New Mexico, and Nevada. Jackling's large-volume mining techniques once again yielded impressive results. The Arizona mine was at Ray, 80 miles southeast of Tucson in the Mineral Creek Mining District. Many directors of Ray Consolidated Copper Company, incorporated in May 1907, were tied to Penrose and the Cripple Creek district, including Sherwood Aldrich, Spencer Penrose, Charles MacNeill, Daniel C. Jackling, Charles Hayden, and Eugene Shove.[37] The immense Ray ore body measured 2.5 miles long, up to a half-mile wide, and 100 to 3,500 feet thick.[38] By 1912 the nearby ASARCO smelter was processing 8,000 tons of Ray ore per day.[39] During its first twenty years the Ray mine produced nearly 50 million tons of ore.[40] By 1956, 107 million tons of ore had been processed, yielding 2.5 billion pounds of copper.[41]

Jackling next developed the Chino Mine, a porphyry copper deposit near Santa Rita, New Mexico. The mine was located 100 miles from Las Cruces where Spencer had begun his business career in 1888. The Chino Copper Company used Jackling's pit-mining techniques on a deposit estimated at 19 million tons of 2.59 percent copper ore. A 3,000-ton-per-day processing plant produced 35 to 40 million pounds of copper annually. Again, most of the directors of the Chino Mine were also directors of the Ray Mine: MacNeill, Jackling, Penrose, Hayden, Aldrich, and A. Chester Beatty.

The MacNeill-Penrose group also ran an open-pit mine and an underground operation in southeast Nevada. Nevada Consolidated was incorporated for $5 million in 1914. Jackling directed this endeavor, transporting ore to the ASARCO mill 80 miles away at McGill. The Nevada operation proved lucrative. The company distributed over $45 million in dividends before it merged with Ray and Chino in 1926.[42] As in the Utah Copper, Ray, and Chino Mines, Penrose was a majority stockholder, and smelting was done by ASARCO.

The relation between Penrose's copper interest and the Guggenheim family enterprises expanded in 1915. The Guggenheims formed Kennecott Copper and the following year acquired a 25 percent interest in Utah Copper. Kennecott, named for a copper property near Kennecott Creek in Alaska, was a holding company for the Guggenheims' international mining properties. Kennecott absorbed the MacNeill-Penrose group's other porphyry companies in 1923 and changed Utah Copper's name to Kennecott Copper Company. Jackling and Penrose continued as corporate directors until their deaths. The Kennecott mine at Bingham Canyon was purchased by Rio Tinto Zinc Corporation in 1989.

Jackling's expertise earned him long-lasting influence at the copper properties and legendary status in the state of Utah. He sat on the Utah Copper/Kennecott Copper board until his death in 1956, serving as president for many years. Until the late 1930s he was chief operating officer of all Kennecott copper properties. When Jackling turned 70, Simon Guggenheim urged the "Copper Prince" to relinquish his decisionmaking authority. Jackling refused and remained involved in decisionmaking until his death.[43] Penrose later recalled: "We all know he was the original founder of the development of Utah Copper. When Mr. Jackling and some of us originally took hold of the Utah properties many mining people did not believe that Mr. Jackling would be able to develop and place the property on a paying basis. They claimed the ores were too low to ever show any profit."[44]

"The father of open-pit mining" received the William Lawrence Sanders gold medal for mining achievement and was honored for making Utah one of the greatest copper-producing regions in the world. The Mining and Metallurgical Society, in an address documented in its November 1926 journal, presented Jackling with a gold medal for combining "imagination and vision to see the economies of large-scale operations with the personality and capacity to enlist the millions of dollars necessary to finance the project . . . the creative and organizing ability and the energy to carry out this ambitious program."[45] The American Institute of Mining and Metallurgical Engineering elected him president in 1938. A heroic-sized bronze sculpture of Jackling stands in the Utah State Capitol. Kennecott Copper commissioned artist Arvard Fairbanks to create the $35,000 sculpture dedicated on August 14, 1954, Jackling's 85th birthday. The copper baron died in 1956, leaving $100,000 to Brigham Young University, $100,000 to the Missouri School of Mines, and $25,000 each to eight other universities. His business papers went to the Stanford University archives in Palo Alto, California.

Like Penrose, Jackling enjoyed a memorable lifestyle. He built a palatial home at 731 East Temple in Salt Lake City and set up his mistress, Helen Blaze, as a madame in the Commercial Street red light district. He showered Helen with gifts including a carriage, horses, and a stable. He escorted her to the Salt Lake Theater, where her expensive gowns and flaming red hair attracted the crowd's attention. Jackling traveled cross-country in his private railroad car, *Cyprus,* visiting the western copper mines and attending Utah Copper/Kennecott Corporation board meetings on Wall Street. He attended class reunions at the Missouri School of

Mines, arriving in a five- or six-car train. He invited students and alumni aboard to enjoy food and drinks.

In 1915 Jackling left Salt Lake City for San Francisco and rented a penthouse suite at the Mark Hopkins Hotel. After he married, he and his wife, Virginia, bought an elegant house in Woodland, California. He purchased a $500,000 yacht, christening it *Cyprus,* and sailed north to investigate mining operations near Juneau, Alaska.[46] *Cyprus* was the largest yacht on the Pacific Coast; it sported ten bedrooms, each with a bath, and required a crew of forty to fifty.[47]

Penrose and Jackling saw each other regularly at board meetings in New York or visiting in San Francisco or Colorado Springs. Jackling served as a director for Penrose's U.S. Sugar and Land Company. Penrose sent Jackling a box of fine cigars each Christmas and gave him bottles from his prized liquor collection.[48] Two weeks after Penrose died in December 1939, a demijohn of Penrose's treasured Hannisville rye arrived at Jackling's home.

Charles MacNeill fared less well than Penrose or Jackling. After advancing as general manager and then vice president at USR&R and Utah Copper, MacNeill stayed involved in mining operations, informing Penrose in lengthy letters. MacNeill manned the Colorado-Philadelphia Company, USR&R, and Utah Copper offices on Wall Street. He invested $350,000 in the Broadmoor Hotel,[49] where he maintained a sixth-floor suite. He frequented the Broadmoor Hotel stock exchange, located where the tavern is today. While Penrose branched into hospitality, transportation, and agriculture, MacNeill squandered his fortune on Wall Street. He died broke on March 18, 1923. Some people blamed his financial losses and premature death on heavy drinking. His widow, Marion, a Rhode Island socialite, married Spencer Willing and traveled extensively in Europe. For years she held stock in several of Penrose's companies and maintained regular correspondence with him.

Penrose's mining ventures provided him with both financial success and industry esteem. Although he remained a lifelong member of the American Institute of Mining Engineers, he refused to be involved in the industry other than owning Utah Copper stock. He refused invitations from Colorado School of Mines President Victor C. Alderson to attend the annual American Mining Congress. Alderson asked Penrose his opinion on mining policies and issues, such as the oil shale industry: "We are very anxious to have your cooperation with others whose judgment will be of greatest assistance in forming this policy."[50] Penrose declined. Instead, he channeled his imagination and investments into new ventures in transportation, hospitality, and agriculture. He had spent nearly twenty years accumulating wealth. Now Penrose turned to the exquisite pleasures of spending his fortune and enhancing Colorado Springs.

NOTES

1. The other is the Great Wall of China.

2. Marshall Sprague, *Money Mountain: The Story of Cripple Creek Gold.* Lincoln: University of Nebraska Press, 1979, pp. 250, 295. District production peaked at $18 million in 1900 and decreased each year thereafter. Annual reduction had dropped to $8 million in 1919.

3. Lynn Robinson Bailey, *Old Reliable: A History of Bingham Canyon, Utah.* Tucson: Westernlore, 1988, p. 18.

4. Ibid., p. 24.

5. Ibid., pp. 42–43; L. F. Pett, *The Utah Copper Story.* Salt Lake City: Kennecott, 1955, p. 3.

6. Ira B. Joralemon, *Romantic Copper—Its Lure and Lore.* London: D. Appleton-Century, 1935, p. 225.

7. Bailey, *Old Reliable,* p. 43.

8. R. Thayer Tutt Family Collection, Stock Certificate Book, 1903–1904.

9. Pett, *Utah Copper Story,* p. 7.

10. Penrose House, Helen Geiger Collection, File 10, letter from Penrose to T. A. Rickard, September 3, 1918.

11. Salt Lake City, Utah State Historical Society, D. C. Jackling file, "Daniel Cowan Jackling" biography.

12. Bailey, *Old Reliable,* p. 42.

13. Clark Spence, *Mining Engineers and the American West—The Lace-Boot Brigade, 1849–1933.* New Haven: Yale University Press, 1970, p. 67.

14. Helen Fairbanks and Charles P. Berkey, *Life and Letters of R.A.F. Penrose, Jr.* New York: Geological Society of America, 1952, p. 305.

15. Penrose House, Helen Geiger Collection, File 10, letter from Daniel C. Jackling to W. H. Leonard, September 3, 1942.

16. Processing ore, whether gold, silver, copper, or other nonferrous metals, involves a series of processes. First, large chunks of ore are sent in hundreds-of-ton quantities through various crushers and mills until the resulting material is as fine as sifted flour. This milled material is then treated in several ways to remove the metal. *Concentration* involves using gravity to pull the heavier metal to the bottom of a liquid solution. *Flotation* mixes the milled ore with oil, floating the metal to the top of the liquid solution. Another technique is adding a variety of chemical reagents that encapsulate the gold, silver, or copper and separate it from the waste product. *Smelting* involves heating ore concentrates to temperatures so high that the molten metal can be retrieved. Most recently, *electrolytic* processes plate the ore to steel wool–like material that is then dissipated through burning at high temperature, leaving the gold behind.

17. George L. Walker, "Facts and Figures About Utah Copper," *Salt Lake Mining Review,* July 15, 1911, p. 2.

18. Leonard J. Arrington and Gary B. Hansen, *The Richest Hole on Earth: A History of the Bingham Copper Mine.* Logan: Utah State University Press, 1963, p. 59.

19. The 1904 sale of the USR&R plants in Colorado to the Guggenheims was part of this financial transaction.

20. Edwin P. Hoyt, *The Guggenheims and the American Dream.* New York: Funk and Wagnalls, 1967, p. 57.

21. A. B. Parsons, *The Porphyry Coppers.* New York: American Institute of Mining and Metallurgical Engineers, 1933. pp. 70–76.

22. Bailey, *Old Reliable,* p. 47.

23. *Mining and Scientific Press,* April 2, 1904.

24. Arrington and Hansen, *The Richest Hole on Earth,* pp. 52–53.

25. Penrose House, Helen Geiger Collection, Penrose Correspondence—Transfer File 38–69, File 5, letter from Penrose to T. A. Rickard, September 3, 1918.

26. Tutt Family Collection, letter from Charles L. Tutt Sr. to Spencer Penrose, August 30, 1904, p. 3.

27. Ibid., letters from Spencer Penrose to Charles L. Tutt Sr., July 30 and August 16, 1904,

28. El Pomar Office, Charles L. Tutt Jr. Collection, File 198, final report of will, March 7, 1910.

29. Penrose House, Spencer Penrose Collection, Box 49, File 214, letter from Charles L. Tutt Jr. to Spencer Penrose, May 27, 1914.

30. Ibid., Helen Geiger Collection, File 7, letter from Spencer Penrose to Boise Penrose, May 12, 1918.

31. Josephine Tutt remained on Coronado Island, where she built a large house.

32. Bailey, *Old Reliable,* pp. 101–109.

33. Ibid., p. 108.

34. *Mining and Scientific Press,* June 18, 1904, p. 420.

35. "Dire Exploration of Copper Trust's Slaves United 24 Nationalities in Bond of Solidarity," *New York Call,* October 6, 1912. Quoted in Ronald C. Brown, *Hard-Rock Miners: The Intermountain West, 1860–1920.* College Station: Texas A&M University Press, 1979, p. 24.

36. Bailey, *Old Reliable,* pp. 98, 101–105, 154.

37. Parsons, *The Porphyry Coppers,* pp. 191, 192.

38. Webster B. Smith, *The World's Greatest Copper Mines.* London: Copper Development Association, 1967, p. 93.

39. Parsons, *The Porphyry Coppers,* p. 198.

40. Ibid., p. 200.

41. Frank J. Tuck, *Stories of Arizona Copper Mines.* Phoenix: Arizona Department of Mineral Resources, 1957, p. 3.

42. Parsons, *The Porphyry Coppers,* pp. 120, 130, 132.

43. Penrose House, Spencer Penrose Collection, Box 11, File 27.

44. Ibid., letters from Spencer Penrose to E. T. Stannard, Kennecott president, March 23 and March 25, 1938.

45. *Engineering and Mining Journal,* Vol. 122, No. 19, November 6, 1926, p. 748.

46. "Lengthening of Jackling Yacht—Feat Ship Cut in Two; Middle Section Inserted," *Salt Lake City Herald-Republican,* July 5, 1914.

47. Millie Robbins, "The Fabulous Life of Daniel Jackling," *San Francisco Chronicle,* February 25, 1959, p. 12.

48. Penrose House, Spencer Penrose Collection, Box 11, File 27, letters from Daniel Jackling to Spencer Penrose, May 2, 1926; December 31, 1924; May 5, 1932; July 9, 1937.

49. Brian Levine, *Cripple Creek Gold—A Centennial History of the Cripple Creek District.* Lake Grove, Ore.: Depot, 1988, p. 34.

50. Penrose House, Spencer Penrose Collection, Box 83, File 352, letter from Victor C. Alderson to Spencer Penrose, September 17, 1918.

William Jackson Palmer was born into a Quaker family on September 17, 1836, and grew up in Philadelphia. He traveled to Europe as a youth, inspecting railroads in France, England, and Wales. Until the Civil War began in 1861, he was the private secretary to J. Edgar Thomson, president of the Pennsylvania Railroad. Palmer joined as a cavalry captain and rose to the rank of brigadier general. He received the Medal of Honor for distinguished military service after surviving a Confederate prisoner-of-war camp. Courtesy Jackson Thode Collection.

5

Colorado Springs

FLUSH WITH UTAH COPPER PROFITS, Spencer Penrose turned his ambition and resources toward transforming Colorado Springs into the Rockies' premier tourist resort. As Penrose noted, General Palmer had founded Colorado Springs as a tourist colony for Britons, affluent eastern investors, and health seekers.

By 1910, however, improved curative measures had led to a decline in the city's tuberculosis treatment industry. Cripple Creek's steady downslide punctured the local economy, as Colorado Springs relied heavily on its role as a mining supply center and its Colorado City neighborhood as an ore-processing hub. Penrose envisioned himself enticing a new class of visitors by developing and marketing the region's many scenic attractions. Once again, he brought new energy and resources to revive a secondhand dream.

His vision for Colorado Springs followed the example of the man who founded the city. Gen. William Jackson Palmer formed the Colorado Springs Town Company and built the Denver & Rio Grande (D&RG) into the Rocky Mountain West's most extensive spiderweb of steel. Like Penrose, Palmer came west from Philadelphia. Born in Delaware in 1836, he grew up in Philadelphia's Germantown neighborhood. During the 1850s Palmer learned the railroad business as secretary to the president of the Pennsylvania Railroad. By touring England, Palmer learned not only industrial technologies, such as narrow-gauge railroading, but also how to promote tourism and cultivate British investors. His dream of building a railroad out west was temporarily sidetracked by the Civil War. Despite his Quaker upbringing, he enlisted in the Union Army. Promoted to general for his heroism, he led 1,200 men of the 15th Pennsylvania Volunteer Cavalry.

A photographer recorded the 1871 platting of Colorado Springs on 10,000 acres of raw prairie surrounding the junction of Monument and Fountain Creeks. Gen. William J. Palmer's town was born as an unpromising collection of shacks under the afternoon shadow of Pikes Peak. Courtesy Special Collections, Tutt Library, Colorado College.

After the war ended in 1865, Palmer went west to build the Kansas Pacific Railroad and stayed to found the Denver & Rio Grande Railroad in 1870. He established Colorado Springs in 1871 as the first major stop on his railroad line. Backed by eastern and English investors, he bought the 10,000-acre town site wrapped around the confluence of Monument and Fountain Creeks.[1] Palmer's Colorado Springs Town Company platted a temperance colony featuring attractive homes, tree-lined streets and parks, and refined residents. Palmer's bride, Queen Mellen Palmer, started the first school and sang operettas for small gatherings at her home.

The general bolstered the city's reputation as a resort by building his posh Antlers Hotel in 1883. He took on two English partners, Drs. William Bell and Samuel Solly, who helped him design the five-story brick-and-shingle building in exuberant Queen Anne style, resplendent with towers, turrets, and bay windows.[2] They named the 75-room hotel

Mary Lincoln "Queen" Mellen posed for this mirror photo at age 20 when she married 34-year-old William J. Palmer, a business associate of her father. To coax his bride away from her family home in New York, Palmer laid out parks, parkways, and 5,000 cottonwoods and built a castlelike home, Glen Eyrie, in beautiful, wooded Queen's Canyon. Palmer hoped his wife would fall in love with the place, but she found his dream city dreary. She went back east to have their child and rarely returned. Courtesy Jackson C. Thode Collection.

Gen. W. J. Palmer used his Civil War experience and manpower to survey and build the Kansas Pacific from Kansas City to Denver. Whereas most rail lines were built east to west, Palmer envisioned a rail line running north to south along the Rocky Mountain Front Range, from Denver to the Rio Grande and the Mexican border. Without a land grant or any federal subsidy, he financed his railroad by town building along the line. Of dozens of towns fathered by Palmer and his railroad, his favorite lay at the eastern base of Pikes Peak. Courtesy Special Collections, Tutt Library, Colorado College.

As this 1876 photograph shows, General Palmer laid out Colorado Springs in a grid, with main streets an ambitious 140 feet wide. In an unusually public-spirited town plan, the Colorado Springs Company set aside two-thirds of the income from land sales for construction of roads, parks, schools, irrigation ditches, trees, and other public improvements. Courtesy Denver Public Library, Western History Department.

for Bell's trophy collection of antelope, deer, and elk heads, prominently displayed in the lobby. Visitors drank in the grandeur of Pikes Peak from the west terrace. Other amenities included a barbershop, Turkish spa, children's playroom, gaslights, and four-room bridal suite.[3] Palmer advertised the Antlers as one of the finest hotels in the country, conveniently located next to the D&RG depot. This trackside site led to a fire that consumed the Antlers in 1898. A cigar-smoking hobo supposedly sparked a blaze that exploded a boxcar of blasting powder and burned down the grand hotel.

The rebuilt Antlers Hotel opened in 1901, an Italian Renaissance masterpiece designed by Denver architects Ernest Phillip Varian and Frederick J. Sterner. The 230-room resort, gray brick under a tile roof, cost $600,000. Wrought-iron balconies, a broad central staircase of Italian marble, and a spacious grand ballroom graced this hostelry, touted as the "best hotel in the west." The Antlers became the hub of Colorado Springs society. Leading socialites such as Mrs. Joel A. Hayes and mining tycoon Verner Z. Reed entertained extravagantly. Charles MacNeill rented a year-round suite. Spencer Penrose patronized the Antlers until he was thrown out for riding his horse up the front steps and into the bar.[4]

Colorado Springs' majestic beauty and dry, sunny climate attracted health seekers as well as tourists. By 1900 nearly half of the city's residents were either tubercular invalids or companions of loved ones seeking the Colorado cure. Affluent invalids stayed at the Antlers Hotel, spas in Manitou Springs,

Helen Hunt Jackson, one of America's foremost woman writers, used this drawing of Colorado Springs for her book *Bits of Travel at Home.* Of her 1873 arrival in the town she later came to love, she wrote: "I had crossed the continent, ill, disheartened to find a climate which would not kill. There stretched before me, to the east, a bleak, bare, unrelieved desolate plain. There rose behind me, to the west, a dark range of mountains, snow-topped, rocky-walled, stern, cruel, relentless. Between lay the town—small, straight, new, treeless." Courtesy Denver Public Library, Western History Department.

COLORADO SPRINGS.

The Denver & Rio Grande Depot, a stylish Queen Anne landmark, survives to this day in downtown Colorado Springs. The historic meeting of Charles Leaming Tutt Sr. and Spencer Penrose took place here in 1892. Courtesy Penrose Public Library.

The key to capturing tourists and investors in new western towns was a grand hotel. Colorado Springs awarded its prime location—at the west end of Pikes Peak Avenue—to the Antlers, built by General Palmer in 1883 and rebuilt extravagantly after an 1898 fire. The hotel's twin towers framed Pikes Peak in an unforgettable image of western hospitality. Courtesy Penrose Public Library.

or Cragmor Sanatorium. Working-class patients lodged at boardinghouses built along Pikes Peak, Kiowa, and Nevada Avenues. Other members of the "one-lunged army" resided at more than thirty Colorado Springs sanatoriums, including the Woodmen of America, Sunnyrest, Glockner, and Union Printers' Home.

Palmer shaped Colorado Springs in many ways. He built a business empire using iron-fisted control over his D&RG railroad and the towns that sprang up along its tracks. Palmer's Tudor-style home at Glen Eyrie became a retreat for the city's social and cultural elite. The general also turned to philanthropy. Determined to make Colorado Springs the most beautiful and refined city in Colorado, he donated more than $500,000 to Colorado College, including its first structure, Palmer Hall, now Cutler Hall. He gave another $100,000 for the college's Palmer Science Building in 1901.[5] The general founded Antlers Park, 753-acre Palmer Park (now Austin Bluffs), and 2-mile-long Monument Park. He gave land to the Colorado Springs Public Library, Cragmor Sanatorium, and Colorado School for the Deaf and Blind. Palmer and his business partner Dr. William Bell also donated 10,000 acres north of Woodland Park as a forestry laboratory for Colorado College.[6]

The city had other benefactors. James J. Hagerman, founding president of the Colorado Midland Railroad and owner of Aspen and Leadville silver mines, built the Colorado Springs Opera House, modeled after Madison Square Theater in New York City.[7] Hagerman also served as a Colorado College trustee and funded two campus buildings.[8] Dr. William Bell, Henry McAllister, and William S. Jackson all helped found Colorado College and gave generously to its construction. Winfield Scott Stratton spent his Cripple Creek millions developing the city's streetcar line, building the elegant five-story Mining Exchange Building, and buying land for the new county courthouse and downtown post office. Funds from Stratton's $6.3 million estate built and operated the Myron Stratton Home for the Infirm and Elderly after the mining millionaire died in 1902.[9]

Palmer remained the city's greatest booster. After he died on March 13, 1909, Colorado Springs memorialized the general with a bronze statue on Platte Avenue showing him astride his beloved black horse, Señor. Palmer's passing left a void Spencer Penrose strove to fill. Penrose's itch to improve Colorado Springs grew from his desire to outshine Palmer.

Speck's newfound interest in philanthropy may also be attributed to his marriage in 1906. Julie Villiers Lewis McMillan was a petite, blonde beauty from a prominent Detroit family. She was born in 1870, the great-granddaughter of Frenchman Louis Villiers, who arrived near the Great Lakes region in 1708. Her father, Alexander Lewis, was an influential businessman and mayor of Detroit from 1876 until 1877. Born in Ontario and privately educated, he arrived in Detroit at age 15. One of the first to see the great possibilities of the Beautiful City at the Straits, in 1862 Lewis became a founder and original president of the Detroit Board of Trade. He served as a commission merchant in flour and grains and a director of the Detroit National Bank and Detroit Fire and Marine Insurance Company. Lewis owned real estate on Woodward Avenue, a factory, and a wharf. He ran for mayor as the reform candidate of the Law and Order Party during a fierce antisaloon campaign to close taverns on Sundays

Colorado Springs outclassed other Rocky Mountain cities with its first-rate liberal arts school, the Colorado College. Founded in 1874, the college occupied Palmer Hall for its first two decades. Courtesy Colorado Springs Pioneer Museum.

and election days. Mayor Lewis served only one term and declined a second nomination.

Lewis married Elizabeth Ingersoll, a devout Episcopalian who had moved with her family from Medina, New York, to Detroit at age eight. Lewis, the "First Gentleman of Detroit," was known for his courtly manners, public spirit, and municipal responsibilities. He served as police commissioner and helped found both the Detroit Public Library and Detroit Museum of Art. Julie's father was particular about his personal appearance, dressing in immaculate frock coat and hat. He never smoked or drank alcohol, not even as medicine. His only vices were passions for whist and for horses. His idea of supreme happiness was driving a fleet black horse, Beauty, up and down Lafayette Avenue with one of his daughters in the sleigh beside him. The Lewis sisters were the belles of Detroit society, and Julie was regarded as the loveliest of the four.[10]

Like Spencer Penrose, Julie enjoyed the finer things in life—art, music, gourmet cuisine, and international travel. She acquired her zest for life and love of luxury at an early age. She grew up in a household overflowing

Daring to be different, Colorado College welcomed young women from the beginning. Here, the Plantagenet Society of Young Ladies drills in front of Palmer (Cutler) Hall in 1892. Their crossed brooms were a symbol of women's empowerment. Courtesy Special Collections, Tutt Library, Colorado College.

Gen. W. J. Palmer blessed Colorado Springs with a 2,000-acre system of parks, including the 735-acre Palmer Park, the 2-mile-long Monument Valley Park, Antlers Park, and the smaller Alamo and Acacia Parks downtown. Palmer gave more than $4 million to the betterment of Colorado Springs, where his bronze equestrian statue was installed in 1929 at the downtown intersection of Nevada and East Platte Avenues. Courtesy Denver Public Library, Western History Department.

The Mining Exchange Building, erected by Cripple Creek millionaire Winfield Scott Stratton, sits at the southwest corner of Pikes Peak and Nevada Avenues. This imposing neoclassical edifice epitomized the rise of Colorado Springs as the major beneficiary of the Cripple Creek gold rush. Soon after its 1901 completion, Penrose and Tutt moved their offices into the building. Courtesy Penrose Public Library.

Lovely, cultivated, and wealthy, Julie Villiers Lewis McMillan had suffered a triple tragedy in 1902 when this portrait was made. Her unusual melancholia reflects the death of her son, James McMillan Jr., that April from appendicitis. A month later tuberculosis killed her husband, and that August her father-in-law died. Four years later she met Spencer Penrose at the Cheyenne Mountain Country Club and set her steady blue gaze on the most eligible bachelor in town.

with French culture, style, and language and a bevy of brothers and sisters. The Lewises were a large and happy family, with a big home at 456 Jefferson, Detroit's most fashionable avenue. They also maintained a summer residence at Grosse Pointe Farms.

Of the large Lewis clan, eight of thirteen survived to adulthood: Ida Frances Lewis, Edgar Louis Lewis, Josephine "Josie" Lewis Carpenter, Harriet "Hattie" Ingersoll Lewis Cameron, Henry Bridge Lewis, Julie Villiers Lewis McMillan Penrose, Marian Lewis Muir, and Ingersoll "Inky" Lewis. As in the Tutt and Penrose families, middle names honored family antecedents. Julie's middle name honored her great-grandfather Villiers, who had been educated in France for the priesthood before seeking his fortune in the wilds of Canada. Villiers himself was nicknamed "St. Louis" because of his great piety. Julie proudly used her middle and maiden names all her life. Her sisters' husbands figured prominently in Julie and Spencer's life. They invested in Penrose businesses and visited Colorado Springs often. Clarence and Josephine Carpenter moved to the city shortly after Julie did, living there the rest of their lives. They now rest at Evergreen Cemetery.

A gregarious social butterfly, Julie captivated Old Detroit society. After a year at a Boston finishing school, Julie made her first grand tour of Europe at age 17. When she returned home she captured Detroit's most eligible bachelor, James Howard McMillan, marrying into a family of wealth, influence, and culture. Jim and Julie had grown up together in the Jefferson Avenue neighborhood. Jim's father, U.S. Senator James McMillan, was the state's most powerful figure.

The millionaire statesman owned the Michigan Car Company, one of the nation's largest makers of railroad cars. McMillan also owned dozens of other railroad, shipping, and industrial businesses. Among them were the Detroit and Cleveland Navigation Company, whose cruise ships sailed the Great Lakes, and a Michigan sugar beet company. He spearheaded development of Belle Isle Park as a pastoral setting for boating, yachting, picnicking, ice skating in winter, and an amusement park. His interest in landscape design gained him leadership of the U.S. congressional committee that implemented Pierre L'Enfant's design for the Capitol Mall. The McMillan Plan is regarded today as one of the country's first comprehensive city plans.[11] The senator also helped plan Detroit's Grace Hospital and the McMillan Building and Shakespeare Library at the University of Michigan in Ann Arbor.

Jim McMillan was the senator's second son, born September 17, 1866. He graduated from Yale in 1888 with a law degree and a fierce reputation on the football field. Afterward he toured Europe. Jim's uncles, Hugh and William, and older brother William preceded him in the family businesses. Jim was delegated miscellaneous business tasks, directorship of the Peninsular Land Company in northern Michigan, and tending to the family yacht, the *Idler*. He married Julie on June 18, 1890, at Christ Episcopal Church in Detroit. The prim-looking, bespectacled young man had quite a match in vivacious Julie. They left on their honeymoon in a private railroad car; Jim later complained to his father that he would have preferred taking the yacht.

The young McMillans moved into a home down the street from their parents. Their two children, Gladys and James II, known as "Jimmie," were born in 1892 and 1894, respectively. Jim enlisted in the Spanish-American War and went to Cuba in 1898. There, as a quartermaster, he set up a camp for yellow fever victims. He contracted malaria, which developed into pulmonary tuberculosis. He returned from his military duty an invalid and in 1900 moved with his wife and children to Colorado Springs to try to regain his health.

Jim and Julie bought an elegant home at 30 West Dale Street, but the Colorado cure failed James McMillan. After his son, Jimmie, had died from appendicitis on April 3, 1902, Jim grew worse. He died on May 9, 1902. Julie returned to Detroit in a rented Pullman coach with two coffins, escorted by grieving relatives.[12] After the funerals, she could no longer bear to remain in Detroit with its many memories. She returned to her new home on West Dale Street. Her childhood friend, Edith Stanton Field, also widowed, became her companion.

After several years, Julie wearied of mourning. She cast her sights on Colorado Springs' most eligible bachelor—tall, handsome, and wealthy Spencer Penrose. Legend has it that she first met the standoffish Philadelphian at a Cheyenne Country Club clambake, where his mining millions had set everyone whispering. She invited him to dinner at her home, and soon Penrose was escorting her to Colorado Springs social affairs. Penrose resisted her feminine advances, planning to remain a lifelong bachelor like his brothers Richard and Boies. But Julie persisted. She sent her butler over with sumptuous dishes and her maid to tidy up his room. After two years Julie escalated their courtship on a transatlantic crossing.[13]

Julie and her friend Edith were en route to Europe to enroll Julie's 14-year-old daughter, Gladys, in a private school in Brussels. Penrose had planned a tour of Europe with his brother Richard. Spencer and Julie met aboard the ship as it steamed away from the dock in New York City. Was it fate or Julie's persistence that threw them together? The answer is uncertain, but Julie determined that she would return from Europe as Spencer's bride.

Penrose gallantly offered to drive Julie and Edith through the south of France in his touring car. Chaperoned by Edith, the couple checked into a Nice hotel, and Julie waited for Spencer to pop the question. Smitten, Spencer asked his brother to seek their father's approval of the match. Richard wrote their father:

[She is] a very good looking and very agreeable woman of about thirty-five years old, a blond of medium size. . . . She has one child, a girl of 14 years old. She comes originally from Detroit, Michigan, and Speck says that she is of one of the best families there. He says he has known her well for several years. Speck seems very much devoted to her and she equally so to him. . . . Speck is peculiarly situated. He can't read much on account of his eye and . . . is not interested in any particular subject that would lead him to seek amusement from literary or scientific sources. He is, therefore, peculiarly dependent on social intercourse. As he himself said to me the other day, he "cannot sit down at eight o'clock in the evening and read until bedtime," nor can he go on forever drinking rum at clubs. Therefore he seems to think his only refuge is to get married. . . . I cannot help feeling that Speck would be very much better off if happily married than in his present condition.[14]

Doctor Penrose granted his approval. Spencer bashfully proposed by dropping a note in Julie's lap as she lounged on the beach on the French Riviera.[15] Spencer and Julie were married in London on April 28, 1906. According to Spencer's grandniece, some members of his family were displeased that he had married a Catholic, even worse, a French Canadian from Detroit.[16] The newlyweds drove through Spain and France in Spencer's touring car, enjoying the best restaurants and finest hotels. "Speck and his wife are here and seem to be very happy," Richard reported to Doctor Penrose. "They are staying at the Hotel Princess, where they have very good apartments. . . . They are starting today on a several weeks' trip to Tours and Vichy, in France, in their automobile. They asked me to go with them, but I thought that perhaps people on a honeymoon were more happy alone, so I am not going."[17] Their continental vacation set the pace for their marriage—Spencer and Julie would return again and again to Europe.

Marriage to Julie made the playboy Penrose a new and better man. By this time his copper investments had made him a millionaire. He was ready to savor life's comforts and pleasures—traveling extensively, shopping for artwork and antiques, entertaining in the lovely home on West Dale. Marriage to Julie also helped Speck view himself in a new light—as a sophisticated, cultured, convivial host. As they savored Europe's best hotels, Penrose began envisioning an elegant inn of his own. His global wanderings through scenic resort towns convinced him that Colorado Springs could be transformed into a world-class tourist spa. This dream of building a magnificent inn attracted Spencer to the scenic Broadmoor area in the foothills southwest of Colorado Springs. There he would build his hotel.

The Penroses bought a rambling residence behind the Broadmoor Hotel in 1916, the El Pomar estate at 1661 Mesa Avenue. Grace Goodyear Depew had built the "Spanish villa" after divorcing her first husband and moving to Colorado Springs from Buffalo, New York, in 1910. To design

El Pomar, a Spanish Mission Revival–style villa snuggled in the hills behind the Broadmoor Hotel, took its name from an apple orchard once on the site. Grace Goodyear Depew built the lovely home in 1909 and sold the estate to Spencer and Julie Penrose for $75,000. The Penroses had the Olmsted Brothers of Brookline, Massachusetts, expand and enhance the surrounding 18-acre gardens, which in 1920 still framed a view of the Broadmoor Hotel on the eastern horizon.

her $200,000 house, Grace hired prominent Philadelphia architect Horace Trumbauer, who had designed palatial mansions in Philadelphia and New-port, Rhode Island, the Philadelphia Ritz-Carlton Hotel, and Philadelphia's Free Library. The rambling, one-story, U-shaped villa featured a Spanish-style courtyard that faced south to capture a sunny exposure and majestic views. El Pomar's white stuccoed walls and red-tiled roof gave the estate a Medi-terranean flair, and the surrounding apple trees gave the place its name, the Spanish word for orchard.

Grace had moved into El Pomar with her second husband, Ashton Potter. She and Ashton plunged into Colorado Springs society. Ashton played polo and poker at the Cheyenne Mountain Country Club and joined Penrose's culinary clan, the Cooking Club. The Potters became close friends of Spencer and Julie's, and the two couples toured the Orient together. The Potters' marital bliss was short-lived, however, and Ashton moved into the chauffeur's cottage. Ashton died in the summer of 1913, Grace a year later.[18] When the Potters' beautiful estate went up for sale, Spencer and Julie bought it.

The Penroses paid $75,000 for El Pomar. This bargain price included a wine cellar replete with 400 bottles of fine liquor, including 100 quarts of Pol Roger, 14 quarts of 1875 Apple Jack, and 18 quarts of absinthe.[19] The Penroses hired Westing, Evans, and Egmore of Philadelphia to refurbish the interior. Belgian black and Vermont Corona marble tiles were laid in the main hall to match the dining room floor. Carpenters installed wooden mantels, cornices, paneling, and moldings shipped from Philadelphia by rail. Acanthus-topped pilasters, Italian carved marble mantelpieces, and crystal chandeliers added elegance. Spencer hired a local craftsman to out-fit the library in ornately carved woodwork: built-in shelving, rich panel-ing, and a fireplace featuring bare-busted maidens. Two library bookcases hid a secret passageway to the wine cellar. Julie ordered a giant Aeolian pipe organ for the main hall and hired local designer Grace Johnson to reupholster furniture and hang new draperies. Julie and Spencer finally had a place to display the hundreds of antiques and pieces of art gathered on their trips abroad.[20] To house their growing collection, they later added a second and third story to the west wing.

To design the grounds, the Penroses hired America's most prominent landscape architecture firm, the Olmsted Brothers. Founder Frederick Law Olmsted Sr. had designed many notable parks and gardens: New York City's Central Park with Calvert Vaux; Prospect Park in Brooklyn, New York; the Mount Royal Park in Montreal; the grounds for the 1893 World's Columbian Exposition in Chicago; and Golden Gate Park in San Fran-cisco. After his death in 1903 the firm became the Olmsted Brothers of Brookline, Massachusetts, directed by his son, Frederick Law Olmsted Jr., and his stepson, John. The firm adorned El Pomar's courtyard with a central fountain and terraced gardens leading up to the bathhouse-pavil-

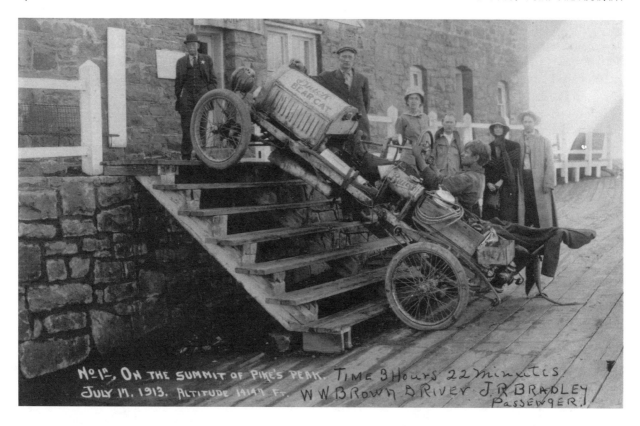

No 15. On the summit of Pike's Peak. Time 3 Hours 22 minutes. July 14. 1913. Altitude 14141 F. W.W. Brown Driver J. R. Bradley Passenger.

After hard hikes and bottom-busting mule rides to the summit of Pikes Peak, many a tourist dreamed of a faster and more comfortable conveyance. After W.W.B. Brown drove his Buick Bearcat up the wagon road to the top of Pikes Peak in 1913, millions of motorists ultimately followed suit. Courtesy Colorado Springs Pioneer Museum.

ion. Under the Olmsted Brothers' supervision, Penrose gardener A. F. Hoffman installed floral terraces, cultivated lawns, and additional apple trees.

While basking in these luxurious surroundings, Penrose was also nourishing several new businesses. He was branching into the auto tourism business to capitalize on Americans' love affair with motorcars. Penrose created the Pikes Peak Automobile Company in 1912 with a fleet of twenty Pierce Arrows to whisk rubberneckers on a dozen different tours of the area's scenic landmarks. Local auto touring companies did a brisk business, with tour operators mobbing passengers disembarking at the train station. Colorado Springs was promoting itself as "the City of Sunshine, the Finest All-Year Playground, Health Resort and Residence City in the Land, the Scenic Roof Garden of the World, and the Motorist's Mecca— at the Junction of the Pikes Peak Ocean-to-Ocean and the Colorado to Gulf Highways."[21] As roads and highways beribboned the state, Penrose envisioned building a highway to the top of Pikes Peak. This vision was jump-started on July 18, 1913, when W. W. Brown and J. S. Bradley drove their Buick Bearcat to the summit, bouncing along the old 1880s wagon road.[22]

Penrose proposed building a paved toll road to speed visitors up the peak for $2.50 per passenger. He calculated that he could make $37,000

Penrose's Pikes Peak Auto Highway Company operated under a lease agreement with the National Forest Service. "Using White buses, which carried 12 to 14 persons, and Pierce Arrow convertibles, it operated quite profitably," William Thayer Tutt recalled, "until the government took the highway back because there was a fight between Mr. Roosevelt, Mr. Penrose, and my father. The Forest Service took the highway over but could not run it very well. During World War II, it was closed for a time. Then we worked out a deal for the City of Colorado Springs to assume the operation of the highway." The City of Colorado Springs reinstated the toll for summer motorists tackling the 14,110-foot peak with a 7,000-foot vertical rise and grades as steep as 11 percent. Drivers often experience broken radiators, burning brakes, or blown engines that give fresh meaning to the old slogan "Pikes Peak or Bust!"

its first year.[23] Pikes Peak had been irresistible to visitors for decades. Its fame was furthered by "America the Beautiful," penned in 1893 by Katherine Lee Bates, a Wellesley College English teacher summering at Colorado College.[24] Visitors could ascend the peak by the Manitou and Pikes Peak Railway, a cog line built by Jerome Wheeler, David Moffat, Major John Hulburt, and mattress tycoon Zalmon Simmons in 1891. Hardier tourists rented burros in Manitou Springs or hiked to the summit on foot. Spencer wanted to offer Pikes Peakers yet another alternative.

He leased the wagon road from the U.S. Department of Agriculture and incorporated his Pikes Peak Auto Highway Company. Then he sold stock to his friends. Penrose, Bert Carlton, and W. A. Otis each bought $20,500 worth of stock; Charles MacNeill invested $10,500; and Eugene Shove $5,000.[25] Construction began in the summer of 1915, and the road opened on August 1, 1916. Its $283,000 cost far exceeded original estimates, but that failed to dampen Penrose's enthusiasm.[26]

As with many of Spencer's endeavors, the Pikes Peak Highway combined pleasure with profit. It was inspired by his infatuation with the automobile. He had purchased four bright yellow Lozier cars for $5,000 apiece and usually took his favorite with him when crossing the Atlantic. He belonged to numerous automobile clubs and sat on the Colorado Good Roads Commission. He also frequented Detroit, the nation's emerging auto capital, where his interest was piqued by conversations with Julie's family.

Penrose opened the "World's Highest Highway" with the Pikes Peak Hill Climb, which inspired syndicated articles on the front pages of

650 newspapers coast to coast. A "noted Colorado Springs sportsman," readers learned, was offering the "richest trophy ever offered for an automobile contest." The Penrose Trophy was custom-made by Philadelphia silversmiths Bailey, Banks, and Biddle.[27] Eastern readers encountered the purple prose of Penrose's publicists: "The Great Spirit, which, according to Indian legend, hovers over the snow-capped summit of Pikes Peak, probably will gasp with wonder in August of this year when hill climbing will be revived as a major automobile sport on the scenic motor highway which leads to the top of the highest pinnacle of the Rocky Mountains."[28]

"The Race to the Clouds" became an annual event and an advertising vehicle for both the highway and the Broadmoor Hotel. Penrose invited politicians, business associates, investors, directors of railroads, owners of mining companies, and his relatives to become *Commissaires Sportifs*. He sent invitations to friends, relatives, neighbors, and some employees. He mailed out hundreds of free passes, encouraging recipients to rent rooms at the Broadmoor.[29] He scheduled important conventions or conferences to coincide with the Pikes Peak Hill Climb after the hotel opened in 1918. Penrose staged a Liberty Bond stunt that sent a World War I tank crawling up the peak in 1918. He published photos across the nation of child actress Shirley Temple throwing midsummer snowballs atop the peak.[30] Speck planned to install a giant searchlight on the summit. He changed his mind after receiving a letter from Frederick Bonfils, *Denver Post* publisher, who advised: "Under no consideration should you place, at your own expense, that great light at the top of Pikes Peak. Colorado Springs and Manitou would derive infinitely more from it than you and they should place that light there and pay for it. It should be a great beacon to attract tourists, and especially automobile tourists, to your city but that would not help Spencer Penrose nor his exquisite Broadmoor Hotel."[31]

The Pikes Peak Highway became the centerpiece of Spencer's "scenic companies." In 1915 he bought the Manitou Incline Railway. He paid $65,000 for the 2,500-foot-long funicular, built in 1907 to haul pipe to the water plant on Mount Manitou. Converted for passenger use, it was one of many funiculars in Colorado in the early 1900s. Others were the Manitou Springs Red Mountain Incline, Golden's Castle Rock Mountain Railway, the Lookout Mountain Scenic Railway, and the Mount Morrison funicular near Red Rocks Park. By the 1920s auto tourism had put most of these funiculars out of business.

The Pikes Peak Highway, meanwhile, competed fiercely for visitors with the Manitou and Pikes Peak Railway. The cog railway put up a fence atop the peak to keep motorists from its site on the eastern side of the summit, which offered a spectacular view of Colorado Springs. Penrose offered to buy out the faltering Cog Wheel Route. He paid a paltry $50,000 for the line after his cutthroat business tactics nearly drove it out of busi-

Spencer Penrose, one of Colorado's most avid motorists, built an auto road up Pikes Peak to test-drive his new automobiles. Constructing this 20-mile road turned into a $283,000 project, but Penrose never flinched. This fabulous Penrose Trophy and auto racing's richest prize lured daring drivers to the first Pikes Peak Hill Climb in 1916.

The Manitou & Pikes Peak Railway was built in 1891 by mattress maker Zalmon "Beautyrest" Simmons, with the help of mules. By the 1920s Simmons was losing money and blamed it on Penrose's auto highway. Penrose bought the cog railway in 1925 for a reputed $50,000 and spent another $500,000 making the cog road a thing of beauty, precision, and predictability. In 1937 he experimented unsuccessfully with winter runs, hoping to turn Pikes Peak into a giant ski area. Since then, the railway has opened as soon as the track can be plowed out in the spring (usually in April) and closes when the snow gets too deep (usually around Halloween). Courtesy c. 1900 photo by J. G. Hiestand, Penrose Public Library; burros from Colorado Springs Pioneer Museum.

ness. Then he spent half a million dollars to rejuvenate the line, bringing in superb Swiss equipment and even Swiss engineers to make it run like clockwork.

Spencer Penrose and others realized that Pikes Peak was Colorado Springs' signature landmark. Its magnificent natural setting fostered the tourism promoted by both Palmer and Penrose. Then and now, the peak elevates local residents. The magical mountain, for all its moods and weather changes, is a steady, inspiring presence visible from anywhere in the city. The landmark provided the ultimate backdrop for Penrose's next project—building a world-class resort hotel.

The Manitou & Pikes Peak Railway still departs from its beautifully preserved original sandstone and shingle depot in the resort town of Manitou Springs. Russell and Thayer Tutt, who supervised the cog route after Penrose's death in 1939, kept the exquisite depot but replaced the old steam equipment with sleek, 52-foot-long diesel cars made by the Swiss Locomotive and Machine Works. The highest scenic mountain railway in the world climbs 8.9 miles on grades as steep as 24.4 percent to the top of 14,110-foot Pikes Peak. Courtesy 1963 photo by Bob McIntyre.

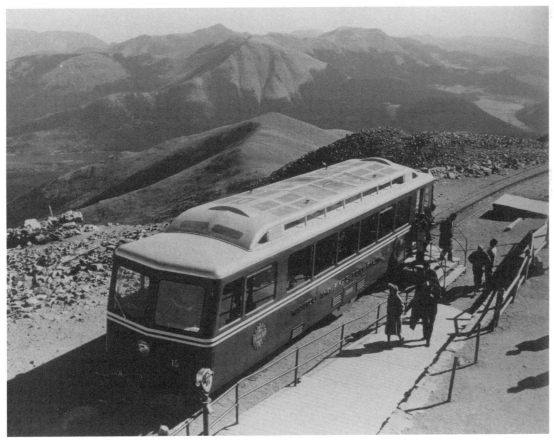

NOTES

1. John S. Fisher, *Builder of the West.* Caldwell, Idaho: Caxton, 1939, p. 181.

2. Dr. William Bell also planned the city of Manitou Springs and for several years was one of its leading citizens.

3. Leland Feitz, *The Antlers Hotel.* Denver: Golden Bell, 1972; and Lester Williams, "The Antlers Conflagration of 1898," in *The Denver Westerners Brand Book,* 1956, pp. 35–36.

4. Lucius Beebe, *The Big Spenders.* Garden City, N.Y.: Doubleday, 1966.

5. J. Juan Reid, *Colorado College: The First Century 1874–1974.* Colorado Springs: Colorado College, 1979.

6. Fisher, *Builder of the West,* pp. 305–306.

7. Henry L. Carter, ed., *The Pikes Peak Region: A Sesquicentennial History.* Colorado Springs: Historical Society of the Pikes Peak Region, 1956, p 18.

8. John J. Lipsey, *The Lives of James John Hagerman.* Denver: Golden Bell, 1968, p. 246.

9. Frank Waters, *Midas of the Rockies.* Denver: Sage, 1949 [1937], pp. 238–239, 271, 283.

10. Jay F. Hunter, *The Genealogy of Marie Muir Lewis and William Howe Muir of Detroit, Michigan.* Detroit: Muir Family, 1991.

11. Jon A. Peterson, "The Nation's First Comprehensive City Plan—A Political Analysis of the McMillan Plan for Washington, D.C., 1900–1902," *American Planning Association Journal,* Spring 1985.

12. Ironically, Senator McMillan died that August; three generations of the McMillan family passed away within five months.

13. Marshall Sprague, *Newport in the Rockies: The Life and Good Times of Colorado Springs.* Chicago: Sage/Swallow, 1980, pp. 244–245.

14. Helen Fairbanks and Charles P. Berkey, *Life and Letters of R.A.F. Penrose, Jr.* New York: Geological Society of America, 1952, letter from R.A.F. Penrose Jr. to R.A.F. Penrose Sr. dated April 5, 1906, pp. 383–385.

15. Sprague, *Newport in the Rockies,* pp. 244–245.

16. Spencer's grandniece Frances Penrose Haythe insists that Spencer's family never approved of his marriage and that his brother Charles forbade Spencer to bring Julie into his house.

17. Fairbanks and Berkey, *Life and Letters of R.A.F. Penrose, Jr.,* letter from R.A.F. Penrose Jr. to R.A.F. Penrose Sr. dated June 4, 1906, pp. 412–413.

18. George F. Goodyear, *Goodyear Family History.* Buffalo, N.Y.: privately printed, 1976. Referenced in Nancy Lyons, *National Register Nomination for El Pomar Mansion.* Denver: Colorado Historical Society, Office of Archeology and Historic Preservation, 1994, Section 8, p. 7.

19. Penrose House, Spencer Penrose Collection, Box 65, File 293, March 1916 inventory.

20. Ibid., 1934 inventory of El Pomar.

21. Ibid., Box 71, File 301, Chamber of Commerce letterhead, 1916.

22. John Fetler, *The Pikes Peak People.* Caldwell, Idaho: Caxton, 1966, p. 247. W. B. Felker and C. A. Yont were the first to conquer the summit by auto in their Locomobile on August 12, 1901.

23. Penrose House, Spencer Penrose Collection, Box 61, File 278.

24. Fetler, *Pikes Peak People,* p. 231.

25. Penrose House, Spencer Penrose Collection, Box 61, File 278.

26. Ibid., letter from Spencer Penrose to R. R. Mullen, May 20, 1936.

27. "'Pike's Peak or Bust' Reward—Trophy of Gold and Silver, Said to Be the Richest Trophy Ever Offered for an Automobile Contest," *Boston Evening Transcript,* April 1, 1916.

28. J. C. Burton, "Autos to Climb Pike's Peak in $6,000 Contest; Four Events Listed for Meet," *Central Press Association,* March 24, 1916. Pikes Peak is not the highest pinnacle in the Rocky Mountains and not even the highest in Colorado.

29. Penrose House, Spencer Penrose Collection, Box 66, File 296.

30. W. J. McGlasson, "'Whippet' Tank Had More Luck With War Than Peak," *Colorado Springs Gazette-Telegraph,* April 25, 1976, pp. 1B, 6B.

31. Penrose House, Spencer Penrose Collection, Box 61, File 278, letter dated May 10, 1921.

The Colorado Springs Company wrote into its town deeds a clause prohibiting the manufacture or sale of liquor. The search for more respectable drinking establishments than this pioneer speakeasy inspired Count James Pourtales, and later Spencer Penrose, to establish the Broadmoor outside the city limits. Courtesy Tom Noel Collection.

6

The Broadmoor

WHILE PENROSE WAS BUSY building transportation systems for tourists, he was also planning a hotel to house them. Early in 1916 he announced plans for a world-famous resort at Broadmoor Lake. Having mastered the gold- and copper-mining industries, he aimed to become one of the country's premier hoteliers. His Broadmoor dream would attract national and international guests and help revive Colorado Springs' sagging economy. It would be his masterpiece, his crowning glory.

Penrose incorporated the Broadmoor Hotel and Land Company in May 1916 and sold stock to Charles MacNeill, Bert Carlton, Charles Tutt Jr., and other associates. Legends linger about what prompted Penrose to build the Broadmoor. Some people said Spencer built the hotel out of spite after the Antlers' management rebuked him for riding his horse into the bar. Others believed he and MacNeill built the hotel so they could hire their friend William Dunning, who had been fired as hotel manager at the Antlers. They said the little *A* in BROᴬDMOOR was intended to insult the Antlers. That styling also created a name that could be trademarked because "Broadmoor" had already been copyrighted.

Spencer's chief motivation may well have been pleasure. A connoisseur of the world's finest hotels, he wanted one of his own. He had tried to buy the Antlers Hotel when it went on the market as part of Palmer's estate. Early in 1916 Penrose offered $87,500 for the Antlers, a price suggested by Charles MacNeill. Palmer's executor, Dr. William Bell, rejected the price, explaining that it had cost $744,000 to build and furnish the Antlers. Bell counteroffered $200,000, but Penrose declined: "I beg to say my associates and myself did everything possible to acquire the Antlers Hotel, in order that Colorado Springs might have a first-class, up-to-date hotel in the future, but, as little attention was paid to our endeavors, we

Count James Pourtales, a wealthy German adventurer, opened the Broadmoor Resort in 1891 at what had been the Broadmoor Dairy Farm. Like a grandiose wedding cake, the count's neoclassical revival Broadmoor Casino sported gobs of architectural frosting. Inside, the count offered European cuisine, fine wines, and Sunday afternoon concerts. Colorado Springs blue noses blasted the Broadmoor as "a sunny place for shady people." Pourtales defended his Sunday "sacred music" concerts, pointing out that Christ himself changed water into wine. Courtesy 1893 photo of Pourtales, Colorado Historical Society; other photos from Colorado Springs Pioneer Museum.

have given up that entirely, and have now plans for building the best hotel in Colorado at Broadmoor."[1]

Like his El Pomar estate, the Broadmoor Hotel was a secondhand dream. Once again Penrose used his drive and his millions to enhance a project begun by someone else. Twenty-five years earlier, a Prussian nobleman named Count James Pourtales had first envisioned a resort hotel on the sunny, scenic farm where dairy cows grazed. Tourist possibilities quickened with construction of a toll road for sightseers wishing to view Cheyenne Canyon's waterfalls and strangely shaped rocks.[2] William J. Willcox's Broadmoor Dairy Farm and Dixon Fruit Farm enjoyed limited success. Willcox sold his farm to Count Pourtales, who thought the panoramic site had potential as a resort. The count formed the Cheyenne Lake, Land, and

Broadmoor Dairy

The Oldest Dairy in Colorado Springs ⁊ Established 1880

Baby cries for it,
Relatives sigh for it,
Old folks demand it,
All the wise ones get it,
Daddy pays for it,
Mother prays for it,
Others crave it,
Only a few don't get it.
Remember, it pays to buy

Phone
Main 155
P. O. Box
1418

ONE OF OUR "DAIRY MAIDS."

**Broadmoor Milk and Cream,
the Purest and the Best**

Improvement Company and dug a lake to reflect the crisp mountain vistas. He divided the land into large residential lots and helped organize the Cheyenne Mountain Country Club. Said to be the second country club in the nation when it opened July 4, 1891, the club offered polo, tennis, shooting, cricket, archery, bowling, and golf. Liquor became a chief

The count dammed Cheyenne Creek to create 10-acre Cheyenne Lake, the centerpiece of the 2,400-acre Broadmoor grounds. In this view from Point Sublime, the emerging oasis around the Broadmoor contrasts with the surrounding prairie. The count planted 10,000 trees and laid out "Broadmoor City," which remained only a dream. Pourtales lost the Broadmoor in the crash of 1893. Pourtales returned to his native Silesia (now Poland), a sadder, wiser, and poorer man. He had sunk $200,000 into the Broadmoor, which languished until Spencer Penrose acquired it in 1916 for $90,000. Pourtales, in his autobiography *Lessons Learned From Experience,* reflected that "Yankees are far too sharp" and Colorado too prone to "stormy conditions, bribery, delayed delivery, strikes, fire, and financial crises." Courtesy Denver Public Library, Western History Department; photo by Louis McClure.

attraction, as the club lay just outside the city limits of Colorado Springs, a dry town. The club gained immediate popularity as a watering hole and playground for the city's socialites but failed to stimulate land sales as the count had hoped.

So Count Pourtales built another attraction next to Cheyenne Lake—an elegant casino patterned after the Imperial Palace in Potsdam, Germany.[3]

The casino languished. When it burned in 1897, the count replaced it with a simpler version. That business failed, too. Disgusted, Pourtales invested instead in the Commonwealth Mine, an Arizona copper property coincidentally owned by Spencer's brother Richard. The count's abundant earnings from this venture enabled him to retire at Glumbowitz, his family estate in Prussia. He sold his Broadmoor real estate and casino to the Myron Stratton Home.[4]

The Stratton Home Estate sold Penrose the Broadmoor casino, lake, and 450 surrounding acres for $90,000.[5] Penrose and MacNeill each invested $300,000. Penrose hired Denver architect Frederick J. Sterner to produce a preliminary plan for the hotel. He rejected Sterner's $1.15 million Italian Renaissance Revival–style proposal as old-fashioned and too expensive. He paid Sterner $20,000, then fired him.[6] Penrose solicited designs from several firms, including Kirkland Cutter of Salt Lake City and William E. Fisher and Arthur A. Fisher of Denver.[7] Several submissions drew inspiration from Venice, with fanciful massing, arched windows covered with striped awnings, towers, and gondoliers floating on the Broadmoor "lagoon." Spencer chose the plan of the New York firm of Warren and Wetmore, which at $600,000 was the lowest bid.[8] Whitney Warren and Charles Wetmore had designed the New York Yacht Club and the 1913 New York City Grand Central Station, done much work for the Vanderbilts, and designed several deluxe New York City hotels including the Biltmore, Ritz-Carlton, Vanderbilt, Belmont, and Commodore.

Warren and Wetmore's design took advantage of the spacious site, far roomier than New York City's cramped avenues. The nine-story central portion was accentuated by a picturesque tower and flanked by four-story wings that could be closed off in winter. Its staggered massing resembled the clustered red-tile roofs of an Italian village and blended with the foothills setting, echoing the mountains rising behind. The lakeside site also enhanced the Mediterranean-style stucco walls and red-tile roof and capitalized on the American infatuation with Spanish colonial influences. The 1915 Panama-California International Exposition in San Diego had reintroduced Spanish-flavored architecture, and stuccoed, red-roofed homes and buildings were rising across the country. The multicolored fresco at the roofline and above the balcony of the Broadmoor exuded an exotic quality. Paul S. Deneville implemented a graffito process that used polychromatic clay baked on with intense heat.[9] An arched colonnade welcomed guests into a lobby rich with paintings and artistic carving.

The wartime shortages of workers and of steel did not daunt Penrose, who was determined to finish the hotel in thirteen months. He broke ground in April 1917 and bet the builders $1,000 each that the Broadmoor Hotel would open by May 15, 1918.[10] The ensuing months were filled with frantic communications between Penrose and the architects, contractor, interior designers, and landscaping firm. Charles Tutt Jr. oversaw construction

BROADMOOR VISIONS: Count Pourtales's casino and hotel became the base for the much more elaborate resort constructed by Spencer Penrose. Four architectural firms submitted proposals to Penrose. He selected the proposal of Warren and Wetmore, who had designed New York's Biltmore, Commodore, Ritz, and Vanderbilt Hotels and Grand Central Station. Their irregular plan used stepped elevations climbing to a slender single tower, an arrangement echoing the surrounding mountains. Low-pitched red tile roofs united the informal collection of shapes that have the feel of a clustered village. The terra cotta walls were painted "Broadmoor pink" to complement the surrounding purple mountain majesty.

details and traveled to New York to meet with Warren and Wetmore. William Dunning organized the hotel departments and ordered stocks and supplies. Story by story the grand building rose, consuming concrete and steel in gargantuan quantities. Much of the stone came from a quarry on Spencer's Turkey Creek Ranch.

Construction costs exceeded $2 million, and furniture and interior decorating cost another $1 million. The project ran over schedule, too. May 15, 1918, passed, and the architect and contractor lost their bets. Penrose later sued the contractor, James Stewart of Salt Lake City, for his late project schedule and cost overruns. Despite myriad design modifications and construction changes, the most expensive being a switch to entirely fireproof building materials, the Broadmoor opened just two months later than Penrose had planned.

The hotel was unveiled on June 29, 1918, with a gala grand opening. The paint had barely dried when invited guests, neighbors, and curious local residents crowded into the hotel. Its 350 guest rooms far outnumbered the Antlers. They found the lobby, halls, restaurants, and guest rooms exquisitely decorated and furnished, reflecting Julie's passion for European decor and art. Penrose had hired an army of Italian artisans to paint frescoes and ceilings reminiscent of the artwork of Italian cathedrals. Westing, Evans, and Egmore—decorators of the Philadelphia Ritz-Carlton—had selected custom-dyed carpeting; wall coverings; hundreds of chairs, tables, beds, and bureaus; and thousands of monogrammed linens and pieces of china and silver. Julie's affection for the Orient was evident in the Palm Court, with bamboo furniture imported from Hong Kong. Her interest in opera inspired the small theater on the first floor. On the dining room's small stage, a hotel orchestra serenaded diners. A swan, Julie's personal trademark, was painted near the elevator and above the fireplace in the center terrace. Several of the graceful white birds also floated on Broadmoor Lake. Charlie and Marion MacNeill designed their own private suites.[11] MacNeill caused a crisis by installing a wood floor in his suite. Penrose, insisting on an entirely fireproof hotel, had the flooring removed. Two other investors, the famous Cripple Creek tycoon Albert "Bert" Carlton and his wife, Ethel, also built a private Broadmoor suite.

On the ground floor a barbershop, brokerage office, drug and cigar store, lace and notions store, boudoir shop, photography studio, and doctor's office catered to guests' wants and needs. The Olmsted Brothers firm designed the circular entry drive curving around a large Italian Renaissance–style stone fountain. Evergreens and flower gardens greeted guests as they entered the drive from Lake Boulevard. Behind the hotel a pedestrian path circled the lake, which was stocked with 10,000 trout. On the south side of the lake, world-renowned golf course architect Donald Ross transformed 135 acres of underbrush, scrub oak, and rolling terrain into one of the West's best and most picturesque golfing havens.

The glorious new hotel fulfilled Spencer and Julie's expectations. "The business of the hotel is going ahead quite steadily," Penrose told Charles Westing a month after the Broadmoor opened. "Last Sunday they had over 247 people, and it is still holding its own. Everyone is enthusiastic about the hotel, and especially about the quality of the menu, and they tell me it is the best American-plan menu they have ever seen. The business is even better than I expected it would be."[12]

Spencer and Julie poured their burgeoning fortune into the Broadmoor as a grand reflection of their personalities and personal tastes. It was a playground for the wealthy, for travelers accustomed to the grand hotels of Europe. Besides being the nucleus of Penrose's many interlocking companies and a venue for his many hobbies, the Broadmoor was a hub for social and athletic activities.

Although the Broadmoor opened in 1918, it was never "finished." The Penroses were continuously refining and expanding their pet project. They nurtured it like a child, adding polo grounds, a rodeo stadium, an ice arena, and a second golf course. The Broadmoor Ice Arena and Golf Course hosted hundreds of state, national, and international athletic events, foreshadowing Colorado Springs' role today as an amateur sports capital.

The Broadmoor gained world acclaim thanks to Penrose's marketing genius. He targeted affluent easterners with advertisements in *Vogue, Vanity*

Penrose adorned the entry under the hotel's port cochere with five busts of Bacchus, the god of wine and fertility. Inside the Broadmoor a grand curving marble staircase, as well as elevators, took guests from the street-level lobby to the mezzanine. Old World cherubs cavorting in the medallion over the lobby elevator were Americanized with feather headdresses and tomahawks. The hotel was a self-contained community with its own power plant, water system, laundry and dry cleaning, greenhouse, garage, carpenter shop, and resident construction crew. The 350-room hotel rose nine stories on a steel skeleton clad in ornate terra cotta, stucco, and plaster trim. The Broadmoor even boasted its own stock exchange, a doctor's office, Turkish baths, a squash court, and a little theater. Courtesy drawings by Vernon Howell Bailey.

Palm trees and bamboo furniture adorned the mezzanine lounge, with its ornate vaulted ceiling. Interior opulence ranged from mural vignettes of classical mythology to the lobby beams, incorporating Colorado scenes such as the Mount of the Holy Cross and the Garden of the Gods. Courtesy drawing by Vernon Howell Bailey.

Fair, Spur, Golf Illustrated, Western Architect, and *Town and Country* that compared the Broadmoor with a graceful Italian villa. An ad in Chicago's *Fashion Art Magazine* touted the tourist mecca as a "Hotel for the Elite . . . situated in the natural playground of America, the Broadmoor attracts the type of people one meets at the Riviera, Monte Carlo, Switzerland, or Cairo." Advertising targeted bored midwesterners seeking solace from scorching summers. Readers of the *New Orleans Times Picayune, St. Louis Post Dispatch,* and *San Antonio Express* were invited to visit "America's Greatest Scenic Resort . . . Noted rendezvous for Polo Players . . . Headquarters for everything that is entertaining." A glossy *Life* advertisement lauded the hotel as "Recreation's Shrine Amid the Rockies." Auto tourists arrived on the newly completed Pikes Peak Ocean-to-Ocean Highway through Colorado Springs, enticed by a photogenic Broadmoor spread in the *Automobile Blue Book.* Spencer sent this spread to Broadmoor neighbors, hotels in surrounding states, and country clubs in Kansas City, Des Moines, Omaha, and Oklahoma City. Penrose also left Broadmoor booklets and photographs in ocean liner salons and grand hotel lobbies as he traveled around the world.

His marketing strategies went beyond newsprint. Laura Gilpin's misty photographs highlighted the hotel in a touring lantern slide show of the Pikes Peak region. Colorado Springs and Denver society editors were invited to the hotel for a St. Patrick's Day ball. Three dozen Denver Press Club members visited for guided tours and a dip in the pool. Prospective brides, gleaned from society columns of midwestern newspapers, received a booklet and a letter telling them: "The Broadmoor would be an ideal place for a honeymoon trip. . . . Should you and your fiancé select [it] for your bridal trip, we are certain that the memories of your stay will never be forgotten."[13]

To carve a niche in the country's lodging industry, Spencer staged a "hotel men's carnival." Two years after the hotel opened he invited forty-five of the country's leading hotel men to the Broadmoor for a free week-long visit in September 1920. Riding to the Rockies in Charles MacNeill's private car, the *Mather,* and other Pullman car palaces, the "Broadmoor Pilgrims" were plied with free-flowing drink, gourmet meals, and dinner at the Cooking Club. Prohibition was ignored at the Broadmoor, where Penrose had stockpiled a vast supply of booze.

The hotel men visited the region's scenic attractions, toured a Cripple Creek gold mine, watched the Western Championship polo games, and played in the Penrose Cup golf tournament. They also cheered on Pikes Peak Hill Climb racers vying for the Penrose Cup and watched airplanes racing from Denver to the Pikes Peak summit.[14] Charles E. Gehring, editor of *Hotel Review,* and Thomas Green, president of the American Hotel Association, cabled Penrose afterward: "[The Broadmoor Pilgrims] send you their renewed appreciation and gratitude for the incomparable entertainment you so magnanimously bestowed upon them while enroute and at the excellent Broadmoor Hotel. Pleasurable memories of this now historic event will ever abide with us and add luster to the name of our beloved host and friend Spencer Penrose."[15]

The following year the Pilgrims presented Penrose with a $2,000 silver replica of the Broadmoor at a New York City banquet in his honor.[16] This confirmed the long shadow Spencer cast back east. Rather than compete with his older brothers—the senator, doctor, and professor—Speck had chosen the business world. He had succeeded, as revealed in this 1921 article by a syndicated New York columnist:

> Spencer Penrose, sometimes of New York and most of the time of
> Colorado Springs, is making his annual pilgrimage to the East shortly.

Everybody in Colorado knows Penrose and almost everybody in New
York. He is a jack of many trades and master of them all.

Just to go the rounds of his clubs would keep the ordinary man busy,
but Penrose finds time on the side to be a mining engineer, a founder
and director of Utah Copper Co.; a pioneer in the Cripple Creek
mining district; president of the Colorado, Midland Terminal Co.; vice
president and director of a dozen other railroads and corporations.

When he comes to New York he is at home in the University, Union
League, Rocky Mountain, Down Town, Bankers, Republican and quite
a number of other clubs of lesser importance. He belongs to more clubs
than that in Philadelphia, where he was born; several in Detroit,
Denver, Paris, and London.

His chief hobby is the Hotel Broadmoor, of Colorado Springs, which
in the past two years has suddenly jumped into popularity with eastern
summer and winter crowds. It is regarded by many as the finest hotel in
America and Penrose also finds time to run it and whoop up the social
life of the city. . . .

Each year he superintends the big roundup, which brings all the
top-notchers in the cowboy and cowgirl world . . . it preserves the halo
of the old west when two-gun men rode the range and Colorado was a
state of trails and hell-roaring mining camps.

The Broadmoor is a sort of a tribute to his love for Colorado. It is
situated on a lake and is a city within itself—operating its own water
system, lighting, etc.

And when Penrose comes to town he goes about his clubs with his
pockets filled with literature telling of the town "that nestles upon the
bosom of old Pike's Peak itself." He lures many tired businessmen away
from their deep cushioned chairs to the boundless west, where they ride
bucking horses, play golf, take a coach over the mountains, and forget
that there is such a thing as prohibition.

He has a personal acquaintance in New York that includes all the
financiers and politicians. After most men leave New York it happens
that in a few years they are forgotten . . . the whirligig of time erases
friendships quickly here.

Yet by sheer force of his personality, Penrose, although only an
occasional visitor, is known widely as any chronic settler in Manhattan.

His favorite poem is Arthur Chapman's "Out Where the West
Begins." He will recite it any time or any place. And before you know it
this unofficial Colorado puffer will have you believing that while New
York is a cozy little city and all that, yet there is only one real spot in
America and that spot is Colorado Springs.[17]

From the start, the Broadmoor attracted the rich and famous. "A great
many well-known people seem to be coming to The Broadmoor," Penrose
told his friend Thomas Green. "They are greatly pleased and are great
boosters for The Broadmoor."[18] Among the first to arrive was the celebrated artist Maxfield Parrish, hired to paint the bewitching Broadmoor
portrait that conveniently transported Pikes Peak to the east side of the
hotel.[19] Penrose convinced New York millionaire John D. Rockefeller Jr.

to pose on horseback for the Broadmoor booklet. Mrs. Rockefeller and daughter Abbey were photographed in a touring car and Standard Oil president A. C. Bedford on the Broadmoor green. Edna Ferber, author of the best-selling novels *Showboat* (1926) and *Giant* (1952), was pictured standing in the Italian fountain. The writer, who came for two weeks and stayed for two months, pronounced the Broadmoor "the most wonderful place of all."[20]

Spencer's greatest publicity coup, however, was enticing world heavyweight boxing champion Jack Dempsey to train at the Broadmoor for his 1926 title defense match against Gene Tunney. Dempsey, a former Victor miner whose fists had earned him international fame, practiced for a week at the golf club. He performed in boxing exhibitions in the hotel ballroom and was honored at a Cooking Club dinner. Milking the event for maximum publicity, Spencer had the "Manassa Mauler" photographed in a range of panoramic poses: riding a horse, fishing for trout in Broadmoor Lake, retreating to the Honeymoon Lodge atop Cheyenne Mountain. Finally, the beleaguered pugilist fled to White Sulphur Springs, West Virginia, to complete his training.[21]

A friendship bloomed between the two men. "You hit the nail on the head when you said I am exceedingly busy. . . . I am—but never too busy to write to a pal," Jack wrote Spencer in the summer of 1927. "I shall have two seats by Monday and want you to come along as my guests. Do not give me any excuses about it because here's your check back again and I won't have it any other way. . . . Best wishes from Estelle and myself to you and Mrs. Penrose, I am, As ever, your pal, Jack."[22] Three years later Spencer invested $50,000 in the Playa de Ensenada hotel and casino Dempsey was developing in Ensenada in Baja California. He and Julie visited the Pacific resort town and even hired an architect to draw blueprints for a bungalow that was never built. Ensenada's charm soured because of a funding shortage and mobster Al Capone's alleged ties to Dempsey's $2 million resort.[23] Penrose refused Dempsey's plea for a $15,000 loan. "It is too bad that your crowd is in such a mess," Penrose told him. "I hope, for the good of everyone, that some arrangement may be made so as to save something out of the wreck."[24] Their friendship waned. Dempsey's manager sent a polite refusal when Penrose asked Jack to referee a 1938 boxing match at the new Will Rogers Stadium.

The Broadmoor attracted celebrities and affluent vacationers, but conventions and conferences were also vital to the hotel's financial success.[25] The first gathering was the American Institute of Mining Engineers (AIME)—of which Penrose was a longtime member—just three months after the hotel opened.[26] The Broadmoor hosted bankers, oilmen, insurancemen, and brokers. Rotarians, fraternities, and sororities came to play at the Broadmoor. The National Garden Council, Colorado State Medical Society, Western Fruit Jobbers Association, Tent and Awning

Jack Dempsey was among the celebrities Spencer Penrose brought to the Broadmoor. The prizefighter trained at the hotel for his 1926 defense of the world heavyweight championship against Gene Tunney, the most famous fight in boxing history. Dempsey, who grew up in Manassa, Colorado, began his pugilistic career in mining camps such as Cripple Creek and Victor, where he posed for this 1914 portrait. Photo by Bill Lehr, courtesy Colorado Historical Society.

Manufacturers, American Institute of Steel Construction, Colorado Bar Association, and National Girl Scout Council all convened at the Broadmoor in its early years.

To lure both businessmen and vacationers to his hotel, Penrose concocted a smorgasbord of sports and other diversions. He revived the high-society sport of polo. A dozen teams converged for tournaments on the three polo fields at the Broadmoor. Thundering hooves, dust rising against a mountain backdrop, the click of the mallet and ball, and polite patters of applause created an unforgettable tableau. Players came from Denver and Wichita Country Clubs, military teams from Fort Riley, Kansas; Fort Sheridan, Wyoming; and Fort Wise, Texas. Homegrown contestants represented the Broadmoor, Pikes Peak, and Cheyenne Mountain Country Club. Oklahoma oilman Ernest Marland brought his two Ponca City teams, filling the hotel's entire Southlake Wing. Broadmoor stables rented polo ponies for $7.50 per game. Society page editors covered the polo season: "smart polo teas, dinners, luncheons, and dances at the Cheyenne Mountain Country club, Broadmoor hotel and Nightclub, and the J. R. Bradley ranch south of town."[27] Penrose rarely missed a game, clad in the riding outfit that became his personal trademark—knee boots, jodhpurs, and tailored coat all custom-ordered from Philadelphia.

Polo playing at the Broadmoor was enhanced by the fine stock of riding horses in the Colorado Springs area. The city was the regional headquarters for the Remount Association, which established a network of breeding stallions available to farmers and ranchers wishing to improve the quality of their horse stock. Penrose's friend Harry Leonard, who owned a ranch north of the city at Pine Valley, helped coordinate the effort. The Remount races, held at the Broadmoor, tested the different breeds of horses against each other to determine which was the fastest and strongest across long distances. Penrose personally financed these competitions and presented the Broadmoor Cup to the winner.[28]

Three polo fields, stables with 100 horses, and 75 miles of riding trails made the Broadmoor neighborhood the center of the Colorado Springs horsey set. The annual Colorado Horse and Colt Show took place at the Broadmoor Westlake Field. The Broadmoor and the Colorado Springs Horse Clubs also practiced there. Local residents, hotel guests, and Penrose himself rode the network of trails on the lower flanks of Cheyenne Mountain. In 1929 he built the Broadmoor Riding Academy west of Broadmoor Lake after studying similar facilities in Detroit and Brooklyn. Touted as Colorado's largest indoor arena, it housed indoor polo, horse shows, and a racetrack. It was also the scene of professional boxing matches arranged by Spencer and the dog shows and flower shows Julie loved.[29] Ten years later Penrose converted the academy into an indoor ice rink that did even more to transform Colorado Springs into the Rocky Mountain center for amateur athletics.

Golf helped publicize the hotel. The $500,000 Broadmoor green was marketed as a "golfer's paradise." A $15,000 salary lured golf champion James Barnes from Philadelphia to "the highest championship golf course in the world."[30] "Long Jim" was immediately sent across the country to play in a series of matches that raised $1 million for the National Red Cross. Representing the soon-to-open Broadmoor Hotel, Barnes played the country's top "golfists" on courses in Washington, D.C., Baltimore, Chicago, Louisville, and elsewhere. The first Broadmoor match in 1918 featured "four of the best golfers in the country." Long Jim teamed up with National Amateur and Open champion Charles "Chick" Evans against Jock Hutchinson and Warren Wood. The event raised $10,000 for the Red Cross and established the Broadmoor links in the world of golf.[31]

The Broadmoor course gained legendary status. The *Philadelphia Inquirer* proclaimed:

> They certainly lived up to that old dictum "spare no expense" when it came to building the new Broadmoor course at Colorado Springs, where our own Jim Barnes now disports himself at brief intervals between playing Red Cross exhibition matches. According to a certain man who insists he is one of the founders, a committee got Donald Ross, the noted links architect, out to Colorado Springs and showed him the site for the proposed new course.
>
> Ross took one look, says this man, and then, turning to Spencer Penrose, a brother of Senator Penrose, principal backer of the project, remarked: "Entirely too small. Won't do at all."
>
> "How much more land do we need?" asked Spencer Penrose.
>
> "About 80 acres," calmly replied Ross.
>
> The other members of the committee nearly fainted, for be it known land at Colorado Springs is worth much real money, but Spencer Penrose never batted an eye. "We will buy it," was his prompt response and buy it he did, the very next morning.[32]

Since its opening day the Broadmoor course has been a major attraction. The Men's Invitational Golf tournament was an annual event from 1921 until 1994. The Broadmoor hosted six Trans-Mississippi Golf Tournaments between 1927 and 1964 and in 1935 was site of the Western Amateur tournament. Golfing legend Jack Nicklaus won his first major tournament on the Broadmoor green, the 1959 U.S. Men's Amateur championship. The Broadmoor links have been the setting for the World Senior Golf Tournament since 1960 and the Olympic Golf Classic during the 1980s and 1990s. The course has been a favorite with celebrity golfers from Jackie Gleason and Bing Crosby to Arnold Palmer and Gerald Ford. The Broadmoor green was expanded, with the West Course designed by Robert Trent Jones Sr., in 1930. Jones further refined the course when he redesigned it in 1965. Broadmoor golfers gained additional turf with the

The oldest building on the Broadmoor grounds was this casino, torn down in 1994 to build the Broadmoor Golf Club and Spa. Courtesy 1990 photo by Tom Noel.

Among Broadmoor golf course caddies, the most memorable was Penrose's pet elephant, "the Empress of India." When she first arrived, the Empress slept in the Broadmoor garage before finding a home at the Cheyenne Mountain Zoo. Courtesy Special Collections, Tutt Library, Colorado College.

1976 creation of a Mountain Course by Ed Seay of the Arnold Palmer Group.

The course stands out in the world of women's golf as well. The first Broadmoor Women's Invitational came in 1942, and renowned Colorado athlete Babe Didrikson Zaharias won the invitational three times during the 1940s. Today the tournament is one of the country's top women's amateur competitions, with many winners going on to play professionally. Three women members of the Broadmoor club are Colorado Golf Hall of Famers: Judy Bell, who in the 1990s became the U.S. Golf Association's first female president; Barbara McIntire, three-time winner of the invitational and winner of numerous amateur titles; and Phyllis Tish Pruce, the 1991 U.S. Senior Women's Amateur champion. In 1995 the Broadmoor hosted the fiftieth U.S. Women's Open.[33]

A new era of sports was launched at the Broadmoor in 1937 when Penrose converted the Riding Academy into an ice arena. Eleven-year-old skater Sonja Henie had captured the world's attention at the World Olympics in Chamonix, France, with her short skirts, light-colored skates, and stunning spins and jumps. Henie won the World Champion title ten straight times from 1927 to 1936. Spencer and Julie were captivated by Henie's professional revue when they saw her in Chicago, and they transformed the riding academy into the Broadmoor Ice Palace. The $200,000 rink was the largest enclosed ice arena west of the Mississippi. It opened January 1, 1938, with a gala ice show and carnival that drew a huge crowd.

Figure skating was in its infancy, remembers Patricia Bates Croke, a local girl whom the *Gazette Telegraph* called "another Sonja" and the "little whiz of the silver blades." Croke reminisced, "I think I was the only child who skated on the opening night of the arena. I had learned to skate on hockey skates on Broadmoor Lake. Dad had to go to Denver to buy me white skates, because there weren't any for sale in Colorado Springs. Mr. Penrose used to come down and watch us practice skating in the arena."[34] Built by Milton J. Strong and decorated with deer, sheep, elk, and buffalo trophy heads, the arena grew into one of the country's leading year-round ice-skating centers. It was second in the country, after Lake Placid, to offer summer skating. Athletes came from throughout the country to rent "patches" of ice at the Broadmoor and practice their jumps and spins.

The Broadmoor Skating Club, begun as the Pikes Peak Skating Club, produced dozens of award-winning skaters. The Broadmoor's first major competition was the 1941 Pacific Coast Championships. Since then, the U.S. Figure Skating National Championships have been skated six times on Broadmoor ice and the World Figure Skating Championships five times. These events outgrew the Ice Palace, renamed Broadmoor World Arena in 1961, but the rink hosted World Junior Figure Skating Championships in 1985, 1990, and 1994.[35]

The Broadmoor Skating Club has produced three Olympic, thirty-five world, two world junior, and sixty U.S. champions.[36] The three Olympic gold medalists are Peggy Gale Fleming, 1968; David Jenkins, 1960; and Hayes Alan Jenkins, 1956. These three skaters also won world championships, as did such Broadmoor stars as Peter and Karol Kennedy, Coleen O'Connor, Edi Scholdan, Cathy Casey, Jill Trenary, and Tim Wood. The club has also been home to noteworthy coaches, including Carlo Fassi who began at the Broadmoor in 1961.[37] The Broadmoor skaters helped groom Colorado Springs' image as a center for amateur athletes, and the United States Olympic Training Center located there in 1977. The club and its supporters also were instrumental in bringing the World Figure Skating

Skating became a year-round activity after the Broadmoor Ice Palace opened January 1, 1938, on the southwest side of Broadmoor Lake. The arena started out as the Broadmoor Riding Academy, designed by Charles Thomas and built in 1928 for indoor polo and other horsey events. A decade later a glistening white parapet was added and the horse arena converted to this ice rink. As a training center, it hosted world champion figure skaters such as Peggy Fleming, Yvonne Boederos, and Jill Trenary. The Palace also hosted ice shows, Colorado College and World Cup hockey, and American, North American, and world figure-skating events. To reflect its growing international status, in 1961 the Ice Palace was renamed the Broadmoor World Arena. Courtesy Pikes Peak Library, Local History Collection.

During this winter golf game, skaters can be seen playing hockey on the frozen Cheyenne Lake. Courtesy Pikes Peak Library District, Local History Collection.

Museum and Hall of Fame to 20 First Street at Broadmoor. The U.S. Figure Skating Association is headquartered in the same facility.

Along with figure skating, the arena hosted regulation hockey, as well as local entertainment and recreation. Home to Colorado College hockey for four decades, it also hosted the NCAA ice hockey championship playoffs from 1948 to 1957. The Colorado College Tigers took the NCAA title in 1950 and 1957. The World and European Ice Hockey Championships were played there in 1962. During the 1970s the Broadmoor hosted the World Cup Hockey games between the United States and the USSR.[38] Local skaters flocked to the ice for carnivals, balls, and dazzling ice revues. Out-of-town visitors came for Denver Day, Pueblo Day, Fremont County Day, and Cripple Creek and Victor Day, advertised in regional newspapers.[39] The facility also housed conference exhibitions, graduation ceremonies, and sporting events such as the 1988 U.S. Boxing Championship.[40]

The Broadmoor Hotel and El Pomar Foundation continued to support the arena and skating club long after Spencer Penrose's death. Hotel president William Thayer Tutt helped raise funds for arena expansions in 1958 and 1968. He was also a major organizer of the arena's national and international hockey competitions.[41] El Pomar, meanwhile, helped fund the expansion of the Skating Museum and contributed $10,000 to the 1994 World Junior Championships. After the aging arena was replaced in 1996 by the seven-story West Towers annex, El Pomar ensured Colorado Springs' skating tradition would continue by donating $31 million for a new facility.[42] "Our club and our training program were without ice," recalls Carolyn Kruse, a longtime director of the Broadmoor Skating Club. "Everyone was scrambling for ice after the Broadmoor World Arena was gone. We would not be here in this form and doing as well as we are doing if El Pomar had not stepped forward to help fund this project."[43] The $57 million three-rink Colorado Springs World Arena, which seats 8,500 people, opened in 1998 on 53 acres near Interstate 25 and Circle Drive.

Besides polo, horseback riding, golf, and skating, Broadmoor guests could pursue less vigorous pastimes. After fishing in well-stocked Broadmoor Lake, guests delighted in having their catch cooked by the Broadmoor chef and served to them on the West Terrace. They strolled through the Broadmoor greenhouse to see the hybrid Penrose carnation. The Broadmoor offered cultural amusement, too. A small orchestra clad in red hunting tuxedos performed in the dining room and small hotel theater. The hotel hired fine musicians, such as guest conductor Edouard Deru, "Violinist to the King and Queen of Belgium." Igor Stravinsky, Vladimir Horowitz, and Sergei Rachmaninoff also performed at the Broadmoor.[44] The little theater featured the Fountain Valley Schoolboys' Chorus, plays by young local thespians, and popular films.

The Broadmoor's genteel amusements, however, did not include gambling. Shortly after opening the hotel, Penrose had invited Vaso Chucovich, once the operator of Denver's notorious Navarre Hotel, to run a gaming room at the Broadmoor. Chucovich declined: "I appreciate, very much, the confidence in me which is implied by this suggestion, but a number of years ago I terminated my connections with this business, and I do not care to resume them."[45] Thus ended the Broadmoor's gaming prospects. Guests amused themselves instead by playing whist and bridge or visiting the poker room at the nearby Cheyenne Mountain Country Club.

Penrose popularized his hotel with local residents, inviting Colorado Springs society to dine in the hotel restaurants, dance in the ballroom, swim in the pool, and sun themselves on the Broadmoor beach. Neighbors strolled around the lake and sipped complimentary coffee served on the West Terrace. Millionaires summering in palatial houses in the Broadmoor neighborhood mingled with the local social elite at the hotel and at the Cheyenne Mountain Country Club. The Broadmoor became the city's social center and Julie Penrose its "dowager queen." Her 1918 "Belgian Fete" on the lakefront initiated an annual series of parties with exotic themes.

The cream of society attended the hotel's annual opening, often staged to benefit a local charity. In June 1933, for instance, Broadmoor guests could revel at the "eleven o'clock festival on the esplanade, twelve o'clock grand opening of the Nightclub, four o'clock in the morning sunrise breakfast, five o'clock preview of the bathing beach and opening of the swimming pool" for a $3 cost. Proceeds went to the Junior League. "All-Night Party at Broadmoor a Huge Success," reported the local newspaper afterward. "Members of the social elite of Colorado Springs, Pueblo, and Denver gathered to celebrate the event. . . . Mrs. Spencer Penrose wore a distinctly Parisenne creation of black cire satin with tulip red slippers."[46]

Spencer and Julie thrived on this whirl of social activity and tried their utmost to ensure that everyone had a good time. The hotel printed a weekly schedule offering sunrise horseback riding, picnics atop Cheyenne Mountain, dancing at the nightclub, and tea on the West Terrace. Dinner dances and carnivals raised funds for the Junior League, Colorado College sororities, and the Broadmoor Art Academy. The Broadmoor was also a favorite for weddings, high school proms, and other local affairs, all diligently reported by society columnists.

Sports and recreation at the Broadmoor drew guests galore, from royalty and political powerhouses to entertainers, musicians, and movie stars. Carmen Miranda, Bing Crosby, Victor Borge, Liberace, Jack Benny, Bob Hope, and Burl Ives entertained at the hotel. "Mickey Rooney was always a fantastic person," recalls longtime Broadmoor employee Russell Freymuth.[47] "It seemed like all the teenage girls were following him around and squealing. He'd take them into the soda fountain and he'd buy them all sodas." Child actress Shirley Temple was photographed shaking hands with Spencer and making snowballs atop Pikes Peak. Clark Gable dropped in while stationed in Pueblo during World War II.

Jimmy Stewart and Gloria Hatrick honeymooned at the hotel in 1949. Edgar Bergen and his daughter Candice visited the Broadmoor, as did Carol Channing and Marlene Dietrich. "When Marlene was here everything had to be white," remembers Freymuth, who worked his way up from busboy to vice president and retired at age 62. "The carpet, the curtains, the bedspread all had to be snow white. We happened to have one suite that was decorated pretty much how she wanted. She performed at the International Center for us. It was a good show, with singing and dancing and supporting actors and musicians."[48]

Other musical guests have included Nat King Cole, Maureen McGovern, Marilyn McCoo, Amy Grant, the Doors, Reba McIntyre, and members of the rock group Jefferson Airplane. Jane Fonda, Ted Turner, Joan Rivers, Mark Harmon, Willard Scott, Rich Little, and Jonathan Winters have been celebrated visitors. Sports greats Joe DiMaggio, Rick "Goose" Gossage, "Sugar" Ray Leonard, Roger Staubach, and Chris Evert have stayed at the Broadmoor. Among the hotel's political visitors were U.S.

On the sandy north shore of Cheyenne Lake, Penrose staged bathing beauty contests to attract publicity to what he touted as the finest beach in the Rockies. Although the beach is gone, Cheyenne Lake is still patrolled by Julie Penrose's beloved swans. Julie adorned the lakefront patio with evergreen cabanas for this August 14, 1918, "Belgian fete" to honor the count her daughter married.

To celebrate repeal of the Prohibition Amendment, Penrose opened the Tavern and adjacent Mayan Room, shown here, which featured an exotic Mayan ZigZag Moderne decor. The Tavern has knotty pine walls, wine bottle chandeliers, and a huge collection of prized liquor bottles lining the walls. Over the back bar the bronze sculpture, "Repeal the 19th Amendment," shows Spencer Penrose in his llama-pulled cart campaigning for a return to happy days. The Tavern served the Broadmoor label scotch whiskey after it passed Spencer Penrose's taste test. Penrose's greatest nightmare was running out of booze. On the eve of Prohibition in 1919, he invested an estimated $250,000 in the finest liquor he could find. He hid several hundred cases in the basement at El Pomar and more of his favorite libations all about the Broadmoor. More liquor supposedly lies in the tunnel from the third basement of the hotel to the island in the middle of Broadmoor Lake.

Senator and future President John F. Kennedy, Vice President Richard Nixon, President George Bush, British Prime Minister Margaret Thatcher, USSR President Mikhail Gorbachev, and Gen. Colin Powell. The hotel has been the site of diplomatic events, including the 1979 NORAD summit and a 1994 meeting with Margaret Thatcher and other world leaders. Portraits of many famous faces hang outside the Starz lounge in the Broadmoor West Tower.

The Broadmoor's fame and popularity fulfilled Spencer Penrose's vision of Colorado Springs as a tourist mecca with the hotel as its centerpiece. It earned him a national reputation as a flamboyant hotelier and bon vivant extraordinaire. Being the host of Colorado's grandest hotel also gave Penrose an outlet for his showmanship. Once standoffish, he basked in the limelight with Julie's guidance to keep him within the bounds of good taste. Showy events like the annual rodeo and Pikes Peak Hill Climb enticed visitors to the region. And each year Penrose unveiled a new attraction—

A fresh, airy appendage to the Tavern opened in 1953 as the Garden Terrace, with monkeys and birds galore. Julie hoped to keep some of the critters in the new restaurant, but the health department said no. With a greenhouse glass roof and slate floor, this restaurant is filled with trees, bougainvillea, azaleas, palms, and other tropicals, which thrive here year-round. Courtesy photo by Bob McIntyre.

Each of the five busts of Bacchus over-looking the Broadmoor's main entry is lascivious in its own way. Courtesy photo by Tom Noel.

Polo Park field with its Moorish-style grandstand, the Broadmoor Beach, the Broadmoor Riding Academy.

In 1925 he blasted a toll road up Cheyenne Mountain. Nicknamed the "World's Wonder Trip" and "Ladder-to-the-Sky," it was patterned after a serpentine road near Nice, France.[49] Some local residents didn't care for Spencer branding the mountain his own, but tourists by the thousands paid a dollar toll to drive to the top. At the summit they visited the Cheyenne Mountain Lodge designed by Charles S. Thomas and Thomas A. McLaren, a Pueblo Revival–style structure with adobelike exterior and protruding wooden vigas. The rustic inn, a favorite with honeymooners, was decorated with Native American handicrafts and rugs and mounted buffalo and elk.

Spencer promoted his new road in several ways. He staged a fabulous dedication complete with an Indian footrace to the top run by five Hopis and five Zunis.[50] The Broadmoor's small zoo, relocated from the hotel grounds to the highway entrance, also lured tourists up the mountain. One scheme failed—lobbying the U.S. government to have Zebulon Pike's remains buried atop Cheyenne Mountain, where Penrose insisted "General Pike located one of the most famous mountains of America, now called 'Pikes Peak.'"[51] When this proposition was spurned, Spencer planned his own burial ground on Cheyenne Mountain. Constructed midway up the mountain in the 1930s, the Will Rogers Shrine of the Sun served as both the Penrose mausoleum and a memorial to the popular cowboy humorist.

Despite ceaselessly promoting, decorating, and expanding their hotel, the Penroses escaped to warmer climes each winter. During these long and frequent absences, Charles "Charley" Tutt Jr., the son of Spencer's Cripple Creek mining and milling partner, became Spencer's right-hand man. Born in 1889, Charley Jr. looked to "Mr. Penrose" for advice and guidance after

his father, Charles Tutt Sr., died in 1909. When Spencer's marriage to Julie failed to produce children to help run his expanding empire, he delegated business responsibilities to Charley Jr. Charles Tutt Sr. had lost much of the family fortune in his unfortunate copper-mining investments at Takilma, Oregon. Charley Jr. lacked the resources to join Charles MacNeill and Albert E. Carlton as Penrose's financial partner. So the Penrose-Tutt relationship remained that of employer-employee as Charley Jr. gradually grew into the role of Penrose's business manager.

Tutt's responsibilities steadily expanded. By the 1920s he was vice president of the Granite Gold Mining, Colorado Midland Railway, Manitou Mineral Water, and Beaver Park Land companies, as well as the half-dozen "scenic companies." He was a director of the Broadmoor Hotel and Land Company, Broadmoor Golf Club, and Broadmoor Polo Club. Tutt was also director of El Pomar Investment Company Penrose formed in 1924 to consolidate his many business holdings. When Penrose formed El Pomar

A 100,000-gallon indoor swimming pool with murals of nude bathers occupied what became the Broadmoor drugstore in 1961 and its new shops.

Foundation in 1937, two years before his death, Charley Tutt was put on that board, too. By the 1930s Charley Jr. was approaching middle age, and his sons William Thayer and Russell were becoming involved in administering the vast Penrose business empire.[52]

Unlike some tycoons who excelled only at making money, Penrose turned to spending his fortune. With business details in the Tutts' capable hands, Spencer and Julie could indulge in the international lifestyle they fancied. They traveled abroad from late autumn through spring each year, returning to prepare for the Broadmoor's busy summer season. Earnings from their copper stock and numerous other investments enabled the Penroses to circle the globe enjoying first-class transportation, five-star hotels, gourmet cuisine, and fine liquor. They bought French perfume and exquisite lingerie, Oriental vases and statuary, and objets d'art of all kinds for their beloved Broadmoor.

NOTES

1. El Pomar Center, Spencer Penrose Collection, Box, 71, File 302, letter from Penrose to Bell, May 23, 1916.

2. Elena Bertozzi-Villa, *Broadmoor Memories: The History of the Broadmoor.* Colorado Springs: Broadmoor, 1993, pp. 10–29.

3. Helen M. Geiger, *The Broadmoor Story.* Denver: A. B. Hirschfeld, 1985, p. 16.

4. Long regarded as a "white elephant," the old Broadmoor casino was moved to make way for the new hotel and converted to a golf club building. It was demolished in the 1990s.

5. Penrose House, Spencer Penrose Collection, Box 71, File 303, telegram from Penrose to MacNeill, May 9, 1916.

6. Ibid., letter to Benjamin C. Allen of Colorado Springs, January 17, 1917.

7. Ibid., Box 93, File 404.

8. Ibid., Box 71, File 303, letter to Benjamin C. Allen of Colorado Springs, January 17, 1917.

9. Bertozzi-Villa, *Broadmoor Memories,* p. 73.

10. Ibid., p. 70.

11. Marshall Sprague, *Newport in the Rockies: The Life and Good Times of Colorado Springs.* Chicago: Sage/Swallow, 1980, p. 259.

12. Penrose House, Spencer Penrose Collection, Box 94, File 409, Penrose to Westing, August 14, 1918.

13. Ibid., Box 123, File 466, letter to Dorothy Lowenhaupt, June 10, 1919.

14. Ibid., Box 98, File 282, letters dated August 27, September 2, September 3, 1920; Broadmoor Scrapbook—1921, "Leading Hotel Men of Country Will Spend Week at Broadmoor," *Denver Post,* undated.

15. Penrose House, Spencer Penrose Collection, Box 98, File 282, Charles Gehring to Spencer Penrose, telegram dated September 1920.

16. Ibid., Broadmoor Hotel Scrapbook—1921, "Gotham Hotel Men Repay Recent Host," unidentified article.

17. O. O. McIntyre, "New York Day by Day—Introducing Spencer Penrose." New York Bureau of the Press, Ritz Carlton Hotel, October 15, 1921. Syndicated

column published in the *Cincinnati Tribune, Asheville Times, Lexington Leader,* and elsewhere.

18. Penrose House, Spencer Penrose Collection, Box 30, File 73, letter dated September 1, 1922.

19. This painting graces the cover of *Broadmoor Memories* and hangs behind the hotel's check-in desk.

20. "'Most Wonderful Place of All,' Edna Ferber Declares; Hopes to Return Annually," *Colorado Springs Gazette-Telegraph,* July 24, 1928.

21. Sprague, *Newport in the Rockies,* pp. 267–268.

22. Penrose House, Spencer Penrose Collection, Box 110, File 426, letter from Dempsey to Penrose, August 27, 1927.

23. "New Mexican Resort Opens Doors," *San Diego Union,* October 3, 1930.

24. Penrose House, Spencer Penrose Collection, Box 110, File 426, letter from Penrose to Dempsey, December 9, 1930.

25. During his lifetime Penrose lost between $75,000 and $150,00 a year operating the hotel. Sprague, *Newport in the Rockies,* p. 272.

26. Penrose was an AIME member for over a decade.

27. Ellen O'Connor, "Formal Opening of Broadmoor Polo Season This Afternoon," *Colorado Springs Gazette-Telegraph,* undated, contained in 1929 Broadmoor scrapbook.

28. Bertozzi-Villa, *Broadmoor Memories,* p. 96.

29. "Polo a Year-Round Reality," *Sunday Gazette-Telegraph,* October 10, 1929; "Broadmoor to Build a Large Riding Academy This Year," *Colorado Springs Gazette,* September 8, 1929.

30. "Jim Barnes Goes West," *New York Times,* February 17, 1918.

31. Helen M. Geiger, *The Broadmoor Story.* Denver: A. B. Hirschfeld, 1985 [1968], p. 130.

32. Quoted in E. C. Hoyt, "'Spare No Expense' Broadmoor Motto," *Colorado Springs Gazette-Telegraph,* May 22, 1918.

33. Sherry Clark, manager, Broadmoor Golf Club, interviewed by Cathleen Norman, April 2, 1997.

34. Patricia Bates Croke, interviewed by Cathleen Norman, April 9, 1997.

35. *Program for the 1994 World Junior Figure Skating Championships.* Colorado Springs: United States Figure Skating Association, 1994, p. 10.

36. Carolyn Kruse, interviewed by Cathleen Norman, April 16, 1997.

37. Diane Lynn Betts, *The Broadmoor World Arena Pictorial History Book.* Colorado Springs: Broadmoor World Arena, 1988, pp. 5–6, 35.

38. Ibid., pp. 12–13.

39. Penrose House, Spencer Penrose Collection, Box 125, File 479, February 1938 newspaper advertisements and coupons.

40. Betts, *Broadmoor World Arena,* p. 22.

41. Ibid., pp. 9–10.

42. Rich Laden, "Arena Gets $1.2 Million From County," *Colorado Springs Gazette-Telegraph,* August 6, 1996.

43. Carolyn Kruse, interviewed by Cathleen Norman, April 16, 1997.

44. Bertozzi-Villa, *Broadmoor Memories,* p. 146.

45. Penrose House, Spencer Penrose Collection, Box 104, File H424, letters from H. H. Tammen to Penrose, August 26, 1918; from V. L. Chucovich to

Penrose, August 28, 1918; from Penrose to V. L. Chucovich, September 30, 1918.

46. Ibid., Broadmoor Hotel Notebook—1933, undated articles from unidentified newspapers.

47. G. Russell Freymuth, interviewed by Cathleen Norman, April 18, 1997.

48. Ibid.

49. Penrose House, Spencer Penrose Collection, photograph of unidentified mountaintop village near Nice.

50. Ibid., Box 79, File 336, letter from Penrose to Devereux, June 8, 1926.

51. Ibid., Box 111, File 428, letter from Penrose to Hubert E. Work, secretary of interior, May 29, 1926.

52. The oldest son, Charles III, distinguished himself as a Detroit automobile engineer and professor at Princeton, returning to the Pikes Peak region fifty years later.

As a young man, Penrose strained his retina while lifting a boat out of the Saint Charles River. By 1906 he was blind in that eye, and had it surgically removed in 1927. He filled the empty socket with a custom-made glass eye, but it was not a perfect solution. "Yesterday afternoon I stopped at your office and experimented with the new eye, which you had made for me," he complained to Kohler and Danz of New York City. "I found it entirely unsatisfactory. The rim was a new shape and different from the one which I bought from you several days ago. . . . The eye I did purchase from you seems allright in color, etc., but it does not stay in place, and if I am not very careful the eye turns up-side-down." Penrose even ordered a red-veined one to match his other eye when he was hung over. When that bloodshot eyeball arrived from Dr. Bruneau, Spencer sent a check for 400 francs and a note saying, "The eye you sent me is quite satisfactory but sometimes it seems a little small."

George Caleb Bingham's 1872 oil painting of Pikes Peak captured the spirit of America's famous mountain. Explorer Zebulon Pike called it "the Great Peak" and calculated its height as 18,581 feet. Prominently sited east of the Front Range, the awesome, solitary peak served as the easternmost sentinel of the Rockies and gave its name to what was first called the Pikes Peak region. The 14,110-foot peak attracted movers and shakers such as William J. Palmer, Spencer Penrose, and Charles L. Tutt, who strove to make the city at its base the health spa and tourist mecca of the Rockies. "View of Pikes Peak" by George Caleb Bingham, oil on canvas, 1872, 1967.27, Amon Carter Museum, Fort Worth, Texas.

Charles M. MacNeill, a shrewd and ruthless businessman, ran Tutt and Penrose's ore-processing operations in Florence, Cripple Creek, and Colorado City. MacNeill came to Colorado from Chicago as a youth and worked in the Holden Smelters in Denver, Aspen, and Leadville. In 1896 he went to work for Tutt and Penrose, putting together a "mill trust" that squeezed most rivals out of business.

The Bingham Copper Mine produced about 17 pounds of copper for each ton of earth. Around 3 billion tons of earth have been excavated from America's largest open-pit mine, which still has enough copper to supply the world well into the twenty-first century. Thanks to silver found in the copper ore, Bingham has also emerged as one of the top U.S. producers of silver. Used by permission of Utah State Historical Society, all rights reserved.

Maxfield Parrish's dreamy painting of the Broadmoor can still be seen behind the hotel's registration desk. Penrose paid the acclaimed artist $2,100 but complained that he put the lake in front of the hotel. Julie explained that Parrish had become one of America's favorite artists by being "fanciful." Photo by Bob McIntyre, Broadmoor Hotel.

Departing guests settle their Broadmoor bill with a cashier while cherubs weep at their departure.

The Pauline Chapel, built in 1919 by Julie Penrose to honor her granddaughter Pauline. Londoner Thomas McClaren, who became a leading Colorado Springs architect, designed the exquisite Spanish Mission Revival–style church. The stout stucco walls enclose a collection of antique religious art, including altar *reredos* from an old Spanish cathedral, an ivory cross from Belgium, and a hand-carved rosewood *pridieu* (prayer desk) from France. A statue of St. Paul resides in a niche beside the entrance. Courtesy Denver Public Library, Western History Department.

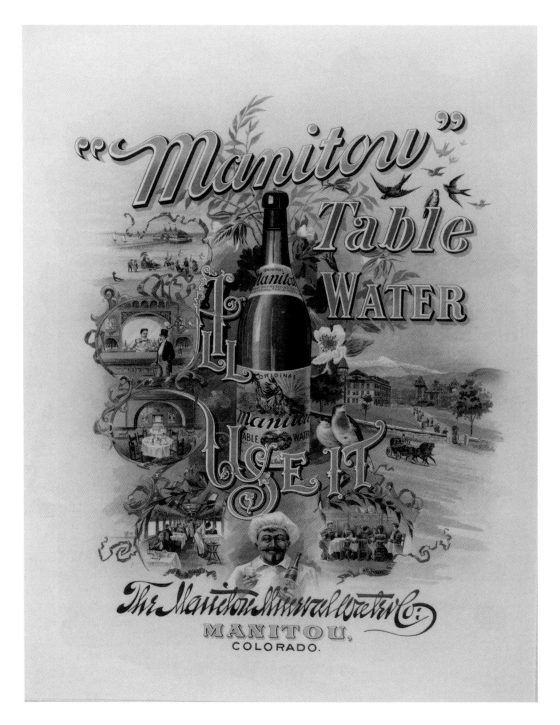

The Penrose-Tutt partnership reemerged with the formation of the Manitou Mineral Water Company, which Penrose bought from his pal, Gov. Oliver P. Shoup, in the late 1920s. Charles L. Tutt Jr. and his son William Thayer managed the company. Penrose, who had little interest in bottled water, used the company to start a wholesale liquor business in scotch whiskey from Scotland, Bordeaux wines from France, and gin from England. The firm helped the Broadmoor get a head start on liquor sales and service following repeal in 1933.

7

The Penrose Lifestyle

ALTHOUGH SPENCER AND JULIE poured their enthusiasm, energy, and money into the Broadmoor Hotel, it was only a home port for their global rambling. Julie, who fell in love with Europe during her grand tour at age 17, could never get enough of the continent. His brother Dick's international travels piqued Spencer's curiosity about exotic countries. Fortunately, the earnings from the Utah Copper stock financed the continual travel that fed the couple's wanderlust.

For nearly three decades they wintered in Europe, sailing across the Atlantic aboard the *Lurline, Europa, Empress of Britain, Lapland, Ile de France,* and other luxury liners. They left Colorado each fall and returned after exploring foreign lands, savoring cuisine, staying at the world's finest inns, and bringing back souvenirs, culture, and entertainment from various parts of the globe. Europe continued to be a magnet, especially after Julie's daughter Gladys married Count Cornet de Ways Ruart in 1914. Through this marriage Spencer and Julie gained a 50-year-old son-in-law, a Belgian count who owned a racehorse and a moldering family chateau, and Brussels became a frequent destination. Belgium's capital city boasted more than 500 breweries, and Spencer may have sampled the local specialty, beer flavored with juniper berries. Julie explored the country's Catholic past—historic cathedrals, monasteries, and convents. She and Gladys shopped at the Saint-Hubert Galleries, the world's first covered shopping arcade.

Spencer and Julie enjoyed the Orient. They traveled to California by Pullman car or private rail coach, then sailed from the West Coast. Sometimes they visited with Daniel Jackling and his young wife, Virginia, in San Francisco. In 1911 they traveled through China, Japan, and the Philippine Islands with Ashton and Grace Potter, original owners of El Pomar.[1]

Wearing a broad-brimmed western hat, sports jacket, riding pants, boots, and a well-waxed moustache, Penrose in his prime pursued an enviable lifestyle. According to a sketch by Forbes Parkhill in the July 24, 1937, *Saturday Evening Post,* Penrose swam and rode a horse daily. "He detested being called a prominent citizen but welcomed the title sportsman. Friends say he is a dreamer who puts up a front of cynicism. He dislikes those who whisper in his presence. He detests dial telephones, which he cannot master."

No matter how late Penrose had been carousing the night before, he arose at dawn to take a walk or horseback ride around the Broadmoor complex. Midmorning, he motored down to the Mining Exchange Building in Colorado Springs to check up on his Utah Copper Company stock. He might lunch at the El Paso Club, then head back to his house for an afternoon nap before dinner and evening festivities. "Any man who works after noon," he quipped, "is a damned fool."

A three-month excursion in 1925 took the Penroses through Honolulu, Shanghai, Hong Kong, Saigon, Singapore, Rangoon, Calcutta, Delhi, and Bombay.

The East Coast was both a destination and a departure point for trips abroad. They passed through Detroit to visit Julie's family or stopped in Philadelphia. There were fewer fraternal hunting trips in the 1920s, but the brothers maintained a regular correspondence. Spencer visited with Charles, a professor at the University of Pennsylvania and president of the Philadelphia Zoo. Dick had returned to the old Spruce Street home and kept busy as a director of the Philadelphia Academy of Natural Sciences and the Fairmont Park Commission and trustee of the University of Pennsylvania and the Philadelphia Free Public Library.

Spencer and Julie particularly loved New York City. Spencer traveled there regularly for Utah Copper Company board meetings, and they passed through frequently on their way to Europe. They enjoyed the entertainment, such as Jack Dempsey's celebrated match in 1926. "Will you kindly reserve for Mrs. Penrose, myself, and maid our regular corner rooms," Penrose asked the manager of the Ritz-Carlton. "We are going to New York for the purpose of attending the Dempsey fight. . . . Mr. Dempsey has been my guest at the Broadmoor since July 1. He is training very hard, running ten to twelve miles in the morning, rowing on the lake, playing eighteen holes of golf and punching a sixty lb. bag for a half afternoon every afternoon."[2]

Julie delighted in New York opera, symphony, and theater. She loved shopping with art dealers like Harold Parsons, who told her: "When you are in New York this winter, I hope you will let me know, and we will go to see some beautiful things. We will look at *every* Renoir in dealers' hands, and I am sure that we can find a lovely one which would give you and your daughter great joy always—and at a sensible price."[3]

During the Broadmoor's slow winter months, the Penroses took cruises overseas. They dressed impeccably, even in the sandy deserts of Egypt. On February 17, 1913, they and a lady friend posed for a portrait with the Sphinx, whose inscrutability intrigued tight-lipped Spencer.

Fleeing the nippy Colorado winters became a habit for the Penroses, shown here on November 20, 1930, prepared to sail to France. Courtesy Denver Public Library, Western History Department.

In Europe the Penroses often lingered in Paris, staying at the Majestic, Plaza-Athene, or Princess Hotel. Julie indulged her taste for French perfume, lingerie, and haute couture. They traveled the continent, cruised the Mediterranean, or sailed up the Nile. Their 1922 tour with Clarence

Hamlin took them to Belgium, the British Isles, Italy, Switzerland, Portugal, Egypt, Palestine, Algeria, and Monaco. "How long do you expect to be in Europe?" exclaimed Speck's friend Fred Bonfils, publisher of the *Denver Post*. "My, what runabouts you and Julie are getting to be! You never stay at home any more."[4]

They often vacationed abroad with Bert and Ethel Carlton or relatives from Detroit and Philadelphia. They spent Christmas 1922 in Paris at the Hotel Plaza–Athens with Henry Blackmer, a leading Colorado financier and oilman, and Charles MacNeill. In March 1924 they planned a trip to Morocco but canceled when Spencer's ulcer flared up. Instead they lounged at Cannes with Gladys and Paul, Mrs. MacNeill, Christine Biddle, and Mrs. and Mrs. Spencer Biddle.

France was their favorite destination. They frequented the French Riviera, especially favoring Nice, scene of Spencer's flustered marriage proposal. The Maritime Alps, which separate France and Italy, reminded them of the Rocky Mountains. The pale stucco walls, red-tiled roofs, and multistoried skylines of Nice and other French villages had influenced their choice of Mediterranean design for the Broadmoor.

To be closer to Gladys, Paul, and their new granddaughter Pauline, in 1929 the Penroses leased an apartment in Paris at 60 Avenue Foch, formerly Avenue du Bois de Boulogne, the city's widest thoroughfare and lined with luxurious residences. The home had an entrance on the avenue and consisted of a hall-gallery, dining room, two drawing rooms, seven bedrooms, six dressing rooms, four bathrooms, four cellars, and five servants' bedrooms on the top floor. Spencer and Julie enjoyed visiting nearby Bois de Boulogne, the former royal hunting ground turned into a sumptuous park. They sampled its grand restaurants, racetracks, flower gardens, small zoo, and horse carriage and walking paths. They wintered in Paris, maintaining bedrooms for Gladys, Paul, and Pauline. The Penroses entertained lavishly at the Parisian apartment, where Spencer kept a well-stocked liquor cabinet guarded year-round by the butler. Julie threw herself into redecorating, repainting, carpeting, and furnishing the place in high style.

In 1934 they bought a cottage near Honolulu between Diamond Head and Koko Head. "We intend to give up our Paris apartment on May 1st," Spencer explained to his friend, New York hotelier Thomas Green. "Therefore in the future we will be much more foot loose. I will not be compelled to come to Paris or go to Phila. except when I want to."[5] Spencer and Julie improved their "little place on the bay," adding a wine room, installing a wooden dance floor, and landscaping the gardens. "We are becoming more and more delighted with the place," he wrote their granddaughter Pauline. "Everything is perfect and we are fixing up the yard. . . . The dance floor has turned out wonderfully successful. . . . Yesterday we were down at the boat to meet Mrs. Carlton and Mrs. Wilcox of Denver, and about eight Philadelphia people."[6] Spencer convinced Julie that they should build a larger house on the other side of the island, but it was not finished when Spencer died in 1939.

In his global travels, Penrose became an epicure of the world's top lodgings. He patronized only his favorites and fraternized with their owners and managers. In New York City he preferred a corner suite at the Ritz-Carlton, designed by Broadmoor architects Warren and Wetmore. In Philadelphia he also preferred the Ritz-Carlton, whose splendid interiors had inspired him to hire Westing, Evans, and Egmore to decorate the Broadmoor. In Denver Spencer and Julie insisted on "our apartment on the second floor," rooms 208 and 210 at the Brown Palace Hotel. In Glenwood Springs, where they retreated to the Hotel Colorado, they demanded a suite overlooking the courtyard. Penrose preferred a corner suite. Aboard a ship they had to have deckside seating and a table at the entrance to the dining salon. All reservations—from Pullman cars to five-star hotels to first-class staterooms—included a smaller room for Julie's French maid.

Penrose monitored his business affairs while away. He dictated lengthy letters to Charley Tutt and other assistants, dashing off telegrams for urgent matters. Morgan-Harjes and Company of Paris forwarded his mail, including subscriptions to the *New York Times, United States News,* and *Boston News Bureau.* Their travels provided marketing opportunities. Wherever he went, Penrose promoted his hotel, displaying Broadmoor booklets on steamships and at each hotel.

Travels doubled as shopping junkets to replenish furnishings and decorative items for the Broadmoor. Julie shopped in Paris and New York for stylish frocks, chic hats, and smart bags and shoes for her Broadmoor Sports Shop. She ordered bamboo furniture for the hotel's Palm Room. She bought Oriental vases and sculptures to decorate El Pomar, the Paris apartment, and the Honolulu cottage. A $2,675 shipment from Peking included a pair of jade birds, a lotus ashtray, a jade boat, and pieces of 380-year-old furniture.[7]

Their travels also provided inspiration for hotel decor and recreation. Julie's love of all things French inspired "Streets of Paris," transforming the hotel courtyard into an old French castle.[8] She poured her passion for the Orient into the "Japanese party" that opened the 1936 Broadmoor season, highlighted by a wisteria bower for 525 dinner guests.[9] Junkets to Hawaii inspired the Jungle Room on the second floor of the Broadmoor Golf Club. The Penroses hired a Hawaiian artist to decorate the nightclub with paper leis, small grass huts, and hula dolls. They imported hula dancer Aggie Auld from Hollywood to swivel her hips in the Jungle Room and invited her to a party at El Pomar "so that we can introduce you to thirty or forty of our dancing friends."[10]

Whether away or at home, Spencer and Julie enjoyed entertaining. "They were always doing something fun," recalls Pat Croke, who grew up

Spring brought the Penroses back to the Broadmoor from their world travels. Upon their return the couple jumped into Colorado Springs social life. For the second annual Sunflower Carnival in 1906, the Tutts and Penroses dressed in summer whites to adorn this float. Courtesy photo by Horace S. Poley.

While posing with tents pitched on Cheyenne Mountain, Spencer and Julie Penrose and their rotund companion, Colorado Governor Oliver Shoup, more than likely found more comfortable quarters that night at the Broadmoor or El Pomar.

To amuse himself and his fellow gourmands, Spencer Penrose founded the Cooking Club in 1912. He modeled it after Philadelphia's Rabbit Club, whose bacchanals he had relished. Chester Alan Arthur II, the playboy son of a U.S. president, served as first president of the club. After first meeting in members' homes, the Cooking Club moved into the rustic clubhouse Penrose built on Cheyenne Mountain next to the zoo. In 1913 Penrose succeeded Arthur and presided for the rest of his life. Penrose, *front and center* with cigar in hand, guided the club's epicureans in the art of fine dining, drinking, and cigar smoking.

in the Broadmoor neighborhood. "They loved people and they had all these fun ideas." They shared with friends an enthusiasm for sports, the arts, travel, gourmet cooking, and expensive drink. Spencer organized monthly gourmet gatherings and elaborate cocktail parties at El Pomar and the Broadmoor. Julie threw dinner parties for Broadmoor neighbors, Detroit relatives, and wives of her husband's friends. More sedate get-togethers included swimming parties, teas, recitals by the hotel orchestra, and parties for neighborhood children.

Spencer's wide circle of acquaintances included members of his forty or so private clubs, ranging from Salt Lake City's Alta Club to the Harvard Engineering Society to Detroit's Yondotoga Club. In his hometown he

Penrose, *left,* posed in 1938 with his longtime chum Harry Leonard at one of his last Cooking Club dinners. Even in death, Penrose sustains the Cooking Club: his will set aside a fund to host January and July banquets for the exclusive male membership. Penrose's spirit still presides over the feast from his empty chair, as a huge gold medallion of Bacchus smiles on the stone fireplace. Each place is set with six liquor glasses and a battery of bottles. The oldest are from Penrose's still unexhausted personal supply.

belonged to the Philadelphia Club, Racquet Club, Country Club, Barge Club, and gourmet Rabbit Club. In New York he was a member of the University Club, Union League, and Rocky Mountain Club, an "Eastern Home of Western Men." In Denver he belonged to the Mile High City's two most prestigious organizations, the Denver Club and Denver Country Club. He was president of Colorado Springs' El Paso Club, the downtown social club where he had roomed during his bachelor days. He served on the boards of the Broadmoor Golf Club and the Cheyenne Mountain Country Club.

Lucius Beebe, chronicler of the rich and famous, relates this tale of Penrose's legendary club life:

> Although he visited San Francisco at only the most infrequent intervals and, at the time of his death at the age of seventy-four in 1939, hadn't seen the Golden Gate in a decade, Spencer Penrose maintained active membership in the Pacific Union, the town's most exclusive and expensive gentlemen's club on the top of Nob Hill, as long as he lived. Asked why he remained a member of a club he never used, Penrose's reply was characteristic: "My God, man!" he said in astonished tones, "I might want a drink out there!"[11]

Penrose used his club memberships to promote his hotel, passing out Broadmoor brochures wherever he went. His favorite organization, the Cooking Club, was his personal creation. Formed in 1912 to solidify bonds between the power elite of Colorado Springs and that of Denver, the club helped satiate his astonishing appetite for food and drink and fondness for fine cigars. It was patterned after Philadelphia's 'Rabbit Club, a favorite of the Penrose men. Each monthly meeting featured an epicurean extravaganza

Russell and Thayer Tutt presided at the Cooking Club under Boardman Robinson's famous lusty-gourmand portrait of Penrose, the club's founder and president-for-life. Penrose also lingers in the slogan he picked for the club:

Good friends, for friendship's sake forebear
To utter what is gossip here
In social chat, lest it may be
Thy tongue do wrong to us and thee.

Bill Tutt, son of Charles L. Tutt II, has presided over the Cooking Club since 1991. He reports: "We have thirty-eight members, half from Colorado Springs and half from the Denver area. The idea is to promote cooperation between the key men in the two communities."

Penrose and several Tutts have graced the membership of the El Paso Club, the oldest (1877) men's social club in the Rockies. The 1883 clubhouse still stands at 30 E. Platte Avenue. Professor James H. Kerr, who taught science at Colorado College, built the Queen Anne–style house with a distinctive crocodile finial atop the corner tower. The El Paso Club moved into the house in 1891, after the City agreed to give it the town's only liquor license. At the billiard tables they still talk about the night Speck Penrose accidentally ripped the felt and spent an unsteady hour trying to pen a letter of apology. Frustrated, he threw the ink well through the window. Courtesy photo by Tom Noel.

prepared by a designated member. Spencer acted as ringleader, enhancing each club dinner with his special hot rum toddy and fine cigars. "I will look after the liquors and I will make a large bowl of the noted Broadmoor hot rum punch," he promised one guest. "This punch is absolutely harmless and will cure all diseases, and is the best foundation in the world to start a meal with."[12] He bragged to Henry Blackmer: "Devereux and I cooked twenty-four ducks, but we did not put them on until after the fish course and I must say they were cooked to perfection, and we had plenty of juices from my big duck press, which I took up to the Club. . . . I gave them plenty of the apple toddy. Everyone drank copiously and every drop was used."[13]

Among the gourmands were Penrose's closest friends and business associates. Charlie MacNeill and Charley Tutt Jr. were officers of the Broadmoor Hotel and Land Company and were involved in other Penrose ventures. Eugene Shove and Clarence Hamlin sat on the boards of Penrose's copper- and gold-mining companies. William Otis was a director of a half-dozen Penrose transportation companies. Albert E. Carlton controlled Cripple Creek's mining, milling, and transportation industries; he also was president of Holly Sugar and a director of Penrose's Garden City Land and Sugar Company. Sugar beet and cement tycoon Claude K. Boettcher had sold Spencer enormous quantities of cement used in the hotel and the Rosemont-Penrose dam. Other influential Denver members included oil baron Albert E. Humphreys Sr., mine manager Bulkeley Wells, Harry Leonard, Horace Devereux, Ashton Potter, Bryant Turner, and Spencer's brother-in-law, Clarence Carpenter. Colorado Governor John A. Love, a former Broadmoor Polo Club employee, and Denver Mayor Quigg Newton later became Cooking Clubbers.

Penrose spearheaded construction of a clubhouse in 1914, a rustic stone lodge on Cheyenne Mountain. He outfitted it with dark wood furnishings and mounted heads of deer, elk, and bighorn sheep that gazed down on the diners. He donated miscellaneous stocks and bonds to help fund club expenses and created an endowment to fund the club's annual Penrose dinner into perpetuity. Each January and July, Spencer posthumously hosts dinner, drinks, and smokes at a memorial banquet featuring his favorite entrees—3-pound steaks and 3-pound lobsters followed by apple brown betty and a toast with his vintage Hennessey scotch.

The Cooking Club still follows time-honored traditions more than sixty years after its founder's death. Seating is still assigned, with an empty chair reserved for Penrose. Cocktails and appetizers precede the gourmet repast, prepared now by retired Broadmoor chefs rather than members. An after-dinner talk is followed by a toast "to the departed members." The men then light up savory cigars. Members take turns sponsoring the meal—planning the menu, selecting the wines, and paying for the repast. Club membership includes Colorado Springs and Denver business leaders, several

Spencer Penrose, Colorado's most notorious tippler, campaigned in his llama-drawn cart for repeal of the Prohibition Amendment. Although a die-hard Republican, Speck supported Democrat Al Smith in 1928 as the "wet" candidate facing the "dry" Republican Herbert Hoover. Penrose even put Franklin D. Roosevelt up at the Broadmoor in 1932 after the president promised to repeal Prohibition.

Prohibition did not dry out Penrose. He stockpiled vast supplies at the Broadmoor and various clubrooms in Philadelphia and New York. Rumor had it that Speck also had hidden a fortune in booze in some of his abandoned Cripple Creek mines. Penrose, quipped one old prospector, was the only man who salted mines with whiskey.

with business ties to Penrose enterprises. Many have served on El Pomar Foundation board, including Karl Eitel, William I. Howbert, William Hybl, Robert V. Menary, Kent Olin, H. Chase Stone, Charles L. Tutt Jr., Russell T. Tutt, William Thayer Tutt, R. Thayer Tutt Jr., Joel A.H. Webb, and Ben S. Wendelken.

During Prohibition the Cooking Club remained a venue for Spencer's enjoyment of liquid refreshment, a pastime that had become increasingly difficult to pursue. When the Volstead Act prohibited sale of liquor in 1919, Penrose launched a vociferous campaign for repeal. He staged repeal campaigns and rallies at the Broadmoor and presided over the Colorado chapter of the Association Against the Prohibition. He turned up at repeal events in a llama-pulled cart and christened the camel at his Broadmoor zoo "Ethel Volstead" after the wife of the Prohibition Act's author. He even threatened to switch his allegiance to the anti-Prohibition Democratic Party, weary of the "pussyfooting and vacillating position the Republican Party has taken upon this all-important subject."[14] Despite his valiant efforts, Spencer waited fifteen long years before repeal allowed him again to serve liquor legally at the Broadmoor.

In anticipation of this red-letter day, Penrose amassed 800 cases of alcohol, which he stored in warehouses back east. This stockpile consisted of liquor inherited from his brothers' estates, spirits purchased abroad, and the contents of the New York University Club's wine cellar, sold to Penrose on the eve of Prohibition. First padlocked in rented warehouses in Philadelphia and New York, 200 cases were moved to the Penrose

Mocking Prohibition at every opportunity, Penrose named this camel Ethel Volstead after the wife of U.S. Senator Andrew J. Volstead, author of the Prohibition Amendment. The Broadmoor's pet chimpanzee, Jemma, rides Ethel in this 1927 photo. Jemma later joined Penrose for a cocktail party toasting the end of the national dry spell. Courtesy Colorado Historical Society.

family home on Spruce Street in the 1920s, filling bedrooms, closets, and cellars. Penrose stored another 600 cases in two rooms at the University Club in Manhattan, paying over $28,000 in rent until repeal came fifteen years later.[15]

Not all of Penrose's liquid assets were back east, however. Vintage alcohol was discovered beneath the outdoor swimming pool at the Broadmoor when it was remodeled in the early 1990s. Tales of illicit liquor hidden in Cripple Creek mine shafts are unproven, but Spencer kept a well-stocked, triple-locked wine cellar at El Pomar, accessed by a stairway hidden behind bookcases in the library. He delighted in sharing this bounty with guests in his home and sent out engraved invitations for El Pomar cocktail parties. Penrose affairs epitomized the riotous gaiety of the Roaring Twenties. The house overflowed with people, and liquor livened up costume parties, all-night parties, and lavish dinner banquets. "I think you and Julie are having some fun out of life, more than anybody I know," Fred Bonfils told Spencer. "I am glad you both have sense enough to enjoy it as you go along."[16]

When repeal finally came, the 800 cases of New York liquor rolled west in two railroad cars. Penrose sold the booze to the Broadmoor for $50,000. Soon the hotel cocktail menu offered an array of whiskeys, fancy cocktails, and prized prewar liquors. Hundreds of bottles from Penrose's vintage collection are still on display in the Broadmoor Tavern.

His mining fortune allowed Spencer to indulge his love for liquor and helped fund his fervent appreciation of gourmet foods, expensive cigars, and tailored clothes. An epicure extraordinaire, he terrorized Broadmoor chefs with his exacting expectations. He pampered his palate with choice foods ordered from back east and served at El Pomar and the Cooking Club. Weekly shipments of butter, scrapple, and sausage came from Philadelphia, as well as box after box of Potomac smoked herring. Speck ordered coffee and gallon tins of olive oil from New York City, ham and bacon from Wisconsin, and hens and fresh eggs from Kansas. He also tickled his palate with Atlantic City oysters by the barrel and Maryland-style diamond-back terrapin at $9 per quart.[17]

Penrose also turned to producing meat, dairy products, and produce at his Turkey Creek Ranch 20 miles south of Colorado Springs on the road to Cañon City. Originally a 320-acre spread, the farm eventually included around 25,000 acres. The Penrose Cattle Company raised pedigreed Hereford cattle and Shropshire sheep. Penrose carefully monitored dairy production and sold milk and butter to the Broadmoor Hotel and the El Paso Club. Spencer sent back east for a special mold so his butter would look like the Philadelphia product he fancied. He cultivated an orchard, but his attempts at brewing applejack went awry.

As a business enterprise, Turkey Creek yielded meager profits but satisfied Spencer's agricultural ambitions frustrated twenty-five years earlier

At his Turkey Creek Ranch, Penrose maintained a model spread, with white painted barns and other outbuildings. Besides his horses, cattle, and hogs, he kept a menagerie of wild animals, including three elk, six black-tailed Michigan deer, a black bear, and a grizzly bear. After he opened the Cheyenne Mountain Zoo in 1926, Penrose moved the more exotic creatures there. He continued to use Turkey Creek Ranch as a place to raise food for the Cheyenne Mountain Zoo. In 1942 the U.S. Army converted the adjacent Cheyenne Valley Ranch to Fort Carson. The army bought 1,135 acres of Turkey Creek Ranch in 1965 and in 1997 opened it to the public as a recreation area. The army is restoring the Penrose ranch house as a visitor's center. Courtesy Pikes Peak Library District, Local History Collection.

in southern New Mexico. He dabbled in ranching and farming with the same thoroughness as in his other businesses. "As soon as you receive this letter I want you to use a full force with three teams and gather in all the crops, and do not stop for Sunday, or any other cause, except bad weather," he instructed farm manager Charles Chess. "I consider it very poor farming not to work on Sundays when your hay crop is on the ground. At El Pomar we got our whole crop in a few days by working overtime and on Sunday, and there is no reason why we should not work on Sundays at Turkey Creek Farm when it is necessary."[18]

The Turkey Creek Ranch provided a retreat from the fishbowl life at Broadmoor. Architects Thomas McLaren and Charles Thomas designed a roomy, U-shaped, Mission Revival dwelling wrapped around an east-facing courtyard. Influenced more by European design than that of the rustic American West, the ranch house featured an English-style great room heated by a massive marble hearth, a butler pantry, three bedrooms for servants, and two padlocked wine cellars. The backyard swimming pool and string of saddle horses provided recreation. In later years the ranch became a pantry for Spencer's burgeoning assortment of exotic animals at Broadmoor. Oats and hay and butchered horsemeat were hauled from Turkey Creek to feed zebras, giraffes, lions, and tigers at his zoo. The U.S. Army purchased the ranch in 1965, and today Fort Carson operates it as a recreation area for military personnel and civilians.[19]

Developing an entire farm to supply his personal table typified the grand scale on which Penrose operated. To satisfy his fondness for fine cigars, he ordered Larranaga Invincibles by the thousands from J. V. Flanigan in New York. Each year he mailed fifty to his closest friends, wrapped in

To raise apples and livestock, Penrose bought the 12,000-acre Turkey Creek Ranch 20 miles south of the Broadmoor and erected a modest Mediterranean-style ranch house in 1912. Two years later Penrose received a fruit distillers' license and permits from the U.S. Internal Revenue Service. He set up a copper still capable of making 20 gallons of apple brandy a day. Turkey Creek beef, lamb, and perhaps the brandy graced the tables at the Broadmoor.

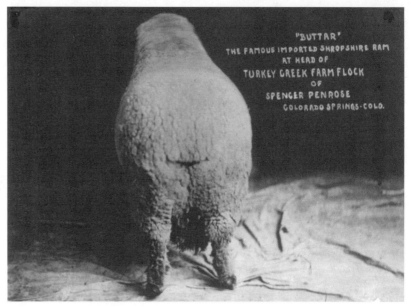

bands printed with "SP" and packed in boxes engraved with "especially selected for Spencer Penrose." Albert Carlton thanked him: "While the wonderful cigars are very much appreciated, your thoughtfulness in remembering me is something that really makes life worthwhile."[20]

Penrose gambled on a large scale, too. He wagered thousands of dollars on his favorite political candidates. His bets on the 1918 election of Governor Oliver Shoup and U.S. Senator Lawrence Phipps exceeded

$12,000. In 1916 he staked thousands against presidential candidate Woodrow Wilson. Spencer's gambling took other forms. He and Julie enjoyed going to the Kentucky Derby in Louisville. At the Broadmoor in 1938 he leased rooms 600 and 602 to E. B. Rossman of Los Angeles for a clandestine gambling operation. Such underground enterprises were not uncommon. Spencer knew Hurlee Inman was running a gambling house in Dr. William Bell's old house in Manitou and that Smiling Charley Stevens and a nephew of Albert Humphreys had similar places in Denver.[21] The Broadmoor venture, however, appears to have been short-lived.

Penrose's extravagant taste extended to his wardrobe as well. His daily outfit of knee boots, jodhpurs, and English riding jacket was custom-ordered from eastern tailors and a New York City bootmaker. He cabled this complaint to Wetzel, Inc., a New York tailor he patronized for decades: "This plaid sporting coat is too big all over. Shoulders slop over and should be raised up. Collar is loose in the back of the neck. Please make changes and return the coat to me here."[22] Spurning off-the-rack clothing, he sent Wetzel a favorite jacket to copy as a pattern and another time left him a French dress shirt to "study as a model." Spencer preferred that his shirts and underclothing come from Philadelphia. "On Saturday I ordered ten suits of underwear from you," he informed Bowker and Bowker on Chestnut Street. "Will you please substitute drawers 37 inches in the waist instead of 38 inches. I find this is my right measurement, which is correct today. Be sure to have the shirts 46 inches, and when you have them ready send by express to me at Colorado Springs."[23]

He was even fussier about his glass eye. As a youth, Penrose strained his retina while lifting a Harvard boat out of the Saint Charles River. The injury hampered his reading and bothered him for years. By 1906 he was blind in that eye. Finally, he had the eye surgically removed in 1927. He scorned an eye patch and filled the empty socket with a custom-made glass eye. Speck even ordered a red-veined one to wear on mornings following a drinking spree. The glass eye, however, was not a perfect solution. "Yesterday afternoon I stopped at your office and experimented with the new eye, which you had made for me," he complained to Kohler and Danz of New York City. "I found it entirely unsatisfactory. The rim was a new shape and different from the one which I bought from you several days ago. . . . The eye I did purchase from you seems allright in color, etc., but it does not stay in place, and if I am not very careful the eye turns up-side-down."[24]

Julie kept an eye on the arts as well. She insisted on only the best orchestras at the hotel and invited the musicians to entertain guests at El Pomar. Her donation of her beautiful house on West Dale helped launch the Broadmoor Art Academy. She was a steady supporter of the Colorado Springs Fine Arts Center. She generously gave to the Central City Opera House for its 1930s revival and bought and restored a small cottage as a personal haven in the crumbling mining town.

At Julie's request, Spencer Penrose hired architect Thomas McClaren to design the Pauline Chapel *(see color insert)* in honor of their granddaughter Pauline, later the Baroness Pauline Francois de Longchamps. Courtesy Denver Public Library, Western History Department.

Her love of material things did not dampen Julie's spiritual nature. After returning to the Catholic faith of her childhood, she shared the Penrose bounty with those less fortunate. She was particularly helpful to boys. "She was tremendously kind," recalled Peter Brown, whose Fountain Valley School education she helped fund. "When I was about six or seven, I was in bed with rheumatic fever. She was worried about me and used to bring me elaborate presents. She brought me a bicycle shaped like an airplane. I had to stay in bed and watch out the window while my brothers peddled around on my new toy. She was very good to me. I think her son Jimmie made her sympathetic with my situation."[25]

A devout Catholic in later life, Julie attended daily Mass. At her request, Penrose hired prominent Colorado Springs architect Thomas McLaren to design a small chapel east of El Pomar. It was built in 1918 as

Speck Penrose spent an estimated $100 million to turn the Pikes Peak region into a recreational haven. In 1914 he and Julie built this $12,000 municipal pool in Monument City Park below 30 W. Dale Street, the first of many Penrose gifts to the city. El Pomar Foundation is working with the City to revitalize and beautify the Monument Park area at the junction of Fountain and Monument Creeks in the heart of downtown. An El Pomar grant initiated planning for a 30-acre park, the prospective hub of a 35-mile greenway system that would transform unkempt creek beds into walkways and parks. Courtesy Library of Congress.

a sign of thanksgiving for the safe release of her daughter Gladys and son-in-law Paul after the two had been placed under house arrest in Belgium during World War I. Named for Julie's granddaughter, Pauline Chapel features thick Spanish Mission–style walls and elaborate baroque entryways and windows. The chapel houses a collection of sixteenth- and seventeenth-century religious artifacts bought by Spencer in Europe at bargain wartime prices. These include a painted triptych from a Spanish cathedral, a gilded reliquary containing a lock of hair from St. Therese, the Little Flower, a bishop's chair from England, and a Madonna and Child painted for the king of Peru. This sacred place provided Julie with spiritual solace in troubled times—during Spencer's illness and death, after Pauline's death, and when Gladys was diagnosed with multiple sclerosis.

Julie's generous spirit also molded Spencer's image of himself as benefactor and philanthropist. Although he remained a pragmatic businessman who kept his hand in numerous projects and his eye on the bottom line, Penrose learned to give. The Penroses donated regularly to dozens of Colorado Springs causes and hosted fundraising events of all kinds at the Broadmoor and El Pomar. They helped pay some of their workers' medical bills and tuition for college-bound children. Their first civic gift was the municipal swimming pool and pavilion, built in 1914 in Monument Park below their home on West Dale.[26] Later they funded the $100,000 Boies Penrose Hall at the Fountain Valley School.

These philanthropic overtures would increase in subsequent years, culminating with the ongoing work of El Pomar Foundation. During the 1920s, however, Spencer focused on an array of successful enterprises. Not only did he dominate Colorado Springs' hospitality, tourism, and transportation industries; he also invested in a variety of commercial schemes ranging from town building to mining, from railroads to sugar beets.

NOTES

1. Penrose House, Spencer Penrose Collection, Box 11, File 30, letter from Penrose to Mr. Stevens, chief boarding officer, U.S. Customer Service, San Francisco, April 17, 1911.

2. Ibid., letter from Penrose to Ritz-Carlton, December 8, 1926.

3. Ibid., Box 65, File 293, letter from Harold W. Parsons, Mar Monte Hotel, Santa Barbara Hotel, September 8, 1941.

4. Ibid., Box 105, File 425, letter dated September 28, 1925.

5. Ibid., Box 30, File 73, letters dated March 19, 1934.

6. Ibid., Box 55, File 243, letter dated January 24, 1936.

7. Ibid., Box 6, File 16, invoice dated April 4, 1935.

8. Ibid., Broadmoor Scrapbook—1933, unidentified article.

9. Ibid., Spencer Penrose Collection, Box 5, File 6, letter from Merton Bogart to Mrs. Willing Spencer, June 15, 1936.

10. Ibid., Box 20, File H455, letters dated May 12, May 20, May 27, and August 28, 1938.

11. Lucius Beebe, *The Big Spenders.* Garden City, N.Y.: Doubleday, 1966, p. 216.

12. Penrose House, Spencer Penrose Collection, Box 10, File 26, letter to A. W. Newberry dated August 28, 1935.

13. Ibid., Box 19, File 50, letter to Henry Blackmer dated October 21, 1929.

14. Ibid., Box 10, File 26, letter dated September 26, 1931.

15. *Empire Magazine*, the *Denver Post,* February 19, 1953, pp. 26–27.

16. Penrose House, Spencer Penrose Collection, Box 105, File 425, letter dated September 28, 1925.

17. Ibid., Box 6, File 16, letters dated September 10, 1910; December 31, 1912.

18. Ibid., Box 46, File 192, dated September 19, 1932.

19. Tom Noel and Cathleen Norman tour of Turkey Creek Ranch with David Thompson and Dennis Kotke, March 10, 1997.

20. Penrose House, Spencer Penrose Collection, Box 63, File 292, letter dated December 16, 1928.

21. Ibid., Box 6, File 6, memorandum dated May 19, 1938.

22. Ibid., Box 42, File 152, telegram dated January 24, 1936.

23. Ibid., letter dated November 1919.

24. Ibid., Box 6, File 16, letter dated December 13, 1933.

25. Peter A.G. Brown, interviewed by Cathleen Norman, April 17, 1997.

26. Penrose House, Spencer Penrose Collection, Box 25, File 89.

8

Sugar and Water, Railroads and Tourists

SPENCER'S COPPER-MINING STOCK MADE HIS FORTUNE and allowed him to try his hand at many other business ventures, most notably mining, transportation, tourism, and agriculture. These ventures had in common the thoroughness Penrose applied to any undertaking. His Colorado investments had begun in the Cripple Creek Mining District with gold mines, railroads, and mills. Penrose applied the same consolidated approach to subsequent enterprises. He not only built the Broadmoor Hotel; he also bought and rejuvenated a half-dozen other tourist attractions to entice visitors to the region and to his resort. He lobbied for paving the Denver–Colorado Springs road in the 1920s to speed auto tourists to his hotel and the region. He sold low-grade ore from his Cripple Creek mine as ballast for the highway, shipping the rock down Ute Pass on his Colorado Midland Railroad.[1] His Pikes Peak empire extended to corporate management and financing. Corporate assets overlapped as well, as one company often invested in another. Financing for his mining and milling operations, sugar beet fields and factories, resort hotel, and water reservoirs continued to come from eastern investors, as well as Cripple Creek cronies like Carlton, MacNeill, and Hamlin.

The three men joined Penrose in mining, milling, transportation, and hospitality firms, as well as farming and ranching. Despite his failed fruit company in Las Cruces in 1889, Penrose never lost interest in agriculture. Spencer expanded Turkey Creek from a 320-acre farm into a 12,000-acre ranch on which he raised livestock and cultivated orchards to stock the pantries at El Pomar and the Broadmoor Hotel. Then he turned south to the sage- and piñon-covered land midway between Cañon City and Pueblo. "A few days ago I happened to be in Grand Junction, and going through the orchards where I noticed a great many orchards have beets planted

Spencer Penrose and Albert E. Carlton bought the Colorado Midland Railroad in 1917, promoting tourism to supplement declining mining revenues. This new Indian logo (*below*) helped the line to draw tourists, such as these wildflower lovers (*right*). Courtesy logo photo by Henry H. Buckwalter, Colorado Historical Society; wildflower excursion photo by Louis C. McClure, Denver Public Library, Western History Department.

between the trees," he told a business associate. "We have several thousand acres of land a good part of which could be very easily planted to beets, and with an abundance of water, I do not see why we should not get a very respectable crop."[2] He incorporated the Beaver Park and Land Company and planned sugar beet fields, orchards, and a farming community named Penrose.

Spencer's Midas touch did not apply to his Beaver Park and Penrose Town Company projects, where his earnings ranged from meager profits to embarrassing losses. He ran his Beaver, Penrose, & Northern Railway south from Penrose to the D&RG line that connected Pueblo and Cañon City. The railway brought prospective land buyers to view sites being sold by the Beaver Land and Irrigation Company.[3] A steam locomotive ran weekly on the 6.5-mile line, supplemented by an automobile outfitted to run on the tracks. The tiny railroad went bankrupt, and Penrose dismantled it. He sold his short-lived Penrose Mercantile Company to a Cañon City lumber dealer. His $1 million investment in the Beaver Creek Reservoir and Penrose town site was lost when a June flood washed out the Beaver Creek Dam in 1921.

Nevertheless, Penrose nursed the Beaver Park Company along, believing "there is a knack in raising beets and perhaps the people at Beaver Park do not know how to raise them to the best advantage, but in time they will learn. It is a good cash crop and the farmers can depend on receiving their money."[4] He never realized his vision of transforming dry and dusty acreage into a productive paradise. To Charley Tutt Jr. he delegated the thankless task of overseeing the company. Around 1,000 acres of Beaver Creek property remained an asset of El Pomar Investment Company until the 1970s when it was sold at a marginal profit.

Cultivating sugar beets in western Kansas yielded slightly better results but only after decades of extensive investment, prolonged risk, and corporate restructuring. Begun about the same time as the Beaver Creek Company, the United States Land and Sugar Company later reorganized as the Garden City Land and Sugar Company. Penrose's Garden City company bought nearly 20,000 acres, acquired extensive Arkansas River water rights, constructed a sugar-processing plant, and built the Garden City Western Railway. By 1920 the company had 17,805 acres planted in beets, alfalfa, wheat, and oats or leased to local farmers.[5] It also owned more than 2,600 pigs, probably raised on beet tops and other waste from the mill that produced white sugar, brown sugar, and molasses. Penrose's sugar company began a gradual turnaround when Bert Carlton took over as president in 1919. Bert was also president and a large stockholder of the Holly Sugar Company, which was ten times larger than the Garden City firm with crops and plants in seven western states. "I have just returned from a twenty-three day trip visiting ten of the eleven Holly factories, traveling 5,645 miles by rail and about 2,000 by auto," Carlton told Penrose in

Penrose, in fur coat *second from right,* and fellow investors pose in front of the Penrose Mercantile Company store in the new town of Penrose, Colorado, on January 28, 1909. Located 30 miles south of Colorado Springs and 15 miles east of Cañon City, this tiny town never became the agricultural Garden of Eden its founder envisioned.

To provide plenty of water for his Pikes Peak empire, Penrose built several dams. This 1912 structure on Beaver Creek provided water for his agricultural colony at Penrose. In 1932 he built Rosemont Dam 18 miles west of the Broadmoor on Beaver Creek. One of the first steel-faced dams constructed anywhere, it provided water for the Broadmoor and residential subdivisions.

1927. "Our plants are operating both as to capacity and extraction as never before."[6] As in their gold-mining investments, the roles of Penrose and Carlton were intertwined. Penrose sat on Carlton's Holly board and owned nearly 8,000 shares of Holly Sugar stock.

Things looked more promising for Penrose's sugar company by 1924. "We had a quite good year at Garden City under our new management, and the prospects from now on are much brighter than they ever were," he informed his brother Richard. "The damn Company has kept me busted for the last fifteen years and I am greatly in debt as a consequence. But it looks now as if we were going to pull out."[7] Five years later he disgustedly rejected Bert's invitation to buy more Holly stock. "If I had never gone into any sugar companies I would have been a great deal better off," he complained to Carlton. "As I have already said, I have lost several hundred thousand dollars in Garden City. . . . I have concluded not to invest any more in sugar stocks as they do not seem to be in my line of business."[8] Nevertheless, Penrose retained ownership of the Garden City Land and Sugar Company, which had dwindled to 8,518 acres by 1937.[9] In the 1940s Charley Tutt Jr.'s son Russell Thayer Tutt took over management of the Garden City companies. The 26,000 acres of Kansas real estate are still held today as an asset of El Pomar Foundation.[10]

Building the town at Penrose, Colorado, and raising sugar beets in west Kansas were both thwarted by a lack of water. Spencer Penrose knew how crucial this natural resource was to mining, agriculture, and land development. To prevent a lack of water from hindering his business interests, he built a series of dams. The Turkey Creek Farm, El Pomar grounds, Broadmoor grounds and golf course, Cooking Club, and Camp Vigil retreat were watered from their own separate reservoirs.

Most of the dam construction was supervised by Milt Strong and overseen by Charley Tutt. The largest project was the Rosemont-Penrose Dam. Penrose boasted to his friend Tom Green, a New York hotelier:

> Our golf course is in perfect shape, much better than ever. This condition has been produced on account of the very big Penrose-Rosemont Reservoir, which was built two years ago, twenty-five miles from the Hotel. This reservoir will hold 500 million gallons of water and at present is filled with over 400 million gallons. Consequently we went through the very serious drought of the past summer in splendid condition. The same can be said of my place, El Pomar, and our polo fields. . . . The reservoir cost an immense amount of money, but we would have been ruined by the drought if we had not had it.[11]

Penrose's relish for dam building continued until Julie intervened. As he was meeting with local rancher and builder Ed Honnen, Julie walked into the room. In response to her protests, he promised, "No more damn dams." Supposedly, his dam construction ended that day.[12] Penrose eventually gave the Rosemont and Cooking Club reservoirs to the city in exchange for 650 water taps on lower Cheyenne Mountain.

The Broadmoor Hotel remained the centerpiece of Penrose's business empire. His deep pockets had funded expansions, improvements, and redecorating and covered operating losses of $75,000 to $125,000 annually. The hotel prospered during the 1920s, but during the Great Depression it

As mining fizzled after 1910, agriculture became Colorado's most important industry. Spencer Penrose joined Albert E. Carlton and other investors in raising the richest agricultural crop of the early 1900s—sugar beets. They formed the Garden City Land and Sugar Company, with 20,000 acres along the Arkansas River in western Kansas. Farmers raised the big, sugar-filled beets, bringing them to the railhead in horse-drawn wagons and trucks. The Garden City Western Railway carried the beets to another Carlton-Penrose operation, the Holly Sugar Company refineries in Holly and other southeastern Colorado towns. As this 1942 billboard suggests, sugar beets continued to pay off during World War II. Only after the war did the sugar beet market turn sour. Courtesy Library of Congress photos by Arthur Rothstein and John Vachon (billboard), railcars by Roger Whitacre.

became a white elephant. "The Hotel Company is passing through a serious situation," Penrose told the hotel groundskeeper in 1932. "See if you cannot reduce this force immediately, and still keep up the work in respectable style. We notice some of your men are rather old and it may be advisable to replace them by younger men."[13] Laying off staff, reducing wages by 10 percent, and closing for the winter season only forestalled the inevitable.

Finally, the Broadmoor Hotel declared bankruptcy on June 12, 1932. El Pomar Investment Company brought a complaint and was awarded a judgment of $2.29 million against the Broadmoor Hotel Company in El Paso County District Court. Charley Tutt Jr. was named the receiver. El Pomar stockholders were informed that "the universal depression of the past two years . . . has rendered it impossible to meet even ordinary operating expenses. . . . The indebtedness greatly exceeds the market value of the property or any value based upon its past or present earning power and there appears to be no equity for stockholders."[14] Much of this debt consisted of loans Penrose made for construction projects and operating costs. Six months later the newly formed Broadmoor Hotel, Inc., headed by Penrose, bought the assets of the Broadmoor Hotel Company for $600,630.76. Corporate directors were Penrose, Tutt, Devereux, Bogart, and Jack Carruthers, Penrose's legal counsel.[15]

Soon after the Broadmoor reorganization, Penrose was plagued by his old nemesis. There were rumors that Broadmoor workers were considering unionizing. "If the unions ever get control of the Broadmoor we will shut down and discharge all of our 500 employees," he informed Tom Green. "[We] will give the hotel to some charitable organization to be used for a children's home and hospital. . . . Life is not worth living if a person cannot run his own business in an honest and honorable way. . . . It is the same old story, over and over again. I believe I told you I have been fighting unions for over forty-five years."[16]

For twenty years Penrose continued the tight-reined control that began when the hotel first opened. Within months of the grand opening he told manager Edward G. Burke:

> It is not only necessary, in my opinion, to watch the time of the employees
> but also to watch their actions, for this reason the back door, or the entrance
> at the covered service driveway, should be guarded day and night. . . .
> The employees, such as this company employs, are of a nature and
> education which, on the average, does not permit them to distinguish
> very clearly between "mine and thine," therefore bulging coat pockets,
> rounded out aprons, suit cases and packages must be inspected.[17]

Concerned about workers' inefficiency, Penrose and the hotel executive committee ordered Milton J. Strong to "keep a large pad on your desk, open for inspection, on all pending jobs . . . make a report every morning to M.H.K. Devereux in regard to the number of your employees and on what jobs they will be employed during that day . . . handle your men more economically and do not move them several times a day from one job to another as has been done in the past . . . all jobs should be finished as rapidly as possible."[18] Penrose's high expectations were legendary. "My understanding about Mr. Penrose is that he was a pretty hard taskmaster," recalls Russell Freymuth, employed at the hotel from 1944 to 1991. "Workers had to be alert at all times because they never knew when he'd be coming around. He might come around riding his horse to check on his mail. Or he might drop into the dining room just to see what was happening, and everything better be perfect. He had a keen eye, he knew when something was out of place."[19]

Despite bankruptcy and union threats, Penrose ran the Broadmoor in grand style. Repeal of Prohibition in 1933 inspired Penrose to begin distributing liquor statewide through his Manitou Mineral Water and Sales Company, which he acquired in 1926 for $425,000.[20] Mineral water sales had been tepid, but liquor distribution went gangbusters. Wet goods sales quickly reached $50,000 a month. The company, Penrose told a friend in June 1935, "is doing an astonishing amount of business, last month . . . over $45,000."[21] The hotel also sold its own line of whiskey and scotch, bottled under the Broadmoor name.

The liquor business, however, nearly sundered the relationship between Penrose and the Tutt family. "I do not like the management," Penrose complained. "Therefore, only yesterday I sold out all my interest to Charley Tutt and his son Thayer Tutt, and from now on I will have no interest in the liquor business."[22] Penrose later reported:

> We are foreclosing on The Manitou Mineral Water Co. and we expect to sell the chattels, furniture, etc., the latter part of this month. . . . The Company really has been busted under "the fine management of Thayer Tutt" as General Manager of the Company. We all had confidence in him, but he handled the property like a schoolboy. The whole trouble was we had a schoolboy to do a man's job and now we are suffering the consequences. Charlie Tutt and Thayer Tutt have moved into town from the Hotel office and now I am trying to build up my organization.[23]

Little did he suspect that one day young Thayer Tutt would become manager of the Broadmoor Hotel. Although Tutt resigned in September 1935, the conflict seems to have quickly blown over. He and Penrose resumed a polite business correspondence within a month. Charley Tutt was back in good graces by the time El Pomar Foundation was formed in 1937 and became one of its first directors.

Penrose's many endeavors involved dynamic partners. These were the men who posed for the camera at the annual Cooking Club meeting and are memorialized in the mural painted inside the Will Rogers Shrine. Most were Colorado Springs businessmen, and several were associates from the Cripple Creek boom. Chief among them was Albert E. Carlton, who came to Colorado to cure his tuberculosis and wound up making millions in Cripple Creek mining, milling, and transportation. Carlton owned the Cresson, Granite, and other gold mines in which Penrose was heavily invested. He was president of several companies in which Penrose held a large interest—Cripple Creek Central Railway, Garden City Land and Sugar Company, Holly Sugar Company, and the Cripple Creek, Victor, and Cañon City National Banks. The fact that the two men owned large shares in each other's companies and served on each other's boards led to a casual intermingling of assets. Carlton once telegrammed Penrose: "Anytime you have $25,000 or $50,000 that is not working, suggest you send it to Cañon City for deposit in open account, subject to your check. Will pay you 3% interest and send you check book."[24] A few weeks later Spencer complied by depositing $25,000 in United States Reduction and Refining Company securities with the Cañon City bank.

Carlton, however, was a reluctant investor in the Broadmoor Hotel. "I have repeatedly denied ever having been conscious of any $100,000 subscription by myself," he told Spencer. "I must be failing fast if such an important matter as a $100,000 subscription to a suburban hotel escaped my memory. . . . I told you I would consider it and do the best I could."[25] Nonetheless, Carlton agreed to be a director of the hotel, and Bert and

In the late 1890s Spencer Penrose, shown here flanked by two associates on a Florence and Cripple Creek caboose, was plotting to monopolize Cripple Creek's railroads. He and his business partners gained control of the Florence & Cripple Creek, Colorado Springs & Cripple Creek District, and Midland Terminal lines, which they consolidated as the Cripple Creek Central.

wife, Ethel, moved into a Broadmoor suite as soon as the hotel opened. The Carltons and Penroses occasionally vacationed together, although, unlike Spencer, Bert seldom took a break from his business. Julie and Ethel Carlton ran the Broadmoor Sport Shop together, relishing their trips to Paris and New York City to buy stylish goods. After Bert died in 1931, Ethel maintained the Carlton's suite at the Broadmoor and traveled around the world with Julie.

Charles MacNeill joined the Tutt and Penrose partnership in 1896 and went on to serve as president of the Chino, Ray, and Nevada Consolidated Copper Companies. MacNeill was a founder and major shareholder in the Broadmoor Hotel. He owned a half-interest in the Manitou Incline and sat on the board of the Garden City Land and Sugar Company. MacNeill alternated his time between his Broadmoor suite and New York mansion, commuting in his private railcar. His notorious drinking contributed to his death in 1923. Despite huge losses on Wall Street, he left his widow financially comfortable. Marion MacNeill later married Willing Spencer of Philadelphia, but she retained large blocks of stock in several mining and tourism companies begun by Penrose and MacNeill.

Penrose also relied on Clarence Hamlin, who had dealt so ruthlessly with the striking Cripple Creek miners in 1903 and 1904. Hamlin became Spencer's attorney and handled numerous lawsuits. He was an original investor in the Broadmoor Hotel and president of the Garden City Land and Sugar Company. He owned and edited both the *Colorado Springs Gazette* and the *Colorado Evening Telegraph,* in which Penrose had a large interest.[26] He was also a director of El Pomar Investment Company, formed in 1924 as a holding company for Penrose business assets.

Other Cripple Creek investors played key roles in Penrose dealings. Eugene Shove owned stock in Penrose-Carlton mines and sat on the boards for the Ray, Nevada Consolidated, and Garden City Land and Sugar Companies. As vice president of Colorado Title and Trust Company, he loaned Penrose capital for various ventures. Henry McAllister Jr., deputy district attorney in Cripple Creek, replaced Hamlin as Penrose's lawyer and was an early director of El Pomar Foundation. Irving Howbert was El Paso County clerk, founder of the Midland Railroad, president of the Colorado Springs & Cripple Creek District (CS&CCD) Railway, and director of several Cripple Creek mines. He, too, sat on several of Penrose's boards.

Spencer's connection with Charles L. Tutt Sr. endured through Tutt's son Charley. Charley's involvement in Penrose's business began during construction of the hotel and gradually expanded. He handled everything from inspecting the quality of sheep manure for the golf course to firing an alcoholic Broadmoor golf professional. He visited the Granite Mine in Cripple Creek with Clarence Hamlin and Horace Devereux to inspect its operation.[27] Charley oversaw the drilling, blasting, and building of roads and dams. At the hotel he orchestrated expansions and improvements, helped select managers, and participated in financial audits.

Charley handled things in Penrose's absence, and his detail-oriented personality meshed well with Penrose's penchant for controlling picayune details. "I think it is very important that the caddies at the Golf Club should be instructed to always put down the divots!" Penrose commanded him. "In France they are very strict on this rule and the caddies pay strict attention to it."[28] During their winter sojourns Tutt cheerfully reported each minute, mundane detail to his employers in lengthy letters that began "Dear Mr. Penrose" and ended with "loads of love to you and Mrs. Penrose." He earned Julie's trust, too, and his role as business manager continued after Spencer's death. Charley Tutt became president of the Broadmoor and El Pomar Investment Company and director of El Pomar Foundation.

Penrose corresponded with some of the state's most influential businessmen. He had been a director of the First National Bank of Denver, whose president, David H. Moffat, also presided over various Colorado mines and railroads. Penrose bought concrete from cement tycoon Claude K. Boettcher to build the Broadmoor Hotel and the Rosemont-Penrose

As Penrose aged, he increasingly entrusted management of his far-flung
business empire to Charles L. Tutt Jr.
Charley, as everyone called the affable
son of Penrose's original partner, presided over the Broadmoor and the Cheyenne Mountain Zoo, where he posed
with these tiger cubs.

dam. Boettcher reciprocated by purchasing $100,000 in hotel stock. Speck's
friends included *Denver Post* publishers Frederick G. Bonfils and Henry
H. Tammen. Bonfils helped Spencer stage the first Pikes Peak Hill Climb
in 1916 and ten years later advised him on finding an elephant for the
Broadmoor Zoo. Spencer paid him back by advertising the hotel in the
Post, the highest-circulation newspaper in the Rocky Mountain empire.
Spencer's high-living lifestyle also appealed to Bonfils and Tammen. "When
you come up be sure and look in on me, as I am hungry to see you Speck.
My best love to you and Julie," Bonfils wrote.[29] Bonfils and Tammen both
enjoyed dinners at the Cooking Club or parties at El Pomar. Tammen told
Penrose: "Agnes and I and the chauffeur [will] arrive Sunday afternoon at
the Broadmoor. Can't just tell how long I can stay, but at any rate I particu-

larly want to come down and say 'hello' to your good wife and you and to breathe the atmosphere in which you live."[30]

The Penrose empire also relied on capable secretaries and assistants. Spencer's secretaries, John A. Hull and Merton Bogart, handled his voluminous correspondence and various business details. Hull handled the Cripple Creek properties and mines through the 1920s, then retired to California. His replacement, Merton Bogart, became a director of El Pomar Investment Company and El Pomar Foundation. These capable assistants orchestrated the couple's travel, updating visas and passports, writing consulates, and reserving berths and suites. They handled shipments of all sorts, ranging from an elephant to a stuffed crocodile to a thousand-pound statue of Buddha. And they dealt with customs officials, paid tariffs, and tracked lost shipments, all under Spencer's meticulous eye. Traffic Manager Fred C. Matthews managed the transportation companies. Penrose personally selected a series of managers for the Broadmoor Hotel: William Dunning, Edward Burke, Alberto Campione, Burton Ogilvie, and Paul Borchert.

An executive committee that included Charles L. Tutt Jr., Merton Bogart, and Horace Devereux oversaw hotel operations. Penrose put Devereux, his close friend and onetime Princeton polo player, on the hotel payroll in the 1930s. Devereux's family had been involved in silver mining in Aspen and in building the Hotel Colorado in Glenwood Springs. After his Cripple Creek stint Horace had a twenty-year career as a mining engineer. Suffering from heart disease, he spent his final years at the Broadmoor serving as Spencer's eyes and ears. As his friend traveled abroad, Devereux dictated long letters about hotel affairs and advised him on his Cripple Creek mines.

By the mid-1920s, Spencer's scenic companies girdled Pikes Peak. These companies included the Pikes Peak Touring Company, Manitou Incline, Pikes Peak Highway, Cog Railway, Crystal Park Toll Road, Cheyenne Mountain Highway, and the Midland Terminal line to Cripple Creek. Never big moneymakers for Penrose, they nonetheless left a lasting mark on the region. After he died they were operated as holdings of El Pomar Investment Company. The Pikes Peak Highway became the property of the City of Colorado Springs, which continues to stage the Pikes Peak Hill Climb every Fourth of July. The Cog Railway, built in 1891, is still operated by the Broadmoor Hotel; El Pomar Foundation retains a 20 percent interest in it. Designated a National Historic Engineering Landmark for the innovative technology used to scale grades up to 25 percent, this "Cog Wheel Route" annually attracts more than 200,000 passengers. The Manitou Incline, however, was dismantled in 1989.

Penrose also toyed with several small railroads. His Beaver, Penrose, & Northern Railway was losing $10,000 a year when he finally abandoned it in 1919. Another unprofitable line was the Grand Junction & Grand

River Valley Railway Company. The "Fruit Belt Route" connected Grand Junction with Fruita, carrying produce and passengers on an 18-mile electric railway. Passenger service stopped in 1928, but freight service continued for seven more years.[31] Spencer also was part-owner of the Chesapeake Beach Railway and Hotel Company, begun by David H. Moffat and backed by Penrose, MacNeill, and Hamlin. The Chesapeake Company included a 25-mile-long railroad serving a hotel, casino, and steamship wharf. Its amusement park offered a 3,000-foot boardwalk, roller coaster, bowling alleys, over-the-water dance pavilion, and saltwater bathing. After attempts to develop a resort subdivision failed, the enterprise was sold in the early 1930s.[32]

Spencer's most profitable railroad was the Cripple Creek Central Railway (CCCR), a holding company for the three lines into the mining district. He had acquired a $200,000 interest in the company in 1906 and, with Carlton and MacNeill, controlled the line as directors and major stockholders.[33] When the railroad's earnings dropped along with declining gold production, the line turned to tourism. Besides touring the mining towns, sightseers could also take underground tours of the El Paso and Granite Mines.

An incident that brought about the 1916 overthrow of CCCR railroad president Henry Blackmer shows how Penrose sometimes did business. "Blackmer . . . has been running the road just to suit himself," Penrose complained to Joel A. Hayes, who later became a CCCR director. "For the past two months he has been practically all the time in New York on an oil consolidation and the road has really been running itself. I intend to put in a big kick against the management, and I believe Blackmer is so busy with other interests that he ought to resign from the Presidency of the board. I am booming Bert Carlton for this position, and have been trying to get him to buy a large interest in the road."[34] The takeover was accomplished within months. Satisfied, Spencer informed the company's New York attorney, Judge Kurnal R. Babbitt, about the resignation of Blackmer, who was replaced by Joel Hayes: "I was elected President of the Road, also of the Midland Terminal, and Hamlin Vice President of both. . . . I am exceedingly happy that this matter has turned out in such a pleasant way. Blackmer seemed perfectly well satisfied with the deal, although he was not very enthusiastic over the price at which we bought his stock."[35]

Mining was a means to an end for Penrose. His earnings had funded his hotel, transportation, and agricultural schemes, as well as an extravagant lifestyle. His interest in mining never waned. He served on the board of Utah Copper/Kennecott Copper until he died in 1939. He dabbled in Alaskan and Mexican gold mines and in Colorado silver and coal mines, with abysmal results. Penrose was a longtime member of the American Institute of Mining Engineers but refused to sit on committees or go to conferences. "We are very anxious to have your cooperation along with

others whose judgment will be of greatest assistance in forming policy," pleaded Victor C. Alderson, an 1885 Harvard graduate and president of Colorado School of Mines.[36] Penrose declined. His interest in copper, however, became a hobby. He collected antique bronze weaponry, which he displayed at the Broadmoor. He insisted on a copper lightning rod for his Will Rogers Shrine and copper fixtures whenever possible at the Broadmoor Hotel. He enthusiastically backed the all-copper houses built near Copperton, Utah, and constructed a similar copper dwelling at Broadmoor.

Penrose's chief mining investments were in his Utah/Kennecott Copper and several Cripple Creek mines. Individuals and companies sought his backing for mining silver, gold, iron, granite, and potash. He spurned thousands of pleas from all over the world. Schemes and propositions flowed in—pencil-scrawled notes, telegrams, dictated letters on engraved

By the 1920s the railroad era was fading fast, and Penrose turned his attention to automobiles, auto tourism, and auto racing. Here he posed shortly before his death in 1939 with the Broadmoor Special #16. Penrose bought his first car in 1902, paying $12,500 for a French Rochet-Schneider. In 1906 he bought four canary yellow Loziers at $5,000 each. At least one would always be working, and he had an extra to ship to Europe when he traveled there.

business letterhead. Claude Boettcher offered stock in the Denver Rock Drill Manufacturing Company. "If I had any available funds it would give me great pleasure to take a block of the stock," Spencer replied. "But at the present time, I am running rather close to the wind on account of some large real estate investments we have been making in the neighborhood of the Broadmoor Hotel."[37] He also declined offers to buy hotels, such as those from the owners of the Hotel Colorado in Glenwood Springs, Mount Princeton Hotel near Salida, and the Ruxton Hotel in Manitou Springs. John Brisben Walker asked for financial backing to build the Mount Falcon Toll Road west of the town of Morrison.[38] Horace W. Bennett needed funds to build a "Tourist's Hotel" in Denver.[39] Penrose said no to them all.

He was a careful steward of his fortune. He distributed his assets among investment houses in New York City and Colorado Springs. In 1924, when his growing empire became unwieldy, he consolidated his interests into El Pomar Investment Holding Company. "My main objective in forming this new Company is that I can manage my business and affairs in a more satisfactory manner during my various absences from the United States," he told the president of Irving Trust Company in New York City.[40] Directors were Charles Tutt Jr., Spencer's secretary John A. Hull, and E. Manns.

Penrose was the sole owner of all El Pomar stock. El Pomar's corporate capital was invested in a variety of enterprises, including the Broadmoor Hotel, Cripple Creek Central Railway, Garden City Land and Sugar Company, Holly Sugar Company, *Colorado Springs Gazette-Telegraph,* and the scenic companies.[41] The New York City firm of Irving Bank–Columbia Trust held securities in four oil companies, the Anaconda and Cresson Gold Mines, two sugar companies, and nearly 200,000 shares of copper stock.[42] Penrose's 1930 gross income of nearly $1 million came from interest and stock dividends on his $9 million in assets plus his $25,000 salary from El Pomar Investment Company. That year, however, Spencer reported a net income of $152,860. Deductions included $212,552 in taxes and insurance, $66,264 in charitable contributions, $393,839 in stock losses, and over $100,000 in business, personal, and traveling expenses.[43]

For a decade El Pomar Investment Company satisfied Spencer's objectives. It simplified managing his assets and profitably increased his holdings. Despite the Broadmoor bankruptcy, failed businesses like the Turkey Creek Ranch, and his 1929 stock market losses, Penrose's earnings grew. So did the amount he paid each year to the Internal Revenue Service.

By the early 1930s all of his brothers had died, and Spencer was battling throat cancer. He realized he must make long-term plans for his estate. Julie had received trust funds and inheritances from both Jim McMillan and the Lewis family. Spencer set up trust funds for Gladys and Pauline, too. He feared his empire might be consumed by estate taxes or squabbled over by shirttail relatives in Philadelphia. He also wanted to ensure that his network of companies and the charitable work begun with Julie would continue.

NOTES

1. Penrose House, Spencer Penrose Collection, Box 73, File 313, letter to A. E. Carlton, December 19, 1921.

2. Ibid., Box 32, File 85, letter to directors, July 19, 1911.

3. *Fort Carson: A Tradition of Victory.* Fort Carson, Colo.: Public Affairs and Information Office, 1972, p. 68.

4. Penrose House, Spencer Penrose Collection, Box 15, File 31, letter to Charles E. White, Mgr. Beaver Park, Co., November 24, 1932.

5. Ibid., Box 48, File 213, September 1, 1920, monthly crop statement.

6. Ibid., Box 63, File 292, letter dated November 6, 1927.

7. Boulder, Colorado, Richard Penrose Collection, Geological Society of America, Penrose material catalogued 12–77, letters to and from Penrose brothers; letter from Spencer to R.A.F. Penrose Jr., May 27, 1924.

8. Penrose House, Spencer Penrose Collection, Box 68, File 300, letter to A. E. Carlton, August 3, 1929; correspondence, July 12, 1916, and December 30, 1924.

9. Ibid., Box 49, File 213, report dated July 3, 1937.

10. R. Thayer Tutt Jr., interviewed by Tom Noel and Cathleen Norman, June 10, 1997.

11. El Pomar Center, Spencer Penrose Collection, Box 30, File 73, letter dated September 4, 1934.

12. R. Thayer Tutt Jr., interviewed by Tom Noel and Cathleen Norman, June 10, 1997.

13. Penrose House, Spencer Penrose Collection, Box 127, File 500H, letter dated April 5, 1932.

14. Ibid., Box 30, File 73, letter dated April 3, 1939.

15. Ibid., Box 127, File 505, articles of incorporation, December 5, 1932.

16. Ibid., Box 98, File 383, letter dated September 3, 1933.

17. Ibid., Box 122, File 463, dated October 12, 1918.

18. Ibid., Box 116, File 440, dated November 12, 1929.

19. Russell Freymuth, interviewed by Cathleen Norman, April 18, 1997.

20. Penrose House, Spencer Penrose Collection, Box 79, File 339, correspondence, May 1926.

21. Ibid., Box 19, File 50, letter to Henry Blackmer, June 19, 1935.

22. Ibid., June 15, 1935.

23. Ibid., July 19, 1935.

24. Ibid., Spencer Penrose Archives, Box 8, File 24, correspondence dated July 9 and July 15, 1915.

25. Ibid., Spencer Penrose Collection, Box 71, File 303, letter from A. E. Carlton to Penrose, January 24, 1917.

26. Ibid., Box 67, File 298, letter to G. C. Hinckley, October 29, 1923.

27. Ibid., Box 84, File 358, letter dated July 26, 1935.

28. Ibid., letter dated March 23, 1929.

29. Ibid., Box 73, File 313, letter from Bonfils to Penrose, April 5, 1927.

30. Ibid., Box 98, File 383, letter dated September 3, 1920.

31. Ibid., Box 44, File 173, railroad business records and correspondence; Tivus E. Wilkins, *Colorado Railroads*. Boulder: Pruett, 1974, pp. 177, 204.

32. Penrose House, Spencer Penrose Collection, Box 44, File 171, annual letter of Chesapeake Beach Railway and Hotel Companies, October 2, 1916.

33. Ibid., Box 20, File 47, May 15, 1906, certificate of purchase.

34. Ibid., Spencer Penrose Archives, Box 46, File 186, letter from Penrose to J. A. Hayes, January 12, 1916.

35. Ibid., Box 20, File 47.

36. Ibid., Spencer Penrose Collection, Box 83, File 352, letter from Alderson to Penrose, September 27, 1922.

37. Ibid., Spencer Penrose Archives, Box 24, File 62, letter dated September 26, 1925.

38. Ibid., letter dated August 12, 1925.

39. Ibid., letter dated November 1, 1916.

40. Ibid., Box 96, File 419a, letter dated December 16, 1924.

41. Ibid., File 419b, list of securities—El Pomar Investment Company, Colorado Title and Trust, October 19, 1925.

42. Ibid., File 419a, statement of securities held by Irving Trust Company, January 22, 1930.

43. Ibid., File 419, year-end audit by John B. Geijsbeek and Company, May 28, 1931.

9

The Penrose Legacy

To perpetuate his love for Colorado Springs and Colorado, Penrose incorporated El Pomar Foundation on December 17, 1937. He created it with a donation of 15,000 shares of stock in El Pomar Investment Company and a check for $129,500. Penrose, Charles Tutt, Irving Howbert, Henry McAllister Jr., and Merton Bogart were the first trustees. The foundation's first gifts established later giving patterns: $45,000 to the Fountain Valley School, $32,000 to the Boys Club, $1,000 to the Junior League, and $500 to a public school in Penrose, Colorado.[1] From his deathbed, Penrose began plans for a cancer care wing to be built at Glockner Hospital. El Pomar grants would help sustain health care, education, and fine arts projects in the Pikes Peak region and around the state. When Spencer died two years later, he left $15 million to El Pomar.[2]

The foundation's chief asset, stock in El Pomar Investment Company, ensured continued maintenance of his scenic companies and hotel. The foundation also perpetuated the image of Spencer Penrose, philanthropist. He had seen other capitalists establish charitable foundations, including the Carnegie Foundation in 1902, Rockefeller Foundation in 1913, and Ford Foundation in 1936. Spencer's friends Albert E. Humphreys and Claude K. Boettcher had set up foundations. Philanthropy was also a Penrose tradition—his brother Charles had endowed the Philadelphia Academy of Natural Sciences and the Philadelphia Zoo. Richard's estate had been divided between the Geological Society of America and the Philosophical Society of America. Julie's generosity toward the Catholic Church, Colorado Springs Fine Arts Center, and Central City Opera Association influenced Penrose, too.

As an umbrella for Spencer and Julie's philanthropy, the foundation followed their traditional giving patterns. They made annual donations of

Cragmor Sanatorium, founded in 1905 as one of America's most elegant havens for tuberculosis patients, put Colorado Springs on the map as a health spa. Julie Penrose, whose first husband died from the deadly disease, favored El Pomar funding for Cragmor. After drugs ended the need for such tuberculosis care centers, Cragmor was reincarnated as the University of Colorado's Colorado Springs (UCCS) campus in 1965. In 1998 El Pomar gave $4 million toward constructing a $28 million, three-story technology and information center, El Pomar Center. Courtesy Pikes Peak Library District, Local History Collection.

$100 or so to the Boy Scouts, Girl Scouts, YMCA, Red Cross, School Milk Fund, Visiting Nurses Association, and dozens of other Colorado Springs charities. They gave to several health-related causes, including $10,000 to the Tuberculosis Society, $5,000 for research at Colorado College, and $25,000 for an expansion of the Cragmor Sanatorium.[3] Penrose had spearheaded a fund drive that raised $217,000 for the local Red Cross during World War I.[4] After Penrose died the foundation funded construction of the Penrose Pavilion Cancer Center at Glockner Hospital.

The Penroses supported education as well. Spencer helped found Fountain Valley Boys School in 1931. He served as a director, funded several scholarships, and built the $100,000 Boies Penrose Memorial Dormitory designed by renowned Santa Fe architect John Gaw Meem in the Pueblo Revival style.[5] Julie delighted in inviting students to lunch or dinner at the Broadmoor and hearing the school choir perform at the hotel's little theater. Fountain Valley School still receives large annual grants from El Pomar. Student scholarships and grants to Colorado College, the University of Denver, and other colleges in the state furthered the Penroses' traditional support of education. Consistent El Pomar grants have also financed maintenance and expansions at the Cheyenne Mountain Museum and Zoo.

Philanthropic causes such as these were the chief purpose of El Pomar, but the foundation also fulfilled Spencer's wish that his Broadmoor attraction network be maintained intact. The labyrinth-like foundation owned the hotel, zoo, scenic companies, $7.4 million in Kennecott Copper stock, and numerous other investments.[6] Earnings from the $15 million Penrose estate funded grants and paid for operation and staffing for El Pomar offices. Early giving averaged about $400,000 per year.[7] Despite receiving letters from across the country, Julie and Spencer limited grants to people

Speck's last project was the Penrose Cancer Pavilion at Glockner Hospital. As
trustees, he selected business colleagues,
doctors, and Sister Anne Hermine,
Glockner's mother superior. After receiving substantial further funding from
El Pomar Foundation, Glockner was
renamed Penrose Hospital. Old
Glockner, shown above in 1956, has
given way to the modern high-rise
Penrose Hospital, the largest health care
center in southern Colorado. Courtesy
Pikes Peak Library District, Local History Collection.

and projects within Colorado, mainly in the Colorado Springs area. The
foundation did likewise.

To help him invest, administer, and disburse foundation funds, Penrose
assembled a board of trustees intimately familiar with the Penrose empire.
Irving Howbert had been El Paso County clerk and president of First
National Bank of Colorado Springs from 1880 to 1888 and 1919 to 1923.[8]

The Fountain Valley School on the southern outskirts of Colorado Springs has received Penrose and El Pomar support since its founding in 1930. Boies Penrose Memorial Hall, shown here shortly after its completion in the 1930s, commemorates Spencer's oldest brother, a U.S. senator. In 2000, El Pomar Foundation gave $750,000 to renovate this hall. John Gaw Meem designed the campus in Pueblo Revival style, epitomized by projecting, round log roof beams (vigas), flat roofs, and adobelike surfaces. *Photo credit:* Laura Gilpin, "Fountain Valley School of Colorado Boies-Penrose Memorial Hall, Dormitory," 1975, M146 H20 *(above)*; Laura Gilpin, "Fountain Valley School Library, Colorado Springs, Colorado," 1975, M146 G8x *(right)*, © 1979, Amon Carter Museum, Fort Worth, Texas, Bequest of Laura Gilpin.

He mined silver in Aspen and gold in Cripple Creek and helped build the Colorado Midland and Colorado Springs & Cripple Creek District railroads.[9] Henry McAllister Jr., a director of the D&RG railroad, was one of Spencer's lawyers.[10] Merton Bogart, Spencer's longtime secretary, worked for the McMillan family in Detroit before Penrose hired him in 1919.[11] Charley Tutt Jr. had helped manage the Penrose empire since the early 1900s.

El Pomar Foundation, Penrose's largest legacy, was just one of several significant "gifts" to Colorado Springs made during his last years. After Spencer Penrose discovered in 1932 that he had throat cancer, he began planning a memorial tomb on Cheyenne Mountain. Penrose hired Charles Thomas, noted Colorado Springs architect, to design a medieval-looking tower on a rocky promontory along the Cheyenne Mountain road.[12] Construction began in 1934 and ended in 1937. The monumental tower cost $250,000 and had a 200,000-pound steel frame faced with 6,500 cubic yards of pink-gray Pikes Peak granite quarried from a single Cheyenne Mountain boulder, according to *Ripley's Believe It or Not*.[13] Manitou green sandstone was used for the steps and viewing platform. The 100-foot landmark could be seen—and heard—from Colorado Springs. It was a "singing tower" with chimes and a vibraharp that could play 125 selections.

Penrose initially planned to name the memorial for himself, but Julie persuaded him to call it the Will Rogers Shrine of the Sun to honor the popular western humorist who had died in an Alaska airplane accident on August 15, 1935.[14] The shrine was dedicated September 5, 1937, during Colorado Springs' Will Rogers Rodeo. The ceremony began with a procession up the Cheyenne Mountain road led by a riderless horse. At the shrine, the address by Colorado College President Thurston Davies was broadcast nationally by the NBC radio network. Rogers's sister, Mrs. McFadden, unveiled a heroic-size bust of the cowboy philosopher, the work of sculptor Jo Davidson. The dedication closed with a nine-gun salute, the "Star Spangled Banner" performed by the Cowboy Band from Abilene, Texas, and the playing of "Taps."[15]

Some people thought it ironic that the great Colorado Springs capitalist devoted his grand landmark to Will Rogers, a humanitarian with a deep empathy for the workingman. Had Spencer hoped to benefit from Rogers's enormous popularity with the working class? Or did he genuinely admire Rogers's rise from Oklahoma ranch boy to international acclaim as an entertainer, syndicated columnist, and Hollywood's highest-paid movie star? Some newspapers called Rogers and Penrose friends, but the two men were never photographed together, and it seems they never corresponded.

If Will Rogers, cowboy humorist and champion of common folk, and Spencer Penrose, ardent capitalist, knew one another, it was a passing acquaintance. After Rogers's only stay at the Broadmoor in 1926, he jabbed at Penrose in his weekly column with his typical tongue-in-cheek wit: "I

This 1937 Dedication Day crowd gathered at Spencer Penrose's monumental tower on a spur of Cheyenne Mountain. He called it the Shrine of the Sun because the 100-foot tower caught the first rays of morning sunshine and the last shafts of light from the west. Like the pharaohs building the pyramids, Penrose built for the ages, constructing granite walls thirty feet thick. Penrose renamed his Shrine of the Sun for Will Rogers and offered to share his tombstone with the aviator. The Rogers family declined but did attend the dedication of the shrine. Two years later Penrose's remains were laid into the chapel floor. Courtesy Ed and Nancy Bathke Collection.

had heard all my life of the beauty of Colorado Springs, and believe me, it had not been overestimated any. Pikes Peak is there for people that like to go up on top of the Woolworth Tower. Fine Hotels there, the Swimming Pools, 4 Polo Fields, Golf Courses, and private fishing lake; all for the Guests. . . . There is a Teepee in every room to make the Osages feel at home."[16] The "Osages" was a reference to one of the Broadmoor's wealthiest guests, Ed Marland, who had made his fortune drilling oil near Ponca City, Oklahoma. Today, Will Rogers's face, with cocked eyebrow and crooked grin, looks out from dozens of photos that hang on the shrine's second and third floors. His voice echoes through the tower in recordings of wit and wisdom.

The story of Spencer Penrose and the history of Colorado Springs unfold on the ground floor below in a nearly life-size mural. Here strut the region's icons—Spanish explorer-priest Sylvestre Velez de Escalante, Lt. Zebulon M. Pike, and Gen. William Jackson Palmer. And here Spencer's accomplishments are depicted in vivid color—the C.O.D. Mine and bespectacled Charles Tutt Sr., the Utah Copper Mine steam shovels, the Pikes Peak Highway, and the Broadmoor Hotel. Looking like they belong in a boardroom or smoke-filled clubroom, Penrose's cronies crowd together—Charles MacNeill, Clarence Hamlin, Bert Carlton, Horace Devereux, and Charles Tutt Sr. and Jr. The mural was painted by Randall Davey, a Santa Fe artist who summered in Colorado Springs from 1924 to 1931, teaching at the Broadmoor Art Academy, playing polo at the Broadmoor, and carousing at Cooking Club dinners.[17] The first-floor chapel has a red granite floor beneath which lie the remains of Spencer and Julie Penrose. Their resting place is decorated with prayer benches from a medieval monastery, an altar of Italian marble, a baroque painting of the Madonna and Child, and a hand-carved crucifix. Beside them lie Spencer's bachelor pals, Harry Leonard and Horace Devereux.

The shrine has remained a familiar Colorado Springs landmark for over sixty years. Its chimes and vibraphone harp ring every quarter hour. Hotel guests and neighbors within a 5-mile radius are regaled with Sunday hymns, patriotic marches on the Fourth of July, carols at Christmastime, and "Happy Birthday" upon request. The End of the Trail Association, endowed by Penrose, looks after the structure's upkeep. And as Penrose would have wanted, the shrine is still free to zoo visitors. Open year-round, it is visited by more than 70,000 people annually.[18] The Cheyenne Mountain road was closed between the shrine and the summit in 1968. The abandoned Cheyenne Mountain Lodge became a target for vandals and arsonists and was demolished in the 1970s. That same decade the road was dedicated as the Russell Tutt Scenic Highway to honor Charles's son, a local civic leader and El Pomar trustee.

Spencer's grand shrine was not his only parting gift to the city. He also constructed the $100,000 Will Rogers Stadium in 1938. Designed by

After completing the Pikes Peak Auto Road in 1916, Penrose built a 7-mile road up Cheyenne Mountain in the 1920s. When he ran into greater trouble and expense than expected, a friend asked him why he was building the road. "I want to get to the top!" Penrose shot back. He always seemed determined to get to the top—even if it cost $1 million, as his Cheyenne Mountain development did. Atop the mountain Penrose built the Cheyenne Mountain Lodge, shown here shortly after opening in the 1920s. It was demolished in 1973.

Cheyenne Mountain Lodge became a mausoleum for Spencer Penrose's pets. After his beloved St. Bernard, Jack, expired, he had the creature stuffed and placed by the lodge fireplace. Jack was eventually joined by a 15-foot boa constrictor. William Thayer Tutt recalled, "One day the head of the zoo called me and said he thought the snake was dead. So I called Mr. Penrose and we went up there. He kicked the snake and said it was indeed dead, so we curled it up in the truck and took it down to Stainsky's taxidermy because he wanted it mounted for the Cheyenne Mountain Lodge. Stainsky got it about half skinned and found the snake was just hibernating. It thrashed his store to pieces. Of course, then it died and was stuffed—a very expensive stuffing." Courtesy Pikes Peak Library District, Local History Collection.

Charles Thomas, the oval-shaped stadium was built by the American Bridge Company on the west side of Broadmoor Lake. It seated 10,000 spectators for regional rodeos, horse shows, sporting events, and "concerts under stars." Professional football games played by Penrose's favorite teams were among the first events. The Pittsburgh Pirates and the Los Angeles Bulldogs were matched on November 11, 1938. The Cleveland Rams played the Philadelphia Eagles on December 3, 1939. The Colorado Springs Chamber of Commerce renamed it the Penrose Stadium to honor "the great builder" a year after his death.[19] In the mid-1970s the structure was moved from its lakeside site to its present address, 1045 West Rio Grande Street. Now known as the El Paso County–Penrose Equestrian and Events Center, it still hosts hunter-jumper horse shows, miniature horse shows, and rodeos, as well as circuses, music concerts, "monster truck" rallies, and motorcycle races.[20]

Penrose also provided for maintenance of the Cheyenne Mountain Zoo so his beloved animals would be cared for after he was gone. He announced this gift to the City on August 19, 1938, to rodeo-goers who had packed the new stadium. The zoo had evolved in twenty-five years from a grizzly bear kept at the Turkey Creek Ranch to a large mountainside park with 291 animals from 75 species.[21] Intended as a unique diversion for hotel guests, Spencer's "Hundred Thousand Dollar Hobby" helped satisfy his urge to keep up with his older brother Charles, president of the Philadelphia Zoo from 1910 until 1925.[22] His Turkey Creek menagerie expanded, and he moved the creatures to the Broadmoor to amuse his guests. He also acquired other exotic animals kept in cages west of the Broadmoor Golf Club. The animals proved more annoying than amusing.

The Will Rogers Stadium opened in 1938 on the west side of Lake Broadmoor. This 1961 photo shows the Ice Palace next to the stadium and the Broadmoor South rising beside the original hotel.

Coyotes howled beneath guests' windows. Seals begged for table scraps. Flamingos snatched food from diners' plates on the West Terrace.[23] Finally, when a young boy was bitten by a monkey and the hotel was ordered to pay an $8,000 settlement to the lad's mother, Penrose moved all his animals to the new zoo grounds on lower Cheyenne Mountain. This relocation also tidied up the Broadmoor grounds for the 1927 Trans-Mississippi Golf Tournament.[24]

Near the entrance to his new Cheyenne Mountain road, Penrose built fences, pens, and cages for the deer, bobcats, mountain lions, seals, badgers, coyotes, pheasants, eagles, a monkey, and a camel. He bought ten buffalo at $75 a head from Yellowstone Park.[25] To procure an elephant in time for the zoo's grand opening, he contacted Fred Bonfils, onetime owner of the Sells Floto Circus. "Now Speck," Bonfils answered him, "I haven't

After a hotel monkey bit a Broadmoor guest, the boy's mother sued for $8,000. Subsequently, Spencer Penrose opened the Cheyenne Mountain Zoo for his hotel menagerie in 1926. Hotel guests were probably relieved to see the monkey go, as well as the boa constrictor that lived in the basement around the hot water pipes, the howling coyotes, the barking sea lions, and the caged creatures by the golf course. Penrose touted Cheyenne Mountain as "the highest zoo in the world" and gave it a particularly fine primate collection to keep the troublesome monkey from getting lonely. Courtesy Penrose Public Library.

forgotten about that elephant at all. In fact, I have gone to considerable trouble about it, because you must have a big fine looking elephant and one that is perfectly docile."[26] A recent trip to India had inspired Spencer's story that his elephant was a gift from an Indian rajah. Actually, she was a 45-year-old female named Tessie, bought for $3,000 from an Arkansas circus company. Spencer turned the four-ton pachyderm into a publicity spectacle. Broadmoor press releases, sent to every mid-sized city between Hot Lick, Arkansas, and Colorado Springs, heralded her passage. A huge

sign on Tessie's freight car proclaimed: "This car contains the Empress of India. The largest elephant in the world. Gift of the Rajah Nagapur of India to Spencer Penrose, Broadmoor Hotel, Colorado Springs."[27] Arriving at the Rockies, the Empress of India led a parade through town. Then Tessie camped out in the Broadmoor garage until her elephant house on the hill was finished.

Tessie was one of many exotic creatures that came to live at the zoo. Growing in Noah's Ark fashion, Speck's zoo acquired a pair of lions, two ostriches, and two cassowaries.[28] Six cinnamon ring-tailed monkeys moved into the new monkey house, and Tessie gained an iguana as a roommate. Spencer ordered two polar bears from New York animal dealer Louis Ruhe and had two musk ox shipped from Ketchikan, Alaska. In 1929 a *Gazette-Telegraph* article reported: "Spencer Penrose Back From Europe With Two Big Lions for His Zoo."[29] Animals were donated, too: a boa constrictor that escaped from a Colorado Springs circus, a grizzly bear from the Honolulu Zoo, a box of foxes from a friend in Santa Fe.[30] Julie's bird collection, evicted from the Broadmoor Garden Room by the state health department, moved up the hill.

Penrose tended his zoo with his customary thoroughness. Each day he rode on horseback to bottle-feed the antelope babies, plan the animals' menus, inspect their cages, and arrange their schedules. "I find many people are disappointed going to the Zoo on Sunday afternoons because the animals are not fed on that day," he informed zookeeper George Noel. "Therefore, please arrange to have the animals fed on Sundays, and do not feed them on Mondays, which will answer our purpose."[31] He used the Turkey Creek Ranch and the Broadmoor kitchen as pantries for the zoo.

Among Penrose's pets, his favorite was Tessie, shown here at the Broadmoor in the 1920s. Supposedly a gift from the rajah of Nagpur, Tessie came with an East Indian elephant tender who spoke no English. Thayer Tutt put her in a hotel warehouse and installed a bed for the tender who insisted on sleeping with her. Penrose used her as a golf course caddie. Between games Tessie amused herself by tossing around old automobile tires stored in the warehouse. When Penrose rode her in a Colorado Springs Shrine parade, Tessie ripped spare tires off the backs of automobiles and flung them into the crowd, smashing shop windows in the process. Shortly afterward, Mr. Penrose retired his beloved elephant to the Cheyenne Mountain Zoo.

Antelope and other hoofed mammals munched Turkey Creek oats and hay, while the lions dined on butchered horses from the farm. The polar bears feasted three times a week on a dish concocted from stale bread and cod liver oil from the hotel kitchen. Spencer even established a cemetery at Turkey Creek for the zoo animals he did not stuff.[32]

He wanted his facility to be one of the best private zoos in the world. He visited zoos all over the country—New York City, Detroit, Chicago, Milwaukee, St. Louis, San Francisco, and Los Angeles. Speck corresponded with zoo directors and personally handled buying, selling, and trading animals. He also toured animal parks in Paris, Hamburg, Berlin, and other cities around the globe. His zoo became intertwined with the hotel and his scenic companies, and he promoted it by publishing photos of himself drinking champagne with the monkey and guests riding Tessie the elephant.

People flocked to the Broadmoor zoo—over 11,000 visited in July 1938.[33] Pierce Arrow touring cars whisked hotel guests up the hill. Tourists motoring up the Cheyenne Mountain road stopped to visit the animals. In 1937 Penrose built a miniature cog train that ran between the hotel and the zoo.[34] The 15-cent admission fee, however, fell far short of covering expenses. To ensure the zoo's longevity, in 1938 Penrose formed the Cheyenne Mountain Museum and Zoological Gardens, to which the hotel company donated the zoo animals, buildings and grounds, and museum.[35] Since then, large and consistent El Pomar grants have helped fund ongoing operation of the zoo. Under the management of Robert Menary from 1939 to 1969, the facility nearly doubled its exhibits and acquired many exotic animals. Today, it has grown to a collection of 500 animals representing 144 species, with an annual budget of more than $2 million and more than 300,000 annual visitors.

The Zoo Special, a miniature train installed in 1937, carried Broadmoor guests to Cheyenne Mountain Zoo. Sometimes the engineer was Spencer Penrose. Courtesy Pikes Peak Library District, Local History Collection.

Penrose also distracted himself with several home improvements at El Pomar. He added curvilinear parapets facing the courtyard, part of the Olmsted Brothers' 1925 design. He and Julie added a second-story bedroom above the west wing, providing downstairs guest bedrooms for visits from Gladys, Paul, and Pauline. A porte cochere was added to the main entrance in 1931. The west wing's third story, designed by Colorado Springs architect Charles Thomas, contained a private suite for Penrose, complete

During the 1930s the Penroses began to fancy Hawaii as a winter getaway. In Honolulu they built an oceanfront villa in a coconut palm grove near Diamond Head.

These downtown cowboys whooping it up for the annual Pikes Peak or Bust Rodeo are a reminder that before gold was discovered at Cripple Creek, the Pikes Peak region was best known as ranching country. Charles L. Tutt Sr. originally came to Colorado Springs in 1884 to ranch, and Spencer Penrose maintained a second home—and cattle business—at his Turkey Creek Ranch. Colorado Springs began staging rodeos back in 1911 in the old Sportsman's Park between North Nevada and North Cascade Avenues. The rodeo died out in 1927 but was resurrected ten years later by Spencer Penrose, who built Will Rogers Stadium to revive the sport.

Colorado Springs' cowtown legacy is perpetuated by this sculpture in front of the Palmer Center, opened in 1991 as the tallest complex in town. Colorado Springs still cherishes its annual Pikes Peak or Bust Rodeo and Parade. Cowboys and cowgals also ye-hawed the 1979 opening of the ProRodeo Hall of Fame and Museum of the American Cowboy. Courtesy 1992 photo by Ron Johnson.

with an X-ray machine. His deteriorating health explains this 1937 addition, which included an elevator.[36]

These final projects were vigorous endeavors that distracted Spencer from the throat cancer that was killing him. He had been diagnosed and successfully treated for the disease in Paris in 1932. Five years later the ailment had come back. Instead of returning to Paris for treatment, he traveled to the Chicago Tumor Institute to see cancer specialists Dr. Henri Coutard and Dr. Max Cutler. He returned to Colorado Springs under the care of Dr. William P. McCrossin. Despite his terminal illness, Speck indulged his appetite for travel and new projects in his last months. In mid-1939 he traveled with Julie to New Zealand. He also had architect Vladimir Ossipoff design a large new $100,000 house in Kailua, Hawaii.[37] In August he hosted the 1939 Will Rogers Rodeo at his new stadium.

That fall Spencer also began planning the Penrose Tumor Institute, a Colorado Springs center for cancer research and treatment. After he died, his foundation funded the $120,000 Penrose Pavilion designed by Burnham Hoyt as a treatment center at Glockner Hospital. The Sisters of Charity of Cincinnati, who had provided care and support during Spencer's illness, ran the center. El Pomar Foundation also provided operational funds for the facility and paid the salary of Dr. Coutard, a specialist from the Chicago Cancer Institute.

Spencer Penrose died December 7, 1939, at his El Pomar home. He was 74. Penrose would have been pleased with the way he was eulogized by the press. The *Gazette-Telegraph* lamented the loss of the Pikes Peak region's "greatest builder and benefactor of the last quarter century."[38] The *Rocky Mountain News* called his death "a distinct loss to the state and the entire West." The *Denver Post* claimed that "Penrose made his mark as a human being as well as a builder and a philanthropist. Money never spoiled him. He was just as plain and unassuming and as approachable when he was rated the second richest man in the state as when he started from scratch in the early day mining camps of Colorado."

Penrose left the bulk of his estate, including the hotel and surrounding 3,000 acres, to El Pomar Foundation. He also bequeathed $200,000 to his granddaughter Pauline; $100,000 each to Merton Bogart, Boies Penrose II, and Sarah Hanna Boies Van Pelt; $50,000 each to Charles L. Tutt Jr. and D. C. Jackling; $30,000 to Clarence Hamlin; and $25,000 to Dr. McCrossin.[39] His will contained no provisions for Julie and his stepdaughter Gladys, who already had large trust funds in their names.

His burial ceremony was attended only by invited guests—close friends and associates. Charles Tutt and Harry Leonard supported Julie on each arm. A small crowd listened to Governor Ralph L. Carr's homage. Then Harry McAllister Jr. read a brief eulogy and recited Alfred Lord Tennyson's poem "Crossing the Bar." Spencer's ashes were interred in the shrine's crypt while the vibraphone played Anton Dvorak's "Going Home." Afterward, around 4,000 people visited the shrine to pay their respects.

Penrose left his financial matters in tidy order, naming his wife and Merton Bogart co-executors of his will. Two weeks after the funeral, Julie was elected president of El Pomar Foundation and the investment company. For 16 more years she administered the sizable Penrose legacy, aided by Irving Howbert, Henry McAllister, Charley Tutt, and Merton Bogart. In 1949 H. Chase Stone replaced Bogart, and in 1954 Charley Tutt's son William Thayer replaced Howbert. With their help, Julie Penrose shouldered the ongoing work of her mate.

NOTES

1. El Pomar Foundation, El Pomar Investment Company Minute Books 1–4, minutes from December 23 and 30, 1937, meetings.

2. "Penrose Will Dividing Estate Value at 16 Million Is Filed," *Denver Post,* December 18, 1939, pp. 1, 2.

3. Penrose House, Spencer Penrose Collection, Box 87, File 378, November 1930.

4. Marshall Sprague, *Newport in the Rockies: The Life and Good Times of Colorado Springs.* Chicago: Sage/Swallow, 1980 [1961], p. 271.

5. Penrose House, Spencer Penrose Collection, Box 117, File 442, correspondence 1931–1935; Hunter S. Frost, *Art, Artifacts, Architecture: Fountain Valley School.* Colorado Springs: Tiverton, 1980.

6. Ibid., Helen Geiger File 20, undated affidavit.

7. Ibid., "El Pomar Foundation—Projected Cumulative Income and Grants," June 1997.

8. Rufus Porter, "Irving Howbert Could Be Called the Man Who Made Colorado Springs," undated clipping in Irving Howbert vertical file, Penrose Library–Local History Center, Colorado Springs.

9. Marshall Sprague, *Money Mountain: The Story of Cripple Creek Gold.* Lincoln: University of Nebraska Press, 1979, pp. 138–143; see also Howbert's autobiography, *Memories of a Life Time in the Pikes Peak Region.* New York and London: G. P. Putnam's Sons/Knickerbocker Press, 1925.

10. McAllister's father, Henry Sr., had been a pillar of the city, serving in General Palmer's 15th Cavalry regiment and helping found both Colorado Springs and Colorado College. Polly King Ruhtenburg and Dorothy E. Smith, *Henry McAllister: Colorado Pioneer.* Freeman, S.D.: Pine Hill, 1972, pp. 9, 42.

11. Merton Bogart worked for the McMillan family from 1913 to 1918 and was hired to work in Penrose's office in May 1919. He became Penrose's secretary in 1925. Biographical Summary, Penrose Library–History Center, Colorado Springs, August 18, 1968.

12. Thomas also designed the Pauline Chapel, Turkey Creek Ranch house, Will Rogers–Spencer Penrose Stadium, and several expansions at El Pomar and the hotel.

13. Penrose House, Spencer Penrose Collection, Box 123, File 468; *Will Rogers Shrine of the Sun on Cheyenne Mountain.* Colorado Springs: End of the Trail Association, 1994.

14. Penrose House, Spencer Penrose Collection, Broadmoor Scrapbook—1935, undated, unidentified newspaper article.

15. *Will Rogers Shrine of the Sun.*

16. Ibid., p. 3; Will Rogers, *Weekly Articles—Volume 2, The Coolidge Years: 1925–1927.* Stillwater: Oklahoma State University Press, 1980, p. 170, article published March 28, 1926. Rogers, the celebrity cowboy humorist, stretched the truth a little in this account; George Guerrero, curator of the Will Rogers Shrine, tour and interview by Cathleen Norman, February 12, 1997.

17. Sprague, *Newport in the Rockies,* p. 266.

18. George Guerrero, interviewed by Tom Noel and Cathleen Norman, July 17, 1997.

19. Penrose House, unidentified article, Broadmoor Scrapbook—1940, Spencer Penrose Collection, Box 12, File 468B.

20. Telephone call to Information Office, El Paso County–Penrose Equestrian and Events Center, by Cathleen Norman, April 5, 1997.

21. Helen M. Geiger, *The Zoo on the Mountain.* Colorado Springs: Cheyenne Mountain Museum and Zoological Society, 1968, p. 23.

22. Frances Haythe Penrose, interviewed by Cathleen Norman, July 19–20, 1997; "Dr. C. B. Penrose Drops Dead in Car. Brother of Late Senator Victim of Heart Attack on Railway Train. President of Zoo, Member Park Commission and Authority on Gynecology," *Philadelphia Inquirer,* February 28, 1925.

23. Geiger, *The Zoo on the Mountain,* p. 10.

24. Penrose House, Spencer Penrose Papers, Broadmoor Hotel and Land Company, Record of Minutes, minutes dated April 28, 1927.

25. Ibid., Spencer Penrose Archives, Box 105, File 425.

26. Ibid., correspondence from John Robinson, owner John Robinson's Circus, March 1, 1926.

27. Ibid.

28. Geiger, *The Zoo on the Mountain,* p. 23.

29. Penrose House, Spencer Penrose Archives, Box 106, File 425, undated clipping.

30. Geiger, *The Zoo on the Mountain,* p. 10.

31. Penrose House, Spencer Penrose Archives, Box 106, File 425, letter dated September 11, 1929.

32. David Thompson and Dennis Kotke, tour of Turkey Creek Ranch, March 10, 1997.

33. Penrose House, Spencer Penrose Archives, Box 105, File 425, August 2, 1938.

34. Mary Stevens Humphreys, *Cog Train to the Zoo.* Woodland Park, Colo.: Mountain Automation, 1990, p. 2.

35. Penrose House, Box 105, File 425, August 2, 1938.

36. Nancy Lyons, *National Register Nomination for El Pomar Mansion.* Denver: Colorado Historical Society, Office of Archeology and Historic Preservation, 1994, Section 7, p. 5.

37. Penrose House, Spencer Penrose Archives, Box 124, File 469, financial statement, October 8, 1939.

38. "Region Mourns Penrose's Death. Foremost Citizen Dies Early This Morning," *Colorado Springs Gazette-Telegraph,* December 7, 1939, p. 1.

39. "Colorado Springs' Foremost Citizen, and the Greatest Builder in the Pikes Peak Region's History," *Colorado Springs Gazette-Telegraph,* December 7, 1939.

10

Julie Villiers Lewis McMillan Penrose

After Spencer's death, Julie took the reins of his three largest interests. She was elected president of El Pomar Investment Company and El Pomar Foundation and vice president of the Broadmoor Hotel. Charles Tutt became hotel president and vice president of El Pomar Company and the foundation. Julie deferred to Tutt in most financial details, but she insisted that everything be done as Spencer would have done it. This meant keeping foundation and corporate assets intact and giving El Pomar grants to projects her husband would have fancied. Julie and Charles and the other trustees decided who would receive the $400,000 to $500,000 given each year.

They followed the mission elucidated in El Pomar's incorporation papers, to give grants "exclusively for charitable uses and purposes as will, in the absolute and uncontrollable discretion of the trustees, most effectively assist, encourage and promote the general well-being of the inhabitants of the State of Colorado." They gave large grants to Spencer's favorite projects—the Cheyenne Mountain Zoo and Fountain Valley School. In 1941 the foundation funded the $128,020 Penrose Pavilion wing at Glockner Hospital in memory of the tycoon.[1]

Under Julie's direction the foundation continued to support the arts. She had acquired her appreciation of culture from her father. Alexander Lewis was among a group of Detroit businessmen who donated land for the Detroit Museum of Art and was an original museum trustee. Her Detroit in-laws, the McMillans, also were supporters of culture in the City by the Straits. In Colorado Julie gave generous donations to the Colorado Springs Fine Arts Center and the Central City Opera. She and Charley Tutt both loved the visual arts, as had Spencer, and the trio had helped organize the Broadmoor Art Academy in 1919. As Colorado's most prominent center

Julie Villiers Lewis McMillan Penrose oversees, in spirit, the Penrose House, where this 1915 portrait by London artist Julian Storey hangs. Her furs commemorate French fur trade ancestors, including founders and mayors of Detroit, her hometown.

for painters, the academy bolstered a small colony of artists and patrons that had flourished since the late 1800s.

Originally named the Colorado Springs Art Society, it had been rechristened when the Penroses gave the group their large, lovely home at 30 West Dale. The spacious residence was readily converted into an art school. The living room became a salon, bedrooms served as studios, and the greenhouse was turned into classrooms and a gallery.[2] The Broadmoor Art Academy's first board of trustees consisted of Julie V.L. Penrose, Anne D. Ritter, David V. Donaldson, Charles L. Tutt Jr., and artist Francis Drexel Smith.[3]

COLORADO·SPRINGS·FINE·ARTS·CENTER
COLORADO SPRINGS

The Colorado Springs Fine Center grew out of Julie Penrose's interest in the arts. She donated her old mansion at 30 West Dale Street as a home for the Broadmoor Art Academy when she and Spencer moved to El Pomar. Julie later agreed to demolish her old house to clear the site for a new Colorado Springs Fine Arts Center in 1926. Despite Spencer's wariness about the "modern" design, Julie and her sister philanthropist, Alice Bemis Taylor, gave famed Santa Fe architect John Gaw Meem artistic freedom. He created a masterpiece in the neo–Pueblo Revival style, expressed in raw concrete and flat-roofed cubes. *Photo credit:* Laura Gilpin, "Colorado Springs Fine Arts Center, front façade, car, and driveway," 1975: M183: G102x, © 1979, Amon Carter Museum, Fort Worth, Texas, Bequest of Laura Gilpin.

Among the nationally acclaimed artists who taught summer classes were Robert Reid and John Carlson, who had studied at the New York Art Students League and exhibited works at the New York Museum of Metropolitan Art and the Chicago Institute of Art. The opportunity to play polo at the Broadmoor lured Santa Fe artist Randall Davey to teach at the academy and to later paint the mural at the Will Rogers Shrine. Boardman Robinson came west to teach at the Fountain Valley School. The widely known cartoonist, muralist, and political radical immediately became a mainstay of the art academy and, subsequently, of the Colorado Springs Fine Arts Center, where he was the art director for most of the 1940s. Noted Colorado photographer Laura Gilpin also worked in a studio at the academy and, with her camera, captured the grounds and classes. The academy served as a venue for Colorado College art lectures, Junior Symphony concerts, ballroom dancing, and productions by the Drama League

Architect John Gaw Meem posed with some of the Mexican American religious art highlighted at the Colorado Springs Fine Arts Center. Hispanic culture, held in contempt by many early Anglo settlers, later gained respect. Artifacts such as these were resurrected and celebrated as beautiful, honest, and indigenous art of the American Southwest. *Photo credit:* Laura Gilpin, "John Gaw Meem & Alice Bemis Taylor, Sancot Collection in Colorado Springs Fine Arts Museum," © 1979, Amon Carter Museum, Fort Worth, Texas, Bequest of Laura Gilpin.

and the Art Academy Players. It was also an ideal setting for teas, garden parties, and elaborate costume balls like the 1928 Lido Ball, with guests dressed in exotic outfits and sipping Leadville Moon—bootleg whiskey—on the sly.[4]

Julie Penrose and Charles Tutt applauded when Alice Bemis Taylor and Meredith Hare expanded the Broadmoor Academy into the Colorado Springs Fine Arts Center in the 1930s. The new center opened in a stunning $400,000 facility built on the site of Julie and Spencer's old home. Designed by famed Santa Fe architect John Gaw Meem, the building integrated southwestern, Modernist, Art Deco, and classical elements in a monolithic poured-concrete structure. The stepped form blends into its spectacular site—a bluff overlooking Monument Valley Park.[5] The center houses a theater and exhibition hall for Alice Bemis Taylor's southwestern art collection, as well as galleries and studios that wrap around a central courtyard. Julie served as a Fine Arts Center trustee until the mid-1940s. Charles Tutt's wife, Vesta, later joined the board.[6] In the ensuing years El Pomar gave generously to the center, including funding pieces for its collections. The foundation helped fund the 1970 construction of the east gallery wing and a $1.2 million expansion in 1984. Recently, El Pomar has contributed to renovating the center's Taylor Museum of Southwestern Art.[7]

Along with Charles and Vesta Tutt and other El Pomar directors, Julie patronized the Colorado Springs Symphony. The Colorado Springs Opera House had become a movie theater, but the resurrection of opera in Central City appealed to both her generosity and her love of fun. She responded generously when approached by Anne Evans. Evans, the daughter of Territorial Governor John Evans, championed restoration of the crumbling old 1878 Opera House, designed by Colorado's first licensed architect, Robert Roeschlaub. Denver's social elite rallied behind Evans. They contributed funds and bought run-down miners' shacks for back taxes, then donated them to the Opera Association. Burnham Hoyt, an acclaimed Denver architect, completed the facility's restoration, and the reborn opera house debuted with *Camille* in June 1932. Each summer, under the auspices of the University of Denver, the venerable venue hosts performances that feature internationally known stars and draw a moneyed, cultured crowd to the old mining town.

Julie Penrose was in her element at Central City. She had acquired her taste for opera at an early age, enjoying performances at the splendid Second Empire–style Detroit Opera House. She sat on the Central City Opera board almost from its inception. She served as its chair for several years and made numerous donations to the association. Anne Evans thanked her in 1937: "I do hope you are going to have a lot of pleasure over the beautiful thing you are doing for Central City. It is the pleasantest thing I have to think about just now."[8] During Julie's twenty-year involvement she donated more than $100,000 to build dressing rooms, restore the balcony, and renovate the Opera House. She gave $15,000 for cushions to soften the opera's hard hickory chairs and $60,000 to build dressing rooms for the cast. These were badly needed, since some cast members had to wait outside the opera building for their cues.[9]

In the late 1940s Julie bought and donated the Penrose complex of three houses across from the Opera House. Fifty years later this gift was remembered well. "Julie was just wonderful to us," said Nancy Brittain, director of development. "The Penrose Complex is one of our nicer properties. We use it as housing for the principal artists and singers. The whole company consists of more than one-hundred people, all housed in properties owned by the Opera Association."[10]

As chair of the opera board, Julie persuaded opera president Frank H. Ricketson Jr. to choose her favorite works and hire her favorite

Boardman Robinson, nationally noted illustrator, muralist, and cartoonist, became the Fine Arts Center's first director in 1939. He painted these five murals over the main entrance as allegorical representations of the five fine arts: sculpture, drama, dance, music, and painting. *Photo credit:* Laura Gilpin, "Colorado Springs Fine Arts Center, Main Entrance detail," 1975, M183, © 1979, Amon Carter Museum, Fort Worth, Texas, Bequest of Laura Gilpin.

In a sleeveless T-shirt, Boardman Robinson supervised this Fine Arts Center class in mural painting. Robinson, the former director of the illustrious New York Art Students League, used his art to champion socialist causes and the working class. Ironically, the Penroses, who abhorred such views, funded Robinson's work and helped Alice Bemis Taylor create a superb Fine Arts Museum. *Photo credit:* Laura Gilpin, "Colorado Springs Fine Arts Center, Class in Mural Painting," 1975, M183 G36m, © 1979, Amon Carter Museum, Fort Worth, Texas, Bequest of Laura Gilpin.

Julie Penrose was the greatest financial benefactress of the Central City Opera House. With Anne Evans and Ida Kruse McFarlane, she restored one of Colorado's best mining-era monuments, evidence that the gold rush also launched a rush to culture. Julie and her friends restored and reopened the old Opera House in 1932 for *Camille,* starring Lillian Gish. Courtesy photo by Louise Pote.

performers. Ricketson called her the "First Lady of Opera west of the Mississippi River." He described Julie, then in her eighties, "as active as a woman of fifty and as attractive as a young matron."[11] Julie adored the operas and arias, the celebrated singers, and the grand old building. She especially enjoyed the swirl of parties and gala gatherings and the Denver friends who flocked to the picturesque mining town. She even purchased a summer home, the former parish house for St. Mary's Catholic Church, so she could entertain.[12] "The Central City operas begin next Saturday, and I am having fun filling up the house with different parties," she wrote longtime friend Camilla Lippincott in 1952. "Jane and Irving Howbert, also the Spragues and the Wilders. In fact, the same old crowd. So I hope we are going to have a jolly time and I wish you were here too."[13]

As a devout Catholic and a preservationist, Julie Penrose worked with El Pomar Foundation to help underwrite the 1950s restoration of St. Mary's Catholic Church in Central City. Erected in 1892 during the flush times, it faded with the town's decline as a gold-mining hub. Since the 1950s rehabilitation, St. Mary's once again offers services. Julie bought the parish house next door and converted it to a summer residence for opera staff. Courtesy 1970 photo by Edward D. White Jr.

Relishing the invigorating infusion of eastern and local talent, Julie befriended artists, composers, and art critics. Julie corresponded with her favorite young singers, sometimes lending them money. She also courted critics, giving her friend, *New York Times* art critic Olin Downes, $5,000 while he was writing a book on opera history. Downes thanked her profusely: "You can't know how I love your proud spirit and your hot heart—you who hold your head so high and your spirit so pure against—I am certain—a thousand and one heavy trials and burdens."[14] Lucius Beebe and Forbes Parkhill, authors of two articles on Spencer Penrose, were also devotees of the Central City Opera. Julie Penrose's support is perpetuated today by continued support from the foundation. "El Pomar still supports our capital projects," added Nancy Brittain. "And we won their Award for Excellence in Arts and Humanities in 1996."[15]

Foundation giving favored education as well as the arts, especially Fountain Valley School and Colorado College. Penrose scholarships went to college students around the state. At Julie's behest, the foundation also gave liberally to Colorado churches large and small, to Catholic schools, and to the Archdiocese of Denver. El Pomar grants helped boost amateur sports in Colorado Springs, especially after Thayer Tutt joined the board in 1954.

These philanthropic endeavors and her board meetings for the zoo, investment company, and Garden City Sugar gave Julie a much-needed distraction in the years that followed Spencer's death. With the onset of World War II, the 1940s were a grim decade worldwide. The war kept Julie from traveling to Europe and left Pauline and Julie's great-grandchildren stranded in Belgium. Gladys and Paul Cornet sought refuge from the upheaval in Europe, first with Julie at El Pomar and then with relatives at Grosse Pointe Farms. After the Cornets were gone, Julie moved from the huge, empty house into the Broadmoor's sixth-floor suite.

Through the foundation she donated El Pomar (called Penrose House since 1999) as a retreat center to the Sisters of Charity of Cincinnati in December 1944. The order had helped care for Spencer during his last days. The sisters ran the center as a retreat for nearly fifty years, aided by a $10,000 annual maintenance fund provided by Julie. In 1992 the foundation reacquired El Pomar for use as a conference center for nonprofit organizations and government agencies. A $3 million project restored the elegant mansion and returned to it several of the Penroses' furnishings and artworks.[16] The lovely European-style gardens, originally designed by the firm of Frederick Law Olmsted Jr., have been restored to their former, formal glory. Renamed the Penrose House in 1999, El Pomar now hosts around 25,000 people each year at meetings, conferences, and seminars.

After moving from El Pomar to the hotel, "Queen Julie" ruled from her apartment on the sixth floor. Like Spencer, she had a meticulous eye for detail and quality, and she alerted hotel management about any deficiencies. She ordered her meals from the Broadmoor kitchen. "It is certainly an easy way to live," she told her granddaughter. "You go down and tell Louis and he gives you a perfectly delicious dinner with no trouble at all. I always was weak on the restaurant end of my life. I hate bothering about the kitchen and I am no good at it, so this arrangement does suit me perfectly."[17] For company she had her French maid, Hermine Weber, who fixed her small snacks, arranged flowers, and doted on the poodles. Hermine styled her hair and helped her dress, enhancing Julie's regal demeanor.

Julie surrounded herself with friends and relatives, including her great-grandchildren, who frequently came from Belgium to visit. "There seems always to be something doing, no matter how hard one tries to get out of it," she wrote her sister, Marian Muir. "One is always up to their neck in cocktail parties."[18] Always the Grande Dame, Julie loved entertaining at

Colorado College continued to receive Penrose and El Pomar Foundation support during the lean years of the Great Depression and World War II. Although many male students went to war, female students kept the college peppy and maintained a Victory Garden on campus. Courtesy Special Collections, Tutt Library, Colorado College.

Julie spent her last Christmas in the Pauline Chapel and at El Pomar surrounded by the Sisters of Charity (*below*). Julie helped the nuns with their heavenly work of teaching, caring for the sick, and comforting the dying. Courtesy Pikes Peak Library District, Local History Collection.

the Broadmoor. She threw cocktail parties and intimate dinners in her beautiful suite, renovated by architect Burnham Hoyt. She had dinner parties for twenty to thirty people in the hotel dining room. "I had a big dinner last night in the new part of the Tavern and we all went up to the apartment afterwards and had great fun," she told Pauline.[19]

Julie delighted in children, especially boys. When her great-grandchildren came from Europe, she entertained them with horseback riding, ice skating, swimming, tennis, and sightseeing excursions to Cripple Creek gold mines. When Patrick and Daniel visited in April 1954, she presented

The Sisters of Charity of Cincinnati took care of Spencer Penrose in his last days and were rewarded in 1944 when Julie Penrose and El Pomar Foundation gave them the Penroses' El Pomar home. The sisters converted it to a retreat center and installed this chapel. Julie smiled on the conversion, which would have astonished her irreligious husband, Spencer, who relied on El Pomar's vast wine cellar for his spiritual inspiration. El Pomar Foundation bought El Pomar estate back from the Sisters of Charity in 1992 and undertook a $3 million restoration that helped earn Penrose House a 1995 listing on the National Register of Historic Places.

The Mediterranean Revival style of Penrose House belies a more formal neo-classicism inside. Floors of Belgian black and Vermont white marble, exquisite woodwork, neoclassical plaster ceiling moldings and trim, and elegant chandeliers characterize the first floor. El Pomar reopened the Penrose Home in 1992 as a center for nonprofit organizations.

them with two big cowboy hats. "The boys are full of pep," she wrote their father, "swimming, diving, and ice skating all the time, and are really doing very well as a reward for good schoolwork."[20] She did not hesitate to advise 16-year-old Mickey: "A bottle of hair tonic was sent you yesterday, as I thought you must be out. It certainly does good work for you, so please use it. It is that low hairline and very heavy eyebrows of yours that

do not give you much of a forehead, so keep up the good work."[21] When
the children returned to Europe, she wrote Daniel: "I went down to Fountain Valley School the other day and saw all the boys. They are a fine-looking
bunch, and I only wish you were among them."[22]

Peter Brown, who grew up in the Broadmoor neighborhood, remembered walking around the lake with Mrs. Penrose and furry little Pitty Pat.
"It was tough keeping up with her," Brown recalled. "She was in vigorous
condition." He also remembered Julie's kindness. "When our family was
going to Cape Cod, she had a monkey and organ grinder come down to
the train station to see us off. . . . I saw more of her when I came back
from college. She was very interested in the Fine Arts Center. We used to
go to luncheons at Mitchell Wilder's house where we would drink wine
and listen to opera."[23]

Julie doted on dogs. "I do not see how anyone can be without a dog,"
she wrote Pauline. "I must say these are the joy of my life, except when

Julie Penrose moved into this Penrose
Suite on the sixth floor of the Broadmoor
and lived there until her death.

Besides the Penrose Suite at the Broadmoor, Julie spent some of her last years at her Cheyenne Mountain retreat, the Shack, surrounded by friends and, in this C. 1950 portrait, by her great-grandchildren and her precious poodle, Pitty Pat.

anybody rings the doorbell there is the most awful barking going on."[24] Julie's favorite was Pitty Pat, the black toy poodle that accompanied her everywhere. She and Spencer had bred and raised larger dogs—pedigreed German shepherds, Old English sheepdogs, and chow chows. But in her later years Julie fancied poodles—Manon, Yalla, and her beloved Pitty Pat. Of the latter Julie told a friend: "She is the most lovely little dog in character and affection that I have ever seen. Everyone in the Broadmoor Hotel just loves her. She is with me about 24 hours of the day and cannot bear to be parted from me. . . . She has been rather fussy about her eating."[25] She had a New York veterinarian clip the dogs and even had Pitty Pat's portrait painted in Paris.

Julie enjoyed sports, especially figure skating and the national and international hockey tournaments Thayer Tutt staged at the Broadmoor. At one game she was hit in the head with a hockey puck and needed nine stitches. She later wrote Pauline: "The hockey is in full swing, and everyone is excited. I am having a dinner tomorrow at the Tavern. I seem to be losing my 'sporting blood.' I am quite content to stay in—I guess it is about time, don't you think?"[26]

In between board meetings and socializing and travel, Julie busied herself with various projects. She built the Carriage House Museum just east of the Broadmoor Hotel for Spencer's collection of antique vehicles. To design this modern structure she hired A. G. Jan Ruhtenberg, a Swedish architect who had studied at Germany's Bauhaus School of Architecture and designed houses for King Gustav V, Greta Garbo, and Nelson Rockefeller.[27] The one-story, $29,000 museum opened in October 1941 and still operates free to the public across the street from the hotel entrance.[28]

Julie entrusted business decisions to the capable directors of the investment company and the foundation, as Spencer had done. These men included Charley Tutt, Henry McAllister, Irving Howbert, and Merton Bogart. Later Tutt's sons, Russell and Thayer, served on the boards. Her personal secretary, Roland W. Giggey, handled personal and business matters. She let the Tutts run the Broadmoor, intervening only if she thought hotel quality was not up to par. She also suggested improvements, such as the 1950s West Terrace cocktail lounge designed by Burnham Hoyt.

By delegating business affairs, Julie was free to resume traveling after World War II. She often vacationed with Ethel Carlton, Henry and Norena Blackmer, Marion and Wilding Spencer, or Detroit relatives. She took along her touring car, shipping it to Europe via ocean liner. A chauffeur and Giggey often accompanied her. She insisted on bringing Pitty Pat, patronizing only ocean liners and hotels that allowed dogs. When her granddaughter's husband, François, and the children moved to London, she spurned England because of "that awful English law on no dogs." Paris was still her favorite destination, where she enjoyed shopping for stylish dresses and hats and bought perfume by the half-liter.

Her passion for all things French was rooted in her Detroit upbringing. The city had been located in French territory, and French blood and taste lingered in many of Detroit's first families. Julie's French heritage became her personal trademark: many people said Julie "brought Paris to the West." Having grown up in frigid Detroit, she also relished snowy weather. Her Detroit origins also explain her fondness for furs: the frosty city is a longtime center for fur trade. Throughout her life Julie maintained an extensive collection, wearing her favorites in several of her portraits.

Like Speck, Julie was fascinated by automobiles. She took her 1949 Packard Super Eight Touring Sedan when she went to Europe. But she especially loved driving around Colorado Springs in her 1950 Jaguar convertible. "I went driving in my little Jaguar with Pitty Pat," she told Pauline. "I love my little English car, a Jaguar. It is a tiny little thing and I am all enclosed in the back with no glass. I am really crazy about it and so is [my chauffeur] Thompson."[29] Her grandchildren loved the sports car, too. She continued to Pauline, "I take them out in my little Jaguar all the time and they love motoring."

Julie's sunset years were not all gaiety. Gladys's health deteriorated because of multiple sclerosis, and Pauline died of brain cancer in 1953. Julie sought spiritual solace at the Pauline Chapel west of the hotel. She often attended daily Mass there and grew close to Pastor Father Louis Hagus and his successor, Father Michael Harrington. Her high regard for the Catholic Church led to generous donations to parishes and parochial schools around the state. In 1955 she built the Pauline Memorial School next to the chapel. Five years later the congregation outgrew its tiny quarters and moved into a large, new church built next door.[30]

When Julie tired of the fishbowl life at the hotel, she hired Jan Ruhtenberg to design a stylish, modern house on Cheyenne Mountain near Spencer's Cooking Club. The $175,000 ten-room house featured walls of cedar logs and glass and a shed roof supported by colored steel columns.[31] Julie decorated "the Shack" with antiques and Oriental art. The three-level structure became her weekend retreat where she housed visitors, threw dinner parties, and entertained foreign dignitaries. "I have been greatly bored lately by having to have two very smart dinners and luncheons for the Italian ambassador and one for the English ambassador," she wrote friends in New York.[32] Charles L. Tutt Jr. and his family moved into the Shack after Julie died. Today it remains a private residence.

Julie V.L. Penrose turned 85 on August 12, 1955. Great-grandchildren Mickey, Daniel, Sybille, Anne, and Patrick arrived from Europe to help her celebrate. She received hundreds of cards and dozens of gifts from well-wishers around the world. She was especially delighted with the poem penned by her friend, popular and prolific Colorado Springs author Marshall "Marsh" Sprague:

> Not Long Ago in a manner adroit
> JULIE was born to the MAYOR OF DETROIT.
> Of this EVENT we are prompted to say
> That was a *very* REMARKABLE DAY.
>
> Though Mr. LEWIS had daughters GALORE
> None had the talents of this one before.
> When a WEEK OLD she sprang out of bed,
> Turned SEVEN CARTWHEELS and stood on her HEAD.
>
> Far off in BOSTON they sent her to school.
> Once she was locked in for breaking a RULE.
> JULIE, desiring a DATE with a SWAIN,
> JUMPED out the window and slid down the DRAIN.

Archbishop Urban J. Vehr said the solemn high requiem Mass for Julie Penrose in the Pauline Chapel at the Broadmoor before her 1956 interment beside her husband, Spencer, in the chapel at the Will Rogers Shrine of the Sun on Cheyenne Mountain. Courtesy Colorado Historical Society.

Touring ABROAD Julie had a fine FLING
Dangling SUITORS like DOLLS on a string—
Poet and painter and BARON AND PRINCE—
EUROPE has never been quite the same since.

JULIE's grown up now. Her girlhood is done.
That doesn't keep her from having her fun.
She's over TWENTY, but NOTE WELL, we pray—
PIKES PEAK AND JULIE WEREN'T BUILT IN A DAY!

The 85-year-old Queen of the Broadmoor spearheaded expansion of the Glockner-Penrose Hospital. El Pomar Foundation agreed to match the first $1.5 million raised in a capital campaign for the new $5.4 million building. Ultimately, $3.2 million was given toward the project. The "biggest check in Colorado philanthropy history" changed the facility's name to Penrose Hospital.[33]

Julie maintained her energetic pace to the end, entertaining friends and dignitaries. She helped select the operas for Central City's 1956 season. And she began planning a February trip to Europe to see François and the children. Two weeks before Christmas 1955, she saw her doctor for a checkup, and he discovered a malignant tumor in her colon. Exploratory surgery at Glockner-Penrose revealed that the cancer had spread to her liver. Julie spent the holiday in the hospital, surrounded by flowers and deluged with get-well gifts, cards, and telegrams. She was conscious until an hour before she died on January 23, 1956, surrounded by nearly twenty friends and family members.

"The legendary lady who gave so much to so many makes her final journey today," announced the *Colorado Springs Free Press*.[34] Nearly 130 people crowded into the memorial service at Pauline Chapel. She was buried at the crypt in the Will Rogers Shrine beside her husband. Colorado Springs Mayor Harry Blunt said: "Her loss will be deeply felt all over the state. She has given so much to so many." Denver Archbishop Urban J. Vehr reflected, "Her benefactions to the city and church have been outstanding. We will all remember her in our prayers."[35]

Julie had outlived most of her siblings, as well as her husband, daughter, and granddaughter. She left $1.2 million and her furs and jewelry, furniture, and art to her great-grandchildren in Belgium.[36] She left bequests to the people who worked for her—Roland Giggey, Hermine Weber, and Paul Baschleben. The remainder of her estate, over $9 million consisting chiefly of Kennecott Copper stock, went to El Pomar Foundation as the Julie Villiers Lewis Penrose Trust. Julie's passing marked the close of the Penrose era, but her spirit and generosity, as well as her husband's, live on in El Pomar Foundation.[37]

NOTES

1. El Pomar Foundation Minute Book—No. 1, December 1937–1942, entries dated July 18, 1940; January 25, 1941.

2. Manly Dayton Ormes, *The Book of Colorado Springs*. Colorado Springs: Dentan, 1933, p. 341.

3. For a lavishly illustrated history, see *Pikes Peak Vision: The Broadmoor Art Academy 1919–1945*. Colorado Springs: Colorado Springs Fine Arts Center, 1989.

4. *Colorado Springs Fine Arts Center: A History and Selections From the Permanent Collection*. Colorado Springs: Colorado Springs Fine Arts Center, 1986, pp. 14–16.

5. Thomas J. Noel, *Buildings of Colorado*. New York: Oxford University Press, 1997, pp. 293–294.

6. Penrose House, Julie V.L. Penrose Collection, Box 9, File 30, letter dated August 8, 1945.

7. *Colorado Springs Fine Arts Center*. Colorado Springs: Colorado Springs Fine Arts Center, 1986, pp. 14–16, donor acknowledgment plaque on east wing.

8. Penrose House, Spencer Penrose Collection, Box 124, File 470, letter dated November 1937.

9. Charles A. Johnson, *Opera in the Rockies—A History of the Central City Opera Association, 1932–1992*. Denver: Central City Opera House Association, 1992, p. 28.

10. Telephone interview with Nancy Brittain, Central City Opera Association, by Cathleen Norman, June 10, 1997.

11. Penrose House, Julie V.L. Penrose Collection, Box 8, File 40, letter from F. H. Ricketson Jr. to Eleanor Steber, November 17, 1955.

12. Johnson, *Opera in the Rockies*, p. 25.

13. Penrose House, Julie V.L. Penrose Collection, Box 7, File 31, letter dated June 20, 1952.

14. Ibid., Box 6, File 29A, letter dated April 20, 1955.

15. *Mrs. Spencer Penrose, Contributions to Central City Opera.* Central City Opera Association Fact Sheet, 1997; telephone interview with Nancy Brittain, June 10, 1997.

16. Noel, *Buildings of Colorado,* p. 302.

17. Penrose House, Julie V.L. Penrose Collection, Box 6, File 31, letter to Pauline, April 25, 1953.

18. Ibid., File 29A, letter from Mrs. Penrose to Marian Muir, October 22, 1955.

19. Ibid., File 31, letter to Pauline, April 25, 1953.

20. Ibid., Box 7, File 31C, April 1954.

21. Ibid., File 29C, letter dated December 15, 1954.

22. Ibid., letter dated October 26, 1954.

23. Peter A.G. Brown, interviewed by Cathleen Norman, April 17, 1997.

24. Penrose House, Julie V.L. Penrose Collection, Box 7, File 31, letter to Pauline, May 13, 1952.

25. Ibid., Box 5, File 27, letter from Mrs. Penrose to Dana Mill, September 7, 1948.

26. Ibid., Box 7, File 31, letter to Pauline, March 17, 1951.

27. Elena Bertozzi-Villa, *Broadmoor Memories: The History of the Broadmoor.* Colorado Springs: Broadmoor, 1993, p. 127.

28. Penrose House, Julie V.L. Penrose Collection, Box 5, File 24, correspondence with Ruhtenberg, November 1941.

29. Ibid., Box 7, File 31, letter to Pauline, May 13, 1952.

30. Dorothy J. Towne, *The Treasures of Pauline Chapel—The Story of a Journey in Faith,* 4th ed. Colorado Springs: Myron J. Tassin, 1984, pp. 5–11.

31. Penrose House, Julie V.L. Penrose Collection, Box 15, File 83, correspondence dated October 1955, referencing article in *Look* magazine.

32. Ibid., Box 6, File 29A, letter to Donald and Zorka M. Oenslager, October 7, 1955.

33. "El Pomar Foundation to Match First $1.5 Million Raised by Public for New $5,394,620 Glockner-Penrose Hospital," *Denver Post,* August 14, 1955, p. 15, c. 2; "Mrs. Penrose Gives Glockner-Penrose Hospital $3,200,000," *Denver Post,* October 2, 1955, p. 17, c. 1; "Mrs. Penrose Presents Biggest Check in Colo. Philanthropic History," *Denver Post,* October 15, 1955, p. 18, c. 6; "Penrose Hospital," *Denver Post,* December 28, 1955, p. 38, c. 4.

34. "Mrs. Penrose Funeral Set at Pauline Chapel," *Colorado Springs Free Press,* January 27, 1956, p. 1, c. 7.

35. "City and Religious Leaders Pay Homage to Mrs. Penrose," *Colorado Springs Gazette-Telegraph,* January 24, 1956, p. 1, c. 8.

36. Penrose House, Julie V.L. Penrose Collection, Box 7, File 29C, letter to François, November 7, 1955.

37. El Pomar Foundation Office, Helen Geiger file on Julie Penrose.

Charles L. Tutt Jr.'s sons Charley, Russell, and Thayer revealed their characters in this 1921 photo. Charles, direct and proper, *on the left,* became an engineer for General Motors. Russell, perceptive and at ease, *in the center,* became the levelheaded, steady manager of finances for the Penrose, Tutt, and El Pomar empire. William Thayer Tutt, casual, wistful, and charismatic, *at right,* became the gregarious, ambitious dreamer who greatly expanded the Broadmoor Hotel complex and other Penrose operations.

11

Continuing the Legacy

In the decades following World War II, Colorado Springs flourished. Servicemen stationed at Camp Carson returned to the Pikes Peak region after the war, bought houses, and settled down to raise families. Local business leaders ensured the city's economic future by courting—and capturing—military installations. After intense lobbying by the Tutts and others, Colorado Springs was chosen as the site of the $200 million Air Force Academy in 1954. The showplace academy, coveted by many other cities, opened four years later.[1] Ent Air Force Base, established in the 1940s, subsequently expanded into the North American Air Defense Command (NORAD) and burrowed into a hollowed-out "cave" in Cheyenne Mountain in the mid-1960s.

Other contemporary forces shaped the city. During the 1960s and 1970s, urban renewal spurred downtown revitalization in Colorado Springs and nationwide. City leaders tore down aging buildings and replaced them with gleaming new high-rises. The $20 million Chase Stone Center, which included the 300-room Antlers Plaza Hotel and sixteen-story Holly Sugar Building, became the anchor for a rejuvenated downtown. To attract clean, well-paying industries, the city offered tax incentives and developed the Pikes Peak Industrial Park near the Garden of the Gods. Computer manufacturing, software development, telecommunications, and defense companies moved to town: Kaman Sciences and Hewlett Packard in the 1960s; Digital Equipment, Texas Instruments, and NCR in the 1970s, and then MacIntosh and MCI.[2]

El Pomar Foundation continued to be Colorado Springs' angel—boosting education, economic development, amateur sports, the arts, health and human services, and youth programs. Between 1955 and 1990 the foundation disbursed over $127 million in grants, contributing to a wide array of projects and causes.[3] A second generation of trustees guided the foundation.[4] Charley Tutt chaired the foundation and investment company during the five years after Julie's death. His sons, Thayer and Russell, joined the board in the mid-1950s, continuing the Tutt family's role as administrators of the Penrose interests. The Tutts sat on the boards of the Broadmoor Art Academy, Colorado Springs Symphony, and Fountain Valley School.

Yet their relationship did not reach beyond the public and professional arenas. The Penroses asked Charles and Eleanor to join them on a Nile cruise and offered Charles use of their Hawaiian cottage. The Tutts, occupied with their growing family and handling the Penroses' business, declined these invitations. Charley Tutt invited the Penroses to the family's fishing retreat at Lake Uneva in Summit County. Spencer and Julie accepted only once or twice, preferring their own mountain retreat at Camp Vigil west of the Broadmoor.

From the time of construction of the Broadmoor in 1916 until Julie Penrose's death in 1956, Charley Tutt remained integral in managing the Penrose empire. Even after resigning from El Pomar Investment Company in the early 1930s, he became a trustee on the original El Pomar Foundation board in 1937. When he resigned from the Cooking Club in the summer of 1939 because of poor health, Penrose asked Charley Tutt to take his place.[5] He also gave Charley half the contents of the El Pomar liquor vaults.[6] At her husband's funeral, Mrs. Penrose leaned on the arm of Charley Tutt. After Spencer was gone, Tutt went with Mrs. Penrose to Hawaii to help her sell the two houses there. Charley, however, was not Spencer's surrogate son, as suggested by Colorado Springs historian Marshall Sprague. The Penroses maintained a certain aloofness from the Tutts. "We were always aware that Mrs. Penrose was our father's employer," recalled John Wood Tutt, Charles's youngest son, in a 1996 interview. Yet Charles Tutt decided that his sons would inherit his role as trusted, capable steward of the Penrose legacy.

Charley and Eleanor Tutt had four children, all born in Coronado, California: Charles Jr. (III), January 26, 1911; William Thayer, March 2, 1912; Russell Thayer, July 27, 1913; and Josephine, June 1, 1919.[7] The children grew up in Colorado Springs in a large two-story house at 1205 Cascade Avenue that the family later donated to Colorado College. "Eleanor Tutt used to make donuts and we'd go over there," remembered Richard Vanderhoof, who lived down the street as a child. "She was a nice lady and wanted to be nice in the neighborhood."[8] Eleanor Armit Tutt was a statuesque brunette as tall as her husband. Her father, Colorado Springs mining attorney John Lees Armit, supposedly introduced the whiskey sour to the Pikes Peak region.[9] She is remembered as an accomplished horsewoman and for christening the Broadmoor Hotel in 1918.

The Tutts sent their three sons to Thacher, the college preparatory school in Ojai, California, where Charley and his brother Thayer had

The Tutt family residence at 1205 North Cascade, with its generous porch and port cochere, is shown here in 1930. The house has been donated to Colorado College for an Alumni Center.

The Tutt family took charge of the Penrose empire after the 1956 death of Julie Penrose. As she and Spencer had no children, she welcomed the Tutts' role in perpetuating the Penrose businesses and philanthropy. Charles is shown here on the porch of the family home at 1205 North Cascade in 1930 with his children, *left to right,* Russell, Josephine, Charles, and Thayer. Courtesy photo by Laura Gilpin.

been educated. Excerpts from the Thacher yearbook, *El Archivero,* reflect the brothers' personalities and hint at their adult vocations. The oldest brother, Charles III, who pursued a lifelong career in automotive engineering, was nicknamed "Dad" and described as "smelling of glue, oil, and wet paint" used in making model airplanes. William Thayer, called "Thay" in the yearbook, "sells stuff" and managed sports teams, foreshadowing his adult enthusiasm for amateur sports. When Eleanor died of appendicitis in March 1925, 12-year-old Russell was sent to Thacher. Russell completed his course work one year early and spent his last year at Thacher reading. He reflected later, "That was one of the most valuable things I've ever done—spending a year in the library."[10] That experience contributed to his love of learning and fervent belief in education.

Although two of the Tutt sons learned the ropes of the Penrose empire, the other children refrained from involvement in the family business. Charles Tutt III graduated from Princeton in 1933 with a degree in mechanical engineering. He went to work for General Motors in sales, auto shows, and the Buick Motor Division research laboratories. He left GM in 1939 to teach at Princeton but returned to Detroit in the 1940s. He taught engineering at the General Motors Institute and eventually became dean of engineering and academic affairs, supervising a faculty of 300. Perhaps Julie's relatives in the Motor City smoothed this Detroit connection. When he retired from GM in 1975, Charles moved back to Colorado Springs. There he shared his love of fishing and his hobby of tying fishing flies with his brothers at the beloved family lodge at Uneva Lake in Summit County and at the Wigwam Club on the South Platte River.

Josephine, Charley and Eleanor Tutt's youngest child, was known for her equestrian skills and for raising Labrador show dogs. A fourth son, John Wood Tutt, was born July 22, 1939, to Charles Tutt II and his second wife, Vesta. John graduated from Brown University in 1961. He is a past trustee of the Colorado Historical Society and a longtime resident of Telluride, Colorado.

William Thayer Tutt, the happy-go-lucky middle brother, replaced Irving Howbert on the El Pomar board in 1954 and remained a trustee for 35 years. His brothers Charles and Russell went east to study engineering at Princeton, but Thayer never went away to college. Instead he toured Europe, staying so long that his father crossed the Atlantic to find him and bring him home. Returning to Colorado, at his father's suggestion he enrolled in night courses in accounting and business administration at Blair's Business College and the University of Denver. During his teens and twenties he held a variety of jobs at the Broadmoor Hotel and in other El Pomar companies, an apprenticeship of sorts.

"My first job was working for the Granite Gold Mining Company, which owned the Ajax Mine and Gold Coin Mine right at the top side of Victor," Thayer recalled. "The housing was terrible and so was the food.

My job was to 'muck' in the Ajax Mine—that meant putting the ore in the mine cars, pushing it to the lift where it was raised to ground level and sorted. Later I was given the opportunity to sort the ore, too."[11] After this brief mining career, Thayer trained as a teller at the Colorado Title and Trust Company, which managed El Pomar assets. He worked on the Cog Railway and on the Manitou Incline, selling tickets and serving as conductor.

Thayer managed liquor distribution through the Manitou Mineral Water and Sales Company, an operation that split off from the Broadmoor. In the early 1940s Thayer worked for the Boettcher and Company Investment firm in Denver, then served as a lieutenant colonel in the Army Air Corps. He returned to work at the Broadmoor in 1948. Rising steadily in hotel management, he succeeded his father as hotel president and chairman of El Pomar Foundation.

Like Spencer Penrose, Thayer Tutt promoted the Broadmoor in national and international circles. After establishing Ski Broadmoor and the Broadmoor Ice Arena, Tutt went after the ultimate winter event—the Olympic Winter Games. He hired Steve Knowlton, a Tenth Mountain Division veteran and champion skier, as the Broadmoor winter sports promoter. Even after Knowlton moved to Denver to found Ski Country USA, he and Tutt staged an impressive campaign to bring the Winter Olympics to Aspen

"My first job," Thayer Tutt recalled, "was working for the Granite Gold Mining Company, which owned the Ajax Mine and Gold Coin Mine right at the top side of Victor. The housing was terrible and so was the food. My job was to 'muck' in the Ajax Mine—that meant putting the ore in the mine cars, pushing it to the lift where it was raised to ground level and sorted. Later I was given the opportunity to sort the ore, too." 1895 photo of Victor with Gold Coin atop hill courtesy Denver Public Library, Western History Department.

During the 1960s the Broadmoor became a winter resort. Thayer and Russell Tutt hired Steve Knowlton, an Army Tenth Mountain Division ski trooper, former national ski champion, and Aspen restaurateur, to help set up the Broadmoor ski area. It opened in 1961 with this chairlift and later installed one of Colorado's first snowmaking machines. After the hotel found the ski area unprofitable, the Vail Ski Corporation and later the City of Colorado Springs tried running it. The ski area closed in the 1970s. Courtesy Pikes Peak Library District, Local History Collection.

and Colorado Springs. Their proposal, which depended on El Pomar and private sources, lost the 1960 Olympics to Squaw Valley, California.[12]

Tutt pushed the idea vigorously, serving on a committee with brewer Joseph Coors, Vail founder Pete Seibert, Donald S. Fowler of United Airlines, and other heavy hitters.[13] Tutt handled hockey and figure skating for the 1976 proposal and served as vice president of the Colorado Olympics Committee, which persuaded the U.S. Olympic Committee (USOC) to make Colorado the U.S. candidate. He wined and dined Winter Olympics decisionmakers at the Broadmoor. And he and his colleagues persuaded

Thayer Tutt, shown here with his step-daughter Tiana Tutt at Ski Broadmoor, dreamed of making Colorado America's ski heaven and began pushing the idea of a Colorado Winter Olympics in the 1960s. With Tutt's support, in 1963 Steve Knowlton became the founding director of Ski Country U.S.A. This Denver-based organization helped to make Colorado America's top ski destination and pushed Colorado as a site for the international Winter Olympics in the 1960s. Although the Winter Olympics have not yet come to Colorado, Tutt's efforts did bring the U.S. Olympic Committee Training Center and Headquarters to Colorado Springs in 1978. Courtesy photo by Bob McIntyre.

the International Olympic Committee (IOC) to accept Colorado's bid on May 12, 1970.

Colorado's Olympic proponents, concludes sports historian James Whiteside, "sincerely believed that the Olympics would be a boon for Colorado, just as members of their class had always believed that their best interests were the state's best interests."[14] Voters saw things differently. They had not been consulted in the original plans and began to ask difficult questions. How much of the cost would be borne by the public (i.e., Colorado taxpayers)? As costs spiraled toward $100 million and it became apparent that taxpayers would cover a majority of the expense, voters balked. On November 7, 1972, 57 percent of Denver voters opposed city funding. Statewide, 60 percent of voters said no. The IOC got the message and moved the 1976 Olympics to Innsbruck, Austria. For his dedication to amateur athletics and the Olympic Games, the IOC gave Thayer Tutt its highest honor, the Olympic Order, in 1987.

Thayer's younger brother Russell became an El Pomar trustee in 1956. After graduating from Princeton University in 1936, he worked in the New York City brokerage firm of Halsey, Stuart, and Company. His position was secured with the help of this recommendation from Spencer Penrose: "I beg to say that I have been associated with Mr. Tutt's father and grandfather for the last forty-five years. The Tutt family is a family of high standing, which originally came from Philadelphia. All the members of his family are reliable and very trustworthy. Therefore, I can take much pleasure in recommending Russell T. Tutt in every way, and I think he has full qualifications to make him a successful bond salesman."[15]

Russell served as an army major during World War II and received the Bronze Star. In the late 1940s he took over management of the Garden City Company, which had begun raising corn, wheat, milo, and soybeans to supplement sugar production. Following the closure of the sugar plant in 1955, the Garden City firm diversified into developing both minerals and real estate and leasing farmland and Arkansas River water rights to local farmers.[16] Today the Garden City property remains a large El Pomar asset.

Russell married Louise Honnen, the daughter of his father's business partner Ed Honnen, on August 12, 1950. They had two children, Margaret, "Marne," born October 11, 1951, and Russell Thayer Jr., born February 27, 1955. In 1955 Russell moved his family from Garden City to the home at 7 Lake Avenue just east of the hotel and joined his father and his brother on the two El Pomar boards.[17]

For five years, Charles and his two sons sat on both boards, managing affairs much as the Penroses had. The senior Tutt groomed Russell and Thayer to be conscientious stewards of Spencer Penrose's legacy. "Always remember," he would remind them, "this is not our money." After their father's death in 1961, the Tutt brothers took charge of the El Pomar interests. Thayer Tutt became foundation chairman and president of the hotel. Russell Tutt chaired El Pomar Investment Company. "Thayer was the promoter and Russell was the fiscal conservative," reported Russell Freymuth, who worked for the Broadmoor for forty-seven years. "Between the two of them," Freymuth said in a 1997 interview, "they formed a good team. They kept each other in check."

William J. Hybl, who joined El Pomar in 1973 and became vice president and executive director, agrees: "Thayer had a great vision without weighing the attendant costs. Russell was terrific, really a very special individual. They made a great team—Russell made sure Thayer's vision didn't cost too much." The brothers didn't always see eye to eye, recalled Hybl: "When I started here, Mr. Wendelken told me that Russ and Thayer would disagree energetically, and the best thing I could do is leave the room. So I did just that."[18]

For twenty-five years the Tutt brothers exerted a strong influence on El Pomar, the hotel, and Colorado Springs. Thayer Tutt, a tireless booster, helped make the city the sports mecca Penrose had envisioned. His nephew, William B. Tutt, recalls Thayer's strategy: "El Pomar and Thayer Tutt in particular had a unique ability for discovering plums that were out there that others were not aware of and being able to get in and convince those groups to move here before the competition was aware."[19] Thayer Tutt convinced a number of athletic organizations to choose Colorado Springs for their headquarters, starting with the U.S. Amateur Hockey Association, the U.S. Figure Skating Association, and the U.S. Olympic Committee. Thayer Tutt used his seat on the board and a $1 million grant from El Pomar to persuade USOC President Philip Krumm, Executive Director Don Miller, and the USOC itself to relocate their headquarters and training center to Colorado Springs.

Bill Tutt remembered:

> The USOC organization was in disarray, and they had outgrown their center in New York. Thayer said, "We need to convince them to move here." It happened quickly in early 1977. We put together a group of civic-minded folks to make presentations for the USOC. They were in Colorado for skating championships at Keystone. There was another proposal there from the board of directors in Milwaukee. We brought in a blue ribbon group of Colorado Springs folks and promised them four things: $1 million from El Pomar for the headquarters, to establish an event that became the U.S. Olympic Festival, the U.S. Olympic training center, and the U.S. Olympic Hall of Fame. They voted ninety-eight to one to come to Colorado Springs.[20]

Thayer Tutt, always fascinated with sports, had become involved in the national and international world of figure skating and ice hockey in the 1940s. "After the war my father wanted me to get things organized and bring some national events here," he recalled. "My father felt we should concentrate immediately on sports, as the hotel was empty during the winter time."[21] Business trips for the Cog Railway took him to the Swiss Locomotive Works in Winterthur, Switzerland. While abroad, he took in international skating competitions, made numerous European connections, and joined the International Skating Union and International Ice Hockey Federation, of which he became president. Thayer secured both U.S. and international competitions for the Broadmoor Ice Palace, including the 1948 and 1949 National Figure Skating Championships, the 1962 World and European Ice Hockey Championship, and U.S.-Russia World Cup Hockey in the 1970s.[22] As president and a director of the U.S. Amateur Hockey Association, he arranged for the NCAA hockey championships held at the Broadmoor from 1948 to 1957.

Other winter sports also captivated Thayer. He sat on the five-person commission that advanced the state's ill-fated bid for the 1976 Winter

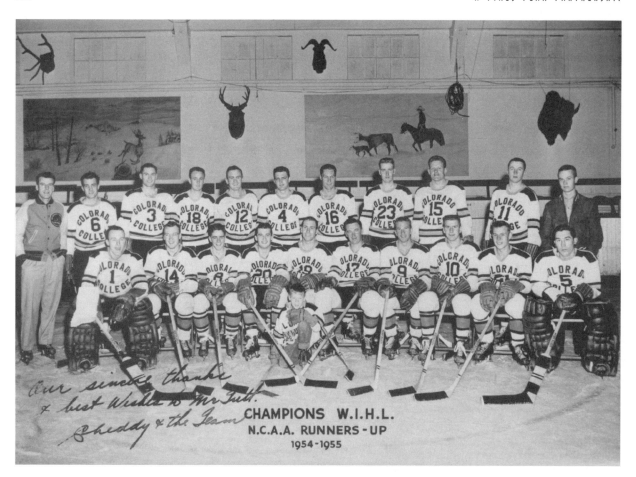

CHAMPIONS W.I.H.L.
N.C.A.A. RUNNERS-UP
1954-1955

Thayer and Russell Tutt helped organize commercially sponsored hockey teams to play at the Ice Palace and persuaded Colorado College (CC) to take up the sport by offering scholarships and free use of the Broadmoor Ice Palace. "Garret Livingston was the first coach, and he was pretty aggressive," Thayer Tutt recalled later. "CC beat Dartmouth and a number of other universities. Hockey became a very popular sport here, and we rebuilt the rink in order to have more seating."

Olympics.[23] His passion for skating spilled into his personal life—his second wife, Kay Servatius, and his third wife, Yvonne Sherman, were both figure-skating champions. Thayer's efforts won him a place in the Colorado Sports Hall of Fame and the U.S. Hockey Hall of Fame.[24]

"Thayer was so busy, busy, busy on so many, many things," reflected Richard Vanderhoof, a longtime family friend.[25] Besides his involvement in the foundation, the Broadmoor, and sports, Thayer sat on the boards of several companies financially connected to El Pomar: Golden Cycle Mining, Kennecott Copper, Denver & Rio Grande Western Railroad, Mountain States Telephone and Telegraph, and First National Bank of Colorado Springs.[26] He was president of the Pikes Peak Rodeo Association and a director of the Colorado Springs Chamber of Commerce. Of course, he was best known as "Mr. Broadmoor," president of the hotel. In the 1960s he spearheaded the expansions necessary for the resort to appeal to the convention crowd. "The International Center was a total change in the scope of marketing the Broadmoor," explained Bill Tutt in a 1997 interview. "Up to that time we had been dependent on the carriage trade. It had

The Broadmoor International Center opened in 1961, transforming an aging hotel into a state-of-the-art convention center with an emphatically modern design—a hyperbolic parabola.

been difficult to book rooms during the winter and slower months. Adding 150 rooms let us get to a competitive size. Adding the International Center and Broadmoor South was a quantum leap in philosophy, commitment, and courage. It let us shift from vacation resort to convention facility." In 1997 Thayer Tutt was posthumously inducted into the Colorado Business Hall of Fame, along with Denver oil, ranching, and railroad mogul Phil Anschutz and historic preservationist–developer Dana Crawford.[27]

Flamboyant and front page, Thayer's showmanship rivaled that of his predecessor, Spencer Penrose. "When Thayer brought in the Russian hockey players, he met them at the airport with limousines and gave them all cowboy hats. They came into the hotel lobby and the Indians were whooping it up," recalled Russell Freymuth. "Monty Montana had ridden his horse halfway up the stairs and threw his lasso down around one of the hockey skaters."[28] Tutt's showy style and his fondness for drink also earned him disapproval. "I think Mrs. Penrose looked upon Thayer as being somewhat of a playboy, and indeed he was," Freymuth said. Thayer married three times, moving into the Broadmoor penthouse suite after his first divorce. Vanderhoof remembers him as a "man's man, a little on the braggadocio side." Tutt is also remembered as a generous employer who knew each of the 300 hotel workers by name and always asked them about their families. "Thayer was very, very close to the employees," Freymuth recalled in 1997.

In contrast to his older brother, Russell Tutt was sedate, conservative, and dignified. He wore several hats in managing the El Pomar dynasty. He

Liquid assets line the entry to the Golden Bee Tavern, a nineteenth-century London pub installed in the basement of the Broadmoor International Center for its 1961 opening. Colorado's finest English-style pub sports an African mahogany back bar and matching side bars with ornate woodwork swirling into human faces and birds beneath the pressed metal ceiling. The haven has its own songbook, as well as imported English ales, porters, and stouts served by the pint and the quart. Courtesy photos by Bob McIntyre.

Broadmoor President Thayer Tutt oversaw the 1962 opening of the Broadmoor South. This nine-story addition designed by Colorado architects Carlisle Guy and Edwin Francis increased hotel rooms from 248 to 392. Courtesy photo by Bob McIntyre.

Thayer Tutt, a compulsive builder like Spencer Penrose, kept expanding the Broadmoor. After opening the hotel in 1918, Penrose had started adding on—a garage, a greenhouse, the Broadmoor stables for 400 mounts, tennis courts, and miles of bridal paths and hiking trials. Tutt added this lakeside swimming pool, designed by Denver architect Burnham Hoyt, in 1946.

provided business acumen as the investment company president, carefully investing and increasing the Penrose millions. He strengthened the company's assets by buying stock in strong U.S. companies and diversifying investments to be less dependent on copper, gold, real estate, sugar beets, and the hotel. At foundation meetings, he quietly helped decide

Catty-corner from the Broadmoor Hotel, El Pomar Foundation's Carriage House Museum is a low-slung modern building open to the public at no charge. Built in 1941 for Penrose's transportation collection, it boasts vehicles dating back as far as this 1863 Concord Stagecoach. Forty antique conveyances include C. L. Tutt's 1906 Renault and Julie Penrose's 1928 custom Cadillac. This V-8 caddy, which averaged only 7 miles to the gallon, has a 35-gallon gas tank.

which organizations would receive the several million dollars in El Pomar grants each year. He was elected director of Centel Corporation and First National Bank of Denver, and director and chairman of the Holly Sugar Company and First National Bank of Colorado Springs.[29] He was both a trustee and chair of the Fountain Valley School, the National Recreation and Park Association, Colorado College, and Cheyenne Mountain Zoo.

Russell Tutt was the financial strategist who guarded El Pomar's assets and sometimes pruned his brother's ambitious plans.

He loved animals and kept a collection of figurines on his desk. A champion of youth organizations, he figured prominently in the construction of the three YMCA/YWCA facilities in Colorado Springs. Russell Tutt was also the self-appointed Tutt family historian, collecting letters, records, and correspondence and having the family genealogy researched and published. In 1998 he was selected to join his brother Thayer and other prominent figures in the Colorado Business Hall of Fame.

Today, a fourth generation of Tutts maintains a continued presence as Colorado business and civic leaders. Russell's son, R. Thayer Tutt, is chief

Brothers Russell, *right,* and William Thayer Tutt brought different perspectives to their Pikes Peak partnership. Russell strove to conserve the Penrose empire, whereas Thayer worked night and day to expand it.

investment officer and president of El Pomar. He has been a trustee since 1983. Russell's daughter, Marne Tutt, graduated from the University of Denver in 1974. She is active in historic preservation and serves on the boards of Historic Denver, Inc., and Colorado Preservation, Inc. The sons of Charles Tutt III are also active in the Colorado Springs business community. Charles Tutt IV, a local entrepreneur, graduated from Michigan State University and worked as director of Food Service for School District 11 in Colorado Springs. He has also served as president of the Pikes Peak Hill Climb Association. During the 1980s William Bullard Tutt, a graduate of Cornell University, was a director of El Pomar Investment Corporation, senior vice president of the Broadmoor Hotel, and

After graduating from Princeton, Russell Thayer Tutt Jr. worked for a New York City brokerage firm. He subsequently became vice president in charge of accounts for the Broadmoor Hotel and was appointed president and chief financial officer (CFO) of El Pomar Foundation. He reports, "When El Pomar sold off the Broadmoor in the 1980s it jumped from 93rd to 67th largest among U.S. foundations. We have diversified our investments and doubled the total assets to more than $400 million. As one of the largest private foundations in the Rocky Mountain West, since 1937 we have given away more than $250 million to Colorado nonprofits."

president of Broadmoor Management Corporation. He has also served on the Executive Board of the U.S. Olympics Committee. Currently, he runs a manufacturing business in Colorado Springs.

The 1980s were pivotal years for El Pomar, marked by the foundation's divestiture of its majority interest in the Broadmoor Hotel. The trustees found themselves operating in an environment greatly changed from the one that prevailed when Spencer Penrose established El Pomar. During the 1960s foundations had been criticized for conducting financial transactions unrelated to charity and for being used as a tax-exempt tool for controlling corporate and other property.[30] Foundations drew criticism because subsequent trustees strayed far from founders' original intent and mission. Their tax-exempt status and operation were also scrutinized thoroughly by the Internal Revenue Service (IRS).

The Tax Reform Act of 1969 regulated foundations and defined how they operated. This watershed law changed the way foundations did business—specifying that they pay out a minimum of 5 percent of their assets to charitable causes, setting standards for reporting foundation earnings and grant-making, and forbidding grants to private individuals. The act also stipulated that tax-exempt nonprofits could not own a majority interest in a business, such as El Pomar's ownership of the Broadmoor Hotel.

"The IRS told foundations that they should be in the business of philanthropy, not the business of business," explained William Hybl, an attorney hired by the foundation in 1973. "We tried to retain ownership of the Broadmoor until just prior to the 20-year transition period [that] expired in May of 1989."[31] Despite a twelve-year effort to secure a permanent exemption for the hotel, Congress failed to soften the law requiring El Pomar to sell the Broadmoor. In summer 1988, Oklahoma Publishing Company of Oklahoma City bought 65 percent of the hotel stock for approximately $50.5 million.[32] The company also bought a majority share of the Cog Railway and Manitou Incline. Two years later, Oklahoma Publishing bought an additional 15 percent of the properties to secure an 80 percent interest that allowed certain tax advantages.

"We picked the new owners ourselves," said Russell Tutt. "They're magnificent people."[33] Edward L. Gaylord was president of the firm. His father, Edward K. Gaylord, an 1897 graduate of Colorado College and a college trustee from 1957 to 1970, was a media magnate who owned the *Colorado Springs Evening Gazette, Colorado Springs Sun, Saint Joseph [Missouri] Evening Gazette,* and *Daily Oklahoman* [Oklahoma City]. The younger Gaylord attended Stanford University and Harvard before beginning his career at Oklahoma Publishing in 1936. He took over the privately held family business after his father's death in 1974. A separate, publicly held company, Gaylord Entertainment Company, also owned the Grand Ole Opry in Nashville, Tennessee, the Opryland Hotel, three country music cable networks, and several television and radio stations in western states. The company also helped preserve the last large undeveloped tract along I-25 between Denver and Colorado Springs—the 22,000-acre Greenland Ranch.[34]

"We think the partnership between the Oklahoma Publishing Company and El Pomar has been a very good one and a very dynamic one," said Steve Bartolin Jr., president of the hotel, in 1997.

> We have taken a great hotel, with a great history and great infrastructure, and reinvested substantially to help it stay competitive in the resort business. We plan on maintaining a balance of history, architectural continuity, and the style of service. It is a very important role to serve as custodian of this heritage. Our goal is to hand down the

Broadmoor in pristine condition to the next generation of employees
and guests. We have been able to build the business level with an
energized marketing effort. The present ratio of hotel guests is approximately 70 percent conferences and conventions and 30 percent social
and family-based customers, a ratio that has been fairly constant for the
past three decades.[35]

The sale of the Broadmoor was painful. For fifty years the hotel had
been the public image and identity of the low-profile foundation, as well as
its most tangible connection to the legacy of Spencer Penrose. Ultimately,
however, selling the Broadmoor proved a financial boon for El Pomar. The
foundation invested proceeds from the sale in blue-chip stocks, and its
assets nearly tripled between 1988 and 1997. Today, El Pomar retains a 20
percent ownership in the hotel, Cog Railway, and Cog Land Company.
William J. Hybl and R. Thayer Tutt still sit on the Broadmoor board. The
new owners have renovated, redecorated, and expanded the hotel. They
replaced the hundred-year-old golf clubhouse with a larger, more spacious
Broadmoor Golf Club and Spa in October 1994 and opened the seven-story
West Towers in May 1995.

Divestiture of the hotel was not the only El Pomar controversy. In the
mid-1980s the IRS challenged the foundation's valuation of the Broadmoor
Hotel at $21.9 million.[36] This valuation had a direct impact on grant dis-
tribution: the hotel comprised 45 percent of the foundation's assets at the
time, and federal law required that foundations disburse a minimum of 5
percent of the fair market value of their assets. The hotel was privately
held, therefore its value was assessed both by an independent firm hired by
El Pomar and by the IRS. A routine IRS audit identified the variance
between the two evaluations, and the foundation reached a compromise
settlement with the IRS. However, the scathing news coverage of the topic
made the trustees realize that El Pomar's low-profile image had left it vul-
nerable to negative publicity. This realization in part influenced changes
that have taken place at the foundation since the 1980s.

During its first fifty years El Pomar Foundation played a behind-
the-scenes role, funding chiefly bricks-and-mortar projects centered in the
Pikes Peak region. During the 1990s the trustees sought ways to better
reach the public and serve the nonprofit arena. They also cultivated a more
public image for El Pomar. The board created various new outreach programs, established the Penrose House for nonprofit organizations, and sponsored the book now in your hands. "We're striving for a greater statewide
presence," said R. Thayer Tutt Jr. "We're trying to raise the image of El
Pomar around Colorado."[37]

Driving through Colorado Springs, one sees many landmarks connected to the Penroses, the Tutts, and El Pomar. On the north side of town
lie the Air Force Academy Visitor Center, Pro Rodeo Hall of Fame, Focus
on the Family headquarters, and the new library and research center at the

Historic preservation of Colorado's important landmarks has been an El Pomar Foundation priority ever since Julie Penrose helped to rescue the Central City Opera House in the 1930s. In more recent years, the terrific growth of Colorado Springs has threatened treasures such as Rock Ledge Ranch in the Garden of the Gods. "Rock Ledge was about to be demolished and subdivided," recalls former Colorado Springs Mayor Eugene McCleary. "We worked with El Pomar, and Russell Tutt gave us a foundation check for $350,000 to buy out the developer and turn the ranch into a city park." The scenic 160-acre, open-space ranch now features a collection of restored structures illustrating Colorado Springs' rapid architectural evolution from log cabins to high-style designs like the restored 1874 Chambers House shown here. Courtesy Penrose Public Library.

George Guerrero, *right,* curator of the Will Rogers Shrine of the Sun, inspects the landmark tower with Russell Thayer Tutt Jr. Restored in the 1990s, the tower is listed on the National Register of Historic Places. Courtesy photo by Robert Middleton.

Following in the footsteps of Palmer and Penrose, William J. Hybl has significantly enhanced the Pikes Peak region. Hybl served in the U.S. Army and the Colorado House of Representatives. As CEO of El Pomar Foundation and the Air Force Academy Foundation and an activist in many other civic and community groups, Hybl has helped to transform Colorado Springs into an amateur athletic hub and nationally noted center for nonprofit organizations. Pictured here as president of the United States Olympic Committee (1991–1992, 1996–2000).

University of Colorado at Colorado Springs, each funded by large El Pomar grants. On the south side are the Broadmoor Hotel, Cheyenne Mountain Zoo, Will Rogers Shrine of the Sun, Penrose House, and Colorado Springs World Arena. To the west are the Pikes Peak Automobile Highway and the Manitou & Pikes Peak Railway. In the heart of the city are the Colorado College campus, the Montgomery Shelter for the hungry and homeless, the Colorado Springs Fine Arts Center, and Penrose Hospital. On the eastern edge lies the U.S. Olympic Complex.

These sites and many others are reminders of the Penroses' enduring effect on the city and the legacy carried on by their foundation. Between 1937 and 2000, more than $250 million in El Pomar grants funded thousands of projects in the city and around the state. "Without Spencer Penrose and the Tutts to follow through, Colorado Springs would not be the type of city it is now," said former Colorado Springs mayor Eugene McCleary. "They were always involved in everything. They were right there and made it possible. El Pomar gifts have always been kind of the keystone for putting together local projects."[38]

Honoring Penrose's original intent—to encourage and promote the general well-being of the inhabitants of the state of Colorado—grant giving continues to focus on education, economic development, amateur sports, the arts, health and human services, and youth. The growth of the foundation's assets during the 1990s allowed El Pomar to make more grants, develop innovative programs, and achieve a broader statewide outreach. Recognizing El Pomar's excellence and innovation, the American Society of Fund Raising Executives gave El Pomar the 1998 National Outstanding Foundation Award.

The foundation's proactive role has earned attention from other non-profit foundations in Colorado. "They're very creative. They are the leader, the most innovative," said Bob Sweeney, president of Denver's Kenneth Kendall King Foundation. "Their fellowship program is unique—preparing young people to be active leaders and directors of foundations. The Awards for Excellence is an incredible program, acknowledging nonprofits around the state. El Pomar is viewed with great respect in the foundation community. They had the money and did the right thing. They've had a big impact on the Rocky Mountain region. You see El Pomar everywhere as a major donor, right there with the Boettcher and Gates Foundations."[39]

El Pomar enters the twenty-first century striving to maintain its leadership role in the foundation world. "One of our goals is to better prepare nonprofits to administer, fund, and manage their organizations," said William Hybl. "We are doing this through a variety of executive, education, and outreach programs—and creative people with good ideas."[40]

NOTES

1. Marshall Sprague, *Colorado: A Bicentennial History.* Nashville and New York: American Association for State and Local History/W. W. Norton, 1976, p. 173.

2. Marshall Sprague, *Newport in the Rockies: The Life and Good Times of Colorado Springs.* Chicago: Sage/Swallow, 1980 [1961], p. 316.

3. Robert Hilbert, interviewed by Cathleen Norman, September 5, 1997.

4. Julie's hope that her oldest great-grandson, Michele, would one day sit on the El Pomar board was never realized because the young baron preferred Brussels to Colorado Springs.

5. Penrose House, Spencer Penrose Collection, Box 84, File 358, letter dated June 21, 1939.

6. Ibid., letter dated October 8, 1939.

7. *The Tutt Family of Virginia, Philadelphia, and Colorado Springs.* Colorado Springs: Russell T. Tutt, 1975, pp. 15–18.

8. Richard Vanderhoof, interviewed by Cathleen Norman, July 22, 1997.

9. Sprague, *Newport in the Rockies,* p. 87.

10. Russell Tutt, interviewed in "The Tutt Legacy." Colorado Springs: Pikes Peak Library District, 1994.

11. "Thayer Tutt Remembers," unpublished memoir of W. Thayer Tutt, Colorado Springs, 1980, p. 2.

12. Stephen A. Knowlton, interviewed by Tom Noel, September 13, 1998.

13. John A. Love, interviewed by Tom Noel, January 24, 1999.

14. James Whiteside, *Colorado: A Sports History.* Niwot: University Press of Colorado, 1999, pp. 145–179.

15. Penrose House, Spencer Penrose Collection, Box 40, File 139, letter to Frank Wood of Halsey, Stuart and Company, May 12, 1936.

16. Eugene Stoeckly, *A Company and Factory—History of the Garden City Company,* unpublished manuscript, pp. 11–14.

17. Michael Churchman, *The Armit Family.* Colorado Springs: self-published, 1978, p. 56.

18. William J. Hybl, interviewed by Tom Noel and Cathleen Norman, April 21 and July 11, 1997.

19. William B. Tutt, interviewed by Cathleen Norman, July 22, 1997.

20. Ibid.

21. "Thayer Tutt Remembers," p. 13.

22. Diane Lynn Betts, *The Broadmoor World Arena Pictorial History Book.* Colorado Springs: Broadmoor World Arena, 1988, pp. 12–13.

23. "Thayer Tutt Selected to Five-Man Colorado Olympic Commission Formed to Further the State's Proposed Bid for the 1976 Winter Olympics," *Denver Post,* December 27, 1964, p. 76, c. 8.

24. "Big Names to Attend 8th Annual Dinner at Which Dowler, Tutt, Wren and Hughes Will Be Enshrined in the Colo. Sports Hall of Fame," *Denver Post,* January 23, 1972; "William Thayer Tutt Selected to Colorado Sports Hall of Fame," *Denver Post,* December 19, 1971; *Colorado Springs Sun,* March 23, 1975, p. 19A.

25. Richard Vanderhoof, interviewed by Cathleen Norman, July 22, 1997.

26. "Tutt Named," *Denver Post,* December 27, 1961, p. 52, c. 6.

27. "Business Leaders Turn Out in Force for Hall of Fame Fete," *Denver Post,* February 9, 1997, p. 8E.

28. G. Russell Freymuth, interviewed by Cathleen Norman, April 18, 1997.

29. "Tutt Named."

30. Merrimon Cuninggim, *Private Money and Public Service: The Role of Foundations in American Society.* New York: McGraw-Hill, 1972.

31. William J. Hybl, interviewed by Cathleen Norman, June 26, 1997.

32. Wayne Hellman, "Broadmoor Sale to Gaylord Completed," *Colorado Springs Gazette-Telegraph,* August 6, 1988, p. A1, c.1; Robert Hilbert, interviewed by Cathleen Norman, September 5 and 8, 1997.

33. "The Tutt Legacy."

34. Elena Bertozzi-Villa, *Broadmoor Memories: The History of the Broadmoor.* Colorado Springs: Broadmoor, 1993, pp. 172–177.

35. Steve Bartolin Jr., interviewed by Cathleen Norman, September 8, 1997.

36. In 1987 El Paso County assessed the Broadmoor at $66.3 million. El Pomar's original estimate had been $21.9 million. El Pomar appealed, placing valuation at $34 million, and the county reduced the 1987 appraisal to $42.5 million. "Local Foundation's Conflicting Estimates of Hotel's Value Raise Issues, Paper Says," *Colorado Springs Gazette-Telegraph,* March 21, 1988, p. B4.

37. Thayer Tutt, interviewed by Cathleen Norman and Tom Noel, June 5 and 10, 1997.

38. Eugene McCleary, interviewed by Tom Noel and Cathleen Norman, March 15, 1996.

39. Robert Sweeney, interviewed by Tom Noel, September 17, 1999.

40. William J. Hybl, interviewed by Tom Noel, April 21, 1999.

A New Beginning by William J. Hybl

FOR NEARLY 100 YEARS, the unique relationship forged between Spencer Penrose and members of the Tutt Family led to the growth and impact of Penrose's ventures throughout the Pikes Peak Region, the state of Colorado and the Rocky Mountain West. Well managed by the inner circle of associates selected by Spencer Penrose, these assets, primarily El Pomar Investment Company, the Broadmoor Hotel and El Pomar Foundation, continued to successfully reflect the design and intent of their founder well beyond his death in 1939. Nearly one hundred years after that December 1892 meeting between Spencer Penrose and Charles Tutt at the Colorado Springs railroad station, however, a series of significant events dramatically altered Penrose's original plans and propelled El Pomar Foundation into a new and exciting chapter in its history of service and support to the people of Colorado.

As noted in this book, in 1988, the Investment Company was dissolved and the Broadmoor Hotel was sold. The central figures in the second generation of "Penrose leadership," and all Trustees of El Pomar Foundation, passed away: Thayer Tutt in 1989, Ben Wendelken in 1991, Russell Tutt in 1992, and Karl Eitel in 1998. At the same time, the sale of the Broadmoor Hotel provided capital to help fuel the growth of the assets of the Foundation, while "intellectual capital" freed from the responsibility of managing the Investment Company and the Broadmoor set the course for the newly autonomous El Pomar Foundation. It is significant to note that of the quarter of a billion dollars given by El Pomar since its inception in 1937, more than half of that amount has been granted since 1990.

Combine these events with our government's realization, at about this same time, that it had neither the fiscal nor human resources necessary to single-handedly solve the nation's social ills and increasing public expectations of accountability by both public and private institutions, and one finds El Pomar Foundation in a challenging new environment that has been accompanied by heightened visibility and a more prominent role in efforts to affect positive change throughout Colorado.

As El Pomar anxiously begins its journey into tomorrow, its direction comes from its past. Spencer Penrose's life, as he lived it and as this book conveys it, provides the principles that will continue to guide his foundation. He clearly saw the future and repeatedly took the necessary risks to secure it. Spencer Penrose was a visionary, and the most important obligation the stewards of his legacy have is to continue to think in ways that others do not and, through the creative use of the resources he left to us, continue to build where others are unable to see opportunity.

This book tells the story of the important relationship between risk and reward that has left an indelible mark on life in the West. Spencer Penrose succeeded in the face of extraordinary challenges. While today's challenges are certainly different, Spencer Penrose's legacy, and that of the individuals who followed in his footsteps, gives those who now lead his foundation the confidence to pursue the future in new and innovative ways that reflect the vision and tenacity of this incredible man.

El Pomar Trustees

Pioneer trustees Spencer Penrose, Julie Penrose, Charles L. Tutt II, Merton Bogart, William J. Howbert, Henry McAllister, and Russell Tutt have been profiled in the text. Since 1949 a second generation of trustees has guided El Pomar. They are profiled here in chronological order.

1949–1966: H. Chase Stone was president of the First National Bank of Colorado Springs and played a large role in bringing Fort Carson and the Air Force Academy to the city. Born May 5, 1900, in Staten Island, New York, Stone graduated from Cornell University and served in both World Wars I and II. He came to Colorado in 1925 to recover from tuberculosis. Stone brought financial skills and a forward-looking attitude to the board. He was a director of El Pomar Investment Company, the Broadmoor, Holly Sugar, and the Garden City Company. Stone was trustee or chair of Fountain Valley School, Colorado College, and Colorado School for the Deaf and Blind. He was also president of the Colorado Springs Chamber of Commerce and the Colorado Springs Sky Sox, a farm team of the Chicago White Sox. His dream of building a downtown financial, commercial, office, and lodging center was realized in 1966. The $20 million Chase Stone Center replaced the historic Antlers Hotel and helped revitalize the city's dying commercial core.

1954–1963: ROBERT V. MENARY was president and manager of the Cheyenne Mountain Zoo for 35 years. He was born in 1893 in San Francisco, where he also grew up. He worked for Matson Steamship, a manufacturer of luxury liners. While living in Hawaii he met and married his wife, Jesse Kennedy. Menary originally moved to Colorado Springs for his health: he had tuberculosis. "Mr. Penrose came to him and asked him personally if he would be a director of the zoo," recalled his daughter, Catherine Calder. "My father knew nothing about animals but knew about management and learned about animals as he went along." He also served on other Penrose-connected boards: the Broadmoor Hotel, El Pomar Investment Company, Fountain Valley School, and, for thirty years, Cheyenne Mountain Country Club.

1961–1975: RAY MONTGOMERY began working in the offices of Spencer Penrose, Charles MacNeill, and Charles Tutt Jr. in 1917 and was Tutt's secretary for forty years. He was born July 16, 1892, in Farmington, Illinois; studied at Kansas State University in Manhattan; and graduated from Blair Business College. He served as a board member for a half-dozen El Pomar–related companies. Montgomery was secretary of the Broadmoor Golf Club for 40 years and an original member of the Broadmoor Pioneer Club founded by Tutt in 1950.

1963–1991: BEN WENDELKEN, regarded as "one of the best legal minds in the West," was born September 10, 1899, in Colorado Springs. He labored as a construction worker building the Broadmoor Hotel in 1916, then served in World War I before going to college. He graduated from Colorado College at age 23 and received a law degree from the University of Michigan. He was admitted to the Colorado Bar in 1925. During his sixty-year career as a trial lawyer, Wendelken handled over 1,000 cases. He was city attorney for Colorado Springs from 1932 to 1947 and the Broadmoor Hotel's corporate lawyer for half a century. "Ben Wendelken was a great influence, a pillar of strength," recalled trustee Karl Eitel. "He was a steadying influence between Russell and Thayer. He also always brought back the fact that we were the trustees and legatees and reminded us to do what Spencer Penrose would have wished."

1969–1989: JOEL WEBB, a member of one of the city's oldest banking families, was born May 2, 1913, in Colorado Springs. His grandfather, Joel Addison Hayes, had been president of the First National Bank of Colorado Springs from 1896 to 1919 and his uncle, Jefferson Hayes Davis, was vice president of the bank from 1930 to 1954. His father was famed tuberculosis physician Dr. Gerald Webb, who invested in several of Spencer Penrose's projects including the Broadmoor Hotel. His maternal great-grandfather was Jefferson Davis, president of the Confederate States of America. Joel Webb started his lifelong career at the First National Bank in 1935, where he worked as a runner while a student at Colorado College. He was elected bank chairman in 1966 and held that position until his retirement in 1975. As an El Pomar trustee, Webb advocated health care, hospitals, and care for the less fortunate.

1975–1998: KARL E. EITEL, hired as resident manager of the Broadmoor in 1961, gained his experience in hotel management at the Cosmopolitan in Denver and the Sir Francis Drake in San Francisco. He was born in Chicago on December 26, 1928, and graduated from Michigan State University in 1951. His business affiliations have included director of the Colorado Springs Chamber of Commerce and several hotel management associations. As hotel manager he organized many national and international events at the Broadmoor. He has served on the boards of Colorado Ski Country,

Inc., Colorado Golf Association, and Fountain Valley School. "Things have changed a lot," reflected Eitel. "Now we are much more pro-active. We reach out into the community and see what we can do rather than wait for people to come to us. In the old days we were good at giving money away—now we have a lot of programs that go out into the community. We also publicize far more than we used to. We want people to know what we are and what we do. El Pomar today is far better known than it was before." The Karl E. Eitel Youth at Risk grants were created by El Pomar Foundation after his death in 1998.

1983– : R. THAYER TUTT JR., born February 27, 1955, in Garden City, Kansas, grew up in Colorado Springs and was educated at Fountain Valley School. He graduated from Princeton in 1977 with a bachelor's degree in geology and from Duke University in 1979 with a master's degree in business administration. He worked in New York, Los Angeles, and Chicago as a loan officer of Citicorp, New York, before joining the board in 1983. "I believe that our stewardship has been as Spencer Penrose would have done it himself. As a board, we have tried to remain consistent with Mr. Penrose's philosophy by supporting only Colorado organizations and also by supporting organizations that the Penroses traditionally supported," explained Tutt. These include the Fountain Valley School, Penrose Hospital, Central City Opera, Cheyenne Mountain Zoo, Colorado Springs Fine Arts Center, Colorado College, and Boys and Girls Clubs. "Recently, our greatest growth in giving has been in our internally generated programs," he continued. "We are creating programs, like our fellowship program and Awards for Excellence. We're doing things that nobody else is doing. We want El Pomar to be the leading advocate for the nonprofit executive." Tutt is director of the boards of the Garden City Company, Broadmoor Hotel, and Manitou & Pikes Peak Railway. He was instrumental in initiating and assisting in writing this history of El Pomar Foundation. Tutt also serves on the boards of the U.S. Olympic Foundation, Cheyenne Mountain Zoo Endowment Fund, Colorado Springs Chamber Foundation, Colorado Springs Fine Arts Center Foundation, the National Recreation Foundation, the Nature Conservancy, and the Colorado Endowment for the Humanities.

1983– : WILLIAM J. HYBL was born in Des Moines, Iowa, on July 16, 1942, and grew up in Pueblo, Colorado. He graduated from Colorado College and received his law degree from the University of Colorado in 1967. After serving in Ethiopia as a captain in the U.S. Army, he became deputy district attorney, then assistant district attorney for the Fourth Judicial District. In 1972 Hybl was elected to the Colorado House of Representatives, where he served as vice chairman of the House Judicial Committee. He joined the Broadmoor Hotel as vice president in 1973 and is currently vice chairman of the hotel board. Hybl was president of the United States Olympic Committee (USOC) during the 1992 Winter Olympics in Albertville, France, and the Summer Olympic Games in Barcelona, Spain. He was reelected president of the USOC for the 1996–2000 quadrennium, which includes the 1998 Winter Olympics in Nagano, Japan, and the 2000 Summer Olympic Games in Sydney, Australia. Hybl is a member of the boards of directors of the First Bank Holding Company of Colorado, the Garden City Company, KN Energy, Inc., and USAA Insurance Company. He is president of the board of the Air Force Academy Association, secretary of Junior Achievement, Inc., and was inducted into the Colorado Springs Sports Hall of Fame in 2000.

Hybl, chairman and chief executive officer of El Pomar Foundation, believes the foundation's most significant accomplishment has been its commitment to promote and support the entire nonprofit community. "We have made a conscientious effort to be part of the nonprofit process in Colorado," he explained. "There are twenty to twenty-five young men and women in our fellowship program. They are going out and becoming an integral part of the leadership in the nonprofit community. We conduct a series of educational programs at the Penrose House Center and throughout the state to enhance the management and financial skills of nonprofit executives. The Awards for Excellence program, which began in 1989, rewards and recognizes nonprofits around the state. Our El Pomar Youth in Community Service now exists in more than ninety high schools. Throughout the state the foundation continues strong support of human services, reflected in the grants that supply goods, services, and support for those least capable of providing for themselves."

1992– : KENT O. OLIN is a 1955 graduate of Ripon College in Ripon, Wisconsin. After serving in the Air Force, he worked for United Bank of Denver from 1957 to 1971, then joined Affiliated Bankshares as executive vice president in 1971. He became president of Affiliated Bankshares' First National Bank in Boulder. He came to Colorado Springs in 1974 to serve as president and chief executive officer (CEO) of First National Bank of Colorado Springs. Olin was president, then CEO, of Affiliated Bankshares of Colorado when that organization was sold to Bank One of Ohio. He retired from the banking industry in 1992. He served as a trustee for Colorado College and as president of the El Paso Club.

1993– : ROBERT J. HILBERT is a native of Denver, Colorado. Since joining the foundation in 1987, he has served as corporate secretary, treasurer, and vice-president for administration. He is responsible for directing the foundation's financial and accounting activities, tax matters, and the internal administrative activities associated with the grantmaking programs, personnel, and office administration. Hilbert is a Certified Public Accountant and a 1970 graduate of the University of Colorado. His professional experience includes revenue agent for the Internal Revenue Service, supervising

tax specialist of Coopers & Lybrand, vice-president and executive director of the Helen K. and Arthur E. Johnson Foundation, secretary-treasurer of the Piton Foundation, and executive vice-president of the United States Olympic Foundation. He is active with the Colorado Association of Foundations and has served on its executive committee. He is also a member of the board and secretary-treasurer of the Colorado Springs World Arena and is a past trustee and board chair of Pikes Peak United Way. He has served as an adjunct professor in the graduate programs for nonprofit management at both the University of Colorado at Colorado Springs and Regis College.

1996– : WILLIAM R. WARD was born May 26, 1942, in Grand Junction and grew up in Pueblo. He graduated from Colorado College in 1964 and received a law degree from the University of Colorado in 1967. He was president of Ward Transport, Inc., a family-owned trucking company, and past chairman of American Trucking Association. The election of Ward, a Denver resident, reflected the foundation's aim to broaden its scope beyond the Pikes Peak region. He has sat on the Highway Legislative Review Committee and the Governor's Transportation Roundtable. He is currently chairman of the Colorado

College board of trustees. "I think El Pomar has worked very diligently to set the stage for nonprofit organizations to serve Colorado in an even greater capacity, making it possible for neighbors to help neighbors," said Ward. "The foundation is part of a wonderful trend toward moving things out of Washington, D.C. I give great credit to Bill Hybl for leadership and vision. El Pomar's gifts and grants have been directed not only for needs of the moment but to build a platform for the future so that nonprofits can be self-sustaining."

1996– : JUDY BELL, El Pomar's first woman director since Julie Penrose forty years earlier, was the president of the United States Golf Association (USGA) in 1996 and 1997. Born in Wichita, Kansas, she played her first Broadmoor Invitational Tournament at age 11 and won that competition in 1957, 1958, and 1960. Bell has competed in thirty-eight U.S. Golf Association events and joined the USGA Executive Committee in 1987. She has been inducted into the Colorado Golf and the Colorado Sports Halls of Fame. Bell served as a director of Bank One from 1982 to 1995. She operates Bell's Deli as well as several other retail businesses in Colorado Springs.

1998– : CORTLANDT S. DIETLER, a Denver native, has often been celebrated as Colorado's "Oil Man of the Year." A graduate of Culver Military Academy and the University of Tulsa, as a youth he worked during the summer in oil field and office jobs with the British-American, Lucey, and Stanolind Oil Companies before serving in World War II. He fought in North Africa, Italy, France, and Germany with the Corps of Engineers. After the war Dietler worked with various pipeline companies in Lebanon, Canada, Wyoming, and Oklahoma before founding his own

company, Western Crude Oil, Inc., in 1951. This was the first of several successful companies he built and then sold. Purchasers included the Permian Corporation in 1960, the Getty Oil Company in 1980, Panhandle in 1994, and Duke Energy in 1997. Cort always plunged back into the oil business, serving as a director of the Forest Oil, Hallador Petroleum, and Key Production Companies.

Besides being chair and chief executive officer of TransMontaigne, Inc., Dietler works with a wide variety of business and civic groups. He is a past director and chair of the Executive Committee of Bank One Corporation. He is a director of the American Petroleum Institute and the Independent Petroleum Association of America. He is a past president and life member of the Rocky Mountain Oil and Gas Association. As a civic activist, his trusteeships include the Buffalo Bill Memorial Association, the Denver Art Museum, the Denver Museum of Natural History, St. Joseph Hospital Foundation, the Western Stock Show Association, and, since 1998, El Pomar Foundation.

1998– : BRENDA J. SMITH, a native of Colby, Kansas, graduated from Palmer High School in Colorado Springs and earned a degree in business administration from the University of Colorado at Colorado Springs. As a specialist in accounting for non-profit and governmental entities, she has worked with a variety of clients. Since 1971 Brenda had been a CPA and audit and consulting partner with Baird, Kurtz, and Dobson. A member of the American Institute of Certified Public Accountants and the Board of Governors of the American Group of CPAs, she served with the Colorado Society of Public Accountants, notably on its Education Standards and Upward Mobility for Women Committees.

Brenda has served as the president of the Colorado Springs Chapter of Executive Women International. She chairs, or has chaired, the boards of the Colorado Springs Chamber of Commerce, the Colorado Springs Chamber of Commerce Foundation, the Colorado Springs Non-Profit Center, and the Colorado Springs Leadership Institute. She has been honored for outstanding contributions to the Chamber of Commerce, the University of Colorado at Colorado Springs, the Pikes Peak Mental Health Center, and the United Way. A member of El Pomar's Awards for Excellence Committee and Advisory Board, she became an El Pomar trustee in 1998. "I am honored to serve as an El Pomar trustee," Brenda reported, "and to learn how much nonprofits strengthen Colorado's economy and reflect a sincere concern for others."

1998– : DAVID J. PALENCHAR, a California native, trained as a pilot and an engineer at the U.S. Air Force Academy. During a career in the U.S. Air Force, David served as a pilot, a professor at the U.S. Air Force Academy, and a foreign policy adviser both in Washington, D.C., and with the State Department in Brussels, Belgium.

Since joining El Pomar Foundation in 1990, David has been engaged in a variety of activities, including overseeing the foundation's grant-making program as vice president for programs. He is also president and CEO of the Colorado Springs World Arena and has served on several community boards, including the Chamber of Commerce, the Colorado Springs Symphony, and the Colorado Springs Sports Corporation. He has also served on the board of the Air Force Academy Foundation, the Colorado Institute of Technology Transfer and Implementation, the Air Force Academy Association of Graduates, Colorado Springs Memorial Hospital, and the Pikes Peak Council of the Boy Scouts of America. David became an El Pomar trustee in 1998.

THE PRESENT BOARD, recently expanded to nine trustees, perpetuates Spencer and Julie Penrose's vision for Colorado Springs, the Pikes Peak region, and the state. "We are trying to carry on their tradition and the legacy," said R. Thayer Tutt Jr. During its first half-century the foundation followed a conservative path. It funded chiefly capital projects and the causes and organizations originally patronized by the Penroses. Today, foundation assets of more than $480 million allow larger numbers and amounts of grants that fund a broad array of programs and projects. While continuing to support its traditional endeavors, El Pomar has taken a more proactive leadership role in Colorado's nonprofit arena. It has initiated a number of innovative outreach programs, such as El Pomar Youth in Community Service (EPYCS), the Awards for Excellence in Nonprofits, the fellowship program, and operation of the Penrose House for nonprofits. Educational sessions conducted by the foundation help empower grant recipients. "I view grants as an investment in these nonprofits rather than just a charitable activity," said Tutt. "Grants are investments with a human touch rather than just giving money away. Training of the leadership is the key to success of nonprofits." Thayer Tutt's great-grandfather, Charles L. Tutt, and Tutt's partner, Spencer Penrose, came to Colorado to make millions. Their legacy has evolved from taking to giving.

Bibliography

MANUSCRIPT COLLECTIONS

Boulder, Colorado. Richard Penrose Collection. Geological Society of America.

Cambridge, Massachusetts. Pusey Library. Harvard University Archives. Rocky Mountain Harvard Club. *Secretary's Reports Nos. I–VII.*

Colorado Springs, Colorado. Broadmoor Hotel Archives.

Colorado Springs, Colorado. Colorado College. Tutt Library. Spencer Penrose, Julie Penrose, Charles L. Tutt, and Russell T. Tutt clipping files.

Colorado Springs, Colorado. Colorado Springs Pioneer Museum. James W. Starsmore Research Center. Spencer Penrose, Julie Penrose, Charles L. Tutt, Tutt Family. *Broadmoor Hotel. El Pomar.*

Colorado Springs, Colorado. El Pomar Foundation Records.

Colorado Springs, Colorado. Penrose House. Helen Geiger (Broadmoor Hotel) Collection, Julie Penrose Collection, Spencer Penrose Collection, Tutt Family Collection.

Colorado Springs, Colorado. Penrose Public Library. Files on Spencer Penrose, Julie Penrose, and Charles L. Tutt.

Cripple Creek, Colorado. Cripple Creek District Museum. Museum archives. Spencer Penrose folder.

Denver, Colorado. Colorado Historical Society. Stephen Hart Library. Cripple Creek and Spencer Penrose clipping files.

Denver, Colorado. Denver Public Library. Western History Collection. Cripple Creek and Spencer Penrose clipping files.

Detroit, Michigan. Detroit Public Library. Burton Historical Collection. James McMillan papers. James McMillan and Alexander Lewis clipping files.

Grosse Pointe Farms, Michigan. Grosse Pointe Historical Society. James McMillan family clipping files and photographs.

Philadelphia, Pennsylvania. American Philosophical Society. R.A.F. Penrose Jr. papers.

Philadelphia, Pennsylvania. Freed Library. Local History Department. Penrose family file and Rabbit Club clipping files.

Philadelphia, Pennsylvania. Historical Society of Pennsylvania. Penrose family pamphlets, articles, and photographs.

Philadelphia, Pennsylvania. National Archives, Mid-Atlantic Region. Philadelphia census records, 1870 and 1880.

Philadelphia, Pennsylvania. Temple University. Paley Library. Temple Urban Archives. Clipping files: Dr. R.A.F. Penrose Sr., Boies Penrose, Dr. R.A.F. Penrose Jr., Dr. Charles Bingham Penrose, Spencer Penrose.

Philadelphia, Pennsylvania. University of Pennsylvania. University Records and Archives. Dr. R.A.F. Penrose Sr., Dr. R.A.F. Penrose Jr., Dr. Charles Bingham Penrose clipping files.

Salt Lake City, Utah. State Historical Society. D. C. Jackling papers, Utah Copper papers.

Salt Lake City, Utah. University of Utah. Marriott Library. D. C. Jackling and Utah Copper clipping files.

BOOKS

Abbott, Carl, Stephen J. Leonard, and David McComb. *Colorado: A History of the Centennial State.* Niwot: University Press of Colorado, 1982.

Abbott, Morris W. *The Pikes Peak Cog Road.* Colorado Springs: Pulpit Rock, 1979.

The American Philosophical Society Year Book. Philadelphia: American Philosophical Society, 1937, 1938, 1958, 1968.

Arrington, Leonard J., and Gary B. Hansen. *The Richest Hole on Earth: A History of the Bingham Copper Mine.* Logan: Utah State University Press, 1963.

Bailey, Lynn Robinson. *Old Reliable: A History of Bingham Canyon, Utah.* Tucson: Westernlore, 1988.

Baltezell, E. Digby. *Philadelphian Gentlemen—The Making of a National Upper Class.* Glencoe, Ill.: Free Press, 1958.

Barker, Ferdinand E. *The World Copper Market: An Economic Analysis.* Cambridge, Mass.: Ballinger, 1974.

Beebe, Lucius. *The Big Spenders.* Garden City, N.Y.: Doubleday, 1966.

Bertozzi-Villa, Elena. *Broadmoor Memories: The History of the Broadmoor.* Colorado Springs: Broadmoor, 1993.

Betts, Diane Lynn. *The Broadmoor World Arena Pictorial History Book.* Colorado Springs: Broadmoor World Arena, 1988.

Bowden, Robert Douglas. *Boies Penrose: Symbol of an Era.* Freeport, N.Y.: Books of Liberties, 1937.

Breckenridge, Juanita L., and John P. Breckenridge. *El Paso County Heritage,* Vol. 1. Dallas: Curtis Media, 1985.

A Brief History of Fort Carson, Colorado—1924–1967. Fort Carson, Colo.: Information Office, July 1968.

Brown, Robert L. *Cripple Creek Then and Now.* Denver: Sundance, 1991.

Brown, Ronald C. *Hard-Rock Miners: The Intermountain West, 1860–1920*. College Station: Texas A&M University Press, 1979.

Buckman, George Rex. *Colorado Springs, Colorado, and Its Famous Scenic Environs*. Colorado Springs: Alley-Allen, 1892.

Burt, Nathaniel. *Perennial Philadelphians*. Boston: Little, Brown, 1963.

Carter, Edward C., III. *One Grand Present—A Brief History of the American Philosophical Society's First 250 Years, 1743–1993*. Philadelphia: American Philosophical Society, 1993.

Carter, Henry L., ed. *The Pikes Peak Region: A Sesquicentennial History*. Colorado Springs: Historical Society of the Pikes Peak Region, 1956.

Carter, Joseph H. *Never Met a Man I Didn't Like: The Life and Writings of Will Rogers*. New York: Avon, 1991.

Centennial: Colorado Springs, Colorado, 1872–1972. Colorado Springs: Pikes Peak Lithographing, 1972.

Chauvenet, Beatrice. *John Gaw Meem, Pioneer in Historic Preservation*. Santa Fe: Historic Santa Fe Foundation/Museum of New Mexico Press, 1985.

Colorado Foundation Directory, 1994–1995. Denver: Junior League of Denver, 1994.

Colorado Springs Evening Telegraph. *Fortunes of a Decade, 1900*.

Colorado Springs Fine Arts Center: A History and Selections From the Permanent Collection. Colorado Springs: Colorado Springs Fine Arts Center, 1986.

Colorado State Business Directories, 1889–1900. Published annually by various companies.

Colorado Viewbook. Colorado Springs: Colorado College, 1997.

Conte, William R. *The Cheyenne Mountain Story*. Colorado Springs: Century One, 1977.

Copper Through the Ages. London: Copper Development Association, 1951.

Criminal Record of the Western Federation of Miners: From Coeur d'Alene to Cripple Creek, 1894–1904. Colorado Springs: Colorado Mine Operators' Association, 1904.

Cripple Creek Mining and Business Directory. Cripple Creek: Hazeltine, 1894.

Cross, Whitman, and R.A.F. Penrose Jr. *Geology and Mining Industries of the Cripple Creek District, Colorado*. Washington, D.C.: U.S. Geological Survey, 17th Annual Report, 1884–1895.

Cuba, Stanley L., with Elizabeth Cunningham. *The Pikes Peak Vision: The Broadmoor Art Academy, 1919–1945*. Colorado Springs: Colorado Springs Fine Arts Center, 1989.

Cuninggim, Merrimon. *Private Money and Public Service: The Role of Foundations in American Society*. New York: McGraw-Hill, 1972.

Davenport, Walter. *Power and Glory, the Life of Boies Penrose*. New York: AMS, 1969 [1931].

Dothard, Robert L. *The David Mills Foundation, 1935–1955*. Montclair, N.J.: Board of Trustees, 1957.

Ellis, Amanda. *The Colorado Springs Story*. Colorado Springs: Dentan, 1954.

Fagan, George V. *The Air Force Academy—An Illustrated History.* Boulder: Johnson, 1988.

Fairbanks, Helen, and Charles P. Berkey. *Life and Letters of R.A.F. Penrose Jr.* New York: Geological Society of America, 1952.

Feitz, Leland. *Cripple Creek! A Quick History of the World's Greatest Gold Camp.* Colorado Springs: Little London, 1974 [1967].

———. *The Antlers Hotel.* Denver: Golden Bell, 1972.

Fell, James E. *Ores to Metals.* Lincoln: University of Nebraska Press, 1979.

Fetler, John. *The Pikes Peak People.* Caldwell, Idaho: Caxton, 1966.

Finlay, George Irving. *Colorado Springs: A Guide Book.* Colorado Springs: Out West, 1906.

The First Twenty-Five Years—The W. K. Kellogg Foundation. Battle Creek, Mich.: Board of Trustees, 1955.

Fisher, Ellen K. *Gates Family Foundation—The First Fifty Years, 1946–1996.* Denver: Gates Family Foundation, 1996.

Fisher, John S. *Builder of the West.* Caldwell, Idaho: Caxton, 1939.

Fort Carson: A Tradition of Victory. Fort Carson, Colo.: Public Affairs and Information Office, 1972.

Fowler, Gene. *Timber Line.* New York: Ballantine, 1960 [1st ed., New York: Covici-Friede, 1933].

Foxhoven, Omer Vincent. *City of God in the City of Gold.* Victor, Colo.: Omer Vincent Foxhoven, 1952.

Freed, Elaine, and David Barber. *Historic Sites and Structures: El Paso County, Colorado.* Colorado Springs: Penrose Public Library, 1977.

Frost, Hunter S. *Art, Artifacts, Architecture: Fountain Valley School.* Colorado Springs: Tiverton, 1980.

Gardener, Mark. *In the Shadow of Pikes Peak: An Illustrated History of Colorado Springs.* Carlsbad, Calif.: Heritage Media, 1999.

Geiger, Helen M. *The Broadmoor Story.* Denver: A. B. Hirschfeld, 1968, 1985.

———. *The Zoo on the Mountain.* Colorado Springs: Cheyenne Mountain Museum and Zoological Society, 1968.

Goln, Jay. *Comprehensive Travel Guide—Philadelphia '93–94.* New York City: Prentice Hall, 1994.

Grimstead, Bill, and Ray Drake. *The Last Gold Rush.* Victor, Colo.: Pollux, 1983.

Hendren, Frederick M. *Pikes Peak Legacy: Historic and Pictorial Highlights of the Region.* Colorado Springs: Great Western, 1984.

Hills, Fred. *The Official Manual of the Cripple Creek District.* Colorado Springs: Fred Hills, 1900.

Hollenback, Frank R., and William Russell Jr. *Pikes Peak by Rail.* Denver: Sage, 1962.

Hough, Henry W. *NORAD Command Post: The City Inside of Cheyenne Mountain: A Pictorial Guide.* Denver: Green Mountain, 1970.

Howbert, Irving. *Memories of a Lifetime in the Pike's Peak Region.* New York and London: G. P. Putnam's Sons, 1925.

Hoyt, Edwin P. *The Guggenheims and the American Dream.* New York: Funk and Wagnalls, 1967.

Humphreys, Mary Stevens. *Cog Train to the Zoo.* Woodland Park, Colo.: Mountain Automation, 1990.

Jameson, Elizabeth. *All That Glitters: Class, Conflict, and Community in Cripple Creek.* Urbana: University of Illinois Press, 1998.

Johnson, Charles A. *Opera in the Rockies—A History of the Central City Opera Association, 1932–1992.* Denver: Central City Opera House Association, 1992.

Jones, Fayette A. *Old Mining Camps of New Mexico—1854–1904.* Santa Fe: Stagecoach, 1964.

Joralemon, Ira B. *Romantic Copper—Its Lure and Lore.* London: D. Appleton-Century, 1935.

Jordan, John W. *Encyclopedia of Pennsylvania Biography,* Vols. 8 and 17. New York: Lewis Historical Publishing, 1917.

Karns, James Merton Lee. *The Impact of Defense Spending in El Paso County, Colorado, 1941–1965.* Norman: University of Oklahoma Press, 1968.

King, Joseph E. *It Takes a Mine to Make a Mine: Financing the Colorado Mining Industry, 1859–1902.* College Station: Texas A&M University Press, 1977.

Kutz, Myer. *Rockefeller Power: America's Chosen Family.* New York: Simon and Schuster, 1974.

Lakes, Arthur. *Geology of Cripple Creek Colorado.* Denver: Chain and Hardy, 1895.

Lamb, Russell, and Dan Harder. *France.* Portland, Ore.: Graphic Arts Center, 1992.

Langdon, Emma. *The Cripple Creek Strike: A History of the Industrial Wars in Colorado—1903–05.* New York: Arno Press and the New York Times, 1969 [1905].

Lavender, David. *The Story of Cyprus Mines Corporation.* San Marino, Calif.: Huntington Library, 1962.

Leach, Josiah Granville. *History of the Penrose Family of Philadelphia.* Philadelphia: William Fell, 1903.

Leaming, George F. *The Copper Industry's Impact on the Arizona Economy.* Marana: Arizona Economic Information Center, 1974.

Lester, Margaret D. *Brigham Street.* Salt Lake City: Utah State Historical Society, 1966.

Levine, Brian. *Cripple Creek—City of Influence.* Cripple Creek: Historic Preservation Department, 1994.

———. *Cripple Creek Gold—A Centennial History of the Cripple Creek District.* Lake Grove, Ore.: Depot, 1988.

Lipsey, John J. *The Lives of James John Hagerman.* Denver: Golden Bell, 1968.

Loe, Nancy E. *Life in the Altitudes: An Illustrated History of Colorado Springs.* Woodland Hills, Calif.: Windsor, 1983.

Luckas, John. *Philadelphia, Patricians and Philistines (1900–1950).* New York: Straus, Farrar, & Giroux, 1981.

Magat, Richard. *The Ford Foundation at Work: Philanthropic Choices, Methods, and Styles.* New York: Plenum, 1979.

Malone, Dumas, ed. *Dictionary of American Biography,* Vols. 12 and 14. New York: Charles Scribner's Sons, 1934.

Marion, John Francis. *Bicentennial City—Walking Tours of Historic Philadelphia.* Princeton: Pyne, 1974.

Mazulla, Fred, and Jo Mazulla. *The First Hundred Years—Cripple Creek and the Pikes Peak Region.* Victor, Colo.: Barbarossa, 1956.

Men of Note Affiliated With Mining and Mining Interests, Cripple Creek District. Colorado Springs: Colorado Springs Mining Investor, 1905.

Miller, Jean Anne. *Architecture at Fountain Valley School: Three Representative Styles of Regional Architecture and the Philosophies of the Architects.* Colorado Springs: Colorado College, 1992.

The Mountain Post—The Home of the Ironhorse Team. San Diego: Military Publishers, 1979.

1995–1996 Colorado Grants Guide. Denver: Denver Community Resource Center, 1995.

Noel, Thomas J. *Colorado: A Liquid History and Tavern Guide to the Highest State.* Golden: Fulcrum, 1998.

————. *Buildings of Colorado.* New York: Oxford University Press, 1997.

Noel, Thomas J., Steve Leonard, and Kevin Rucker. *Colorado Givers: A History of Philanthropic Heroes.* Niwot: University Press of Colorado, 1998.

O'Connor, Harvey. *The Guggenheims: The Making of an American Dynasty.* New York: Covici-Friede, 1937.

Oldach, Denise R.W., ed. *Here Lies Colorado Springs: Historical Figures Buried in Evergreen and Fairview Cemeteries.* Colorado Springs: City of Colorado Springs, 1995.

Ormes, Manly Dayton. *The Book of Colorado Springs.* Colorado Springs: Dentan, 1933.

Parrish, Thomas C. *Colorado Springs: Its Climate, Scenery, and Society.* Colorado Springs: Gazette Print, 1889.

Parsons, A. B. *The Porphyry Coppers.* New York: American Institute of Mining and Metallurgical Engineers, 1933.

Penrose, Charles. *A Text-Book of Diseases of Women.* Philadelphia: W. B. Saunders, 1904 [1897].

Penrose, George H. *A Genealogical Chart, Supplement to the Penrose Family.* New York: Knickerbocker, ca. 1920.

Perennial Philadelphians: Anatomy of an American Aristocracy. The Leisure Class in America Series. New York: Arno, 1975.

Peters, Edward Dyers. *The Practice of Copper Smelting.* New York: McGraw-Hill, 1911.

Peterson, Richard N. *The Bonanza Kings. The Social Origins and Business Behavior of Western Mining Entrepreneurs, 1870–1900.* Norman: University of Oklahoma Press, 1992.

Pett, L. F. *The Utah Copper Story.* Salt Lake City: Kennecott, 1955.

Philadelphia City Directories. Philadelphia: 1861, 1865, 1870, 1875, 1880.

Pikes Peak Vision: The Broadmoor Art Academy 1919–1945. Colorado Springs: Colorado Springs Fine Arts Center, 1989.

Porter, Darwin, and Danforth Prine. *Frommers 96 Paris.* New York: Simon and Schuster/Macmillan, 1995.

Portrait and Biographical Record of the State of Colorado. Chicago: Chapman, 1899.

Pourtales, Count James. Trans. Margaret Woodbridge Jackson. *American Adventure: Lessons Learned From Experience.* Colorado Springs: Colorado College, 1955.

Powell, Allen Kent, ed. *Utah History Encyclopedia.* Salt Lake City: University of Utah Press, 1994.

Proceedings: The American Philosophical Society. Philadelphia: American Philosophical Society; Vol. 48, 1909; Vol. 72, 1933.

Read, Thomas T. *Recent Copper Smelting.* San Francisco: Mining and Scientific Press, 1914.

Reid, J. Juan. *Growing Up in Colorado Springs: The 1920s Remembered.* Colorado Springs: Century One, 1981.

———. *Colorado College: The First Century 1874–1974.* Colorado Springs: Colorado College, 1979.

Rickard, Thomas A. *The Utah Copper Enterprise.* San Francisco: Thomas Rickard, 1919.

Rickard, Thomas A., and George Rex Buckman. *The Official Manual of the Cripple Creek District.* Colorado Springs: Fred Hills, 1900.

Rogers, Will. *Weekly Articles*—Vol. 2, *The Coolidge Years: 1925–1927.* Stillwater: Oklahoma State University Press, 1980, p. 170. Article published March 28, 1926.

Rouse, A. L. *The Cornish Jacks: The Cornish in America.* New York: Charles Scribner's Sons, 1969.

Ruhtenberg, Polly King, and Dorothy E. Smith. *Henry McAllister: Colorado Pioneer.* Freeman, S.D.: Pine Hill, 1972.

Sargeant, William A.S. *Geologists and the History of Geology,* Vol. 3. New York: Arno, 1980.

Smith, Webster B. *The World's Greatest Copper Mines.* London: Copper Development Association, 1967.

Social Register. New York: Social Register Association, 1997.

Society Blue Book of Colorado Springs and Vicinity. Colorado Springs: Blue Book Publishing, 1903.

Spence, Clark. *Mining Engineers and the American West—The Lace-Boot Brigade, 1849–1933.* New Haven: Yale University Press, 1970.

Sprague, Marshall. *Newport in the Rockies: The Life and Good Times of Colorado Springs.* Chicago: Sage/Swallow, 1980 [1961].

———. *Money Mountain: The Story of Cripple Creek Gold.* Lincoln: University of Nebraska Press, 1979 [original edition, Boston: Little, Brown, 1953].

———. *Colorado—A Bicentennial History.* Nashville and New York: American Association for State and Local History and W. W. Norton, 1976.

———. *El Paso Club: A Century of Friendship, 1877–1977.* Colorado Springs: El Paso Club, 1976.

———. *Cheyenne Mountain Ranch: An Uncommon History.* Colorado Springs: n.p., 1970.

Stern, Robert A.M., Gregory Gilmartin, and John Montague Massengale. *New York 1900—Metropolitan Architecture and Urbanism 1890–1915.* New York: Rizzoli International, 1983.

Stoeckly, Eugene. "A Company and Factory—History of the Garden City Company." Unpublished ms.

Stone, Wilbur F. *History of Colorado.* Chicago: S. J. Clarke, 1918.

Sullam, Joanna, Charlie Waite, and John Ardagh. *Villages of France.* London: Weidenfeld and Nicolson, 1988.

Sutulov, Alexander. *Copper Porphyries.* San Francisco: Miller-Freeman, 1975.

Talmadge, Marian, and Iris Gilmore. *NORAD: The North American Air Defense Command.* New York: Dodd, Mead, 1967.

Tatman, Sandra L., and Roger W. Moss. *Biographical Dictionary of Philadelphia Architects.* Boston: G. K. Hall, 1985.

Tauranac, John. *Elegant New York—The Builders and the Buildings, 1885–1915.* New York: Abbeville, 1985.

Taylor, Robert Guilford. *Cripple Creek Mining District.* Palmer Lake: Filter, 1973.

Tenney, Edward P. *The New West, as Related to the Christian College.* Cambridge: Riverside, 1878.

Thode, Jackson C., ed. *The Denver Westerner Brand Book.* Boulder: Johnson, 1972.

Toll, Jean Barth, and Mildred S. Gillan. *Invisible Philadelphia—Community Through Voluntary Organizations.* Philadelphia: Atwater Kent Museum, 1995.

Tuck, Frank J. *Stories of Arizona Copper Mines.* Phoenix: Arizona Department of Mineral Resources, 1957.

Tutt, William Thayer. "Thayer Tutt Remembers." Unpublished ms., Colorado Springs, 1980.

Twain, Mark. *Roughing It.* Hartford, Conn.: American Publishing, 1872.

Ubbelohde, Carl, Maxine Benson, and Duane A. Smith. *A Colorado History.* Boulder: Pruett, 1972.

United States Olympic Committee—97/98 Fact Book. Colorado Springs: Public Information and Media Relations Division of the United States Olympic Committee, 1997.

The Utah Copper Story. Salt Lake City: Kennecott Copper, 1955.

Walters, J. Wesley. *Biography of the Late Boies Penrose and Family.* Philadelphia: J. Wesley Waters, 1939.

Waters, Frank. *Pike's Peak: A Family Saga, an Epic Journey of the American Soul.* Chicago: Sage, 1971.

———. *Midas of the Rockies.* Denver: Sage, 1949 [1937].

Weed, Walter. *The Copper Mines of the World.* New York: Hill, 1907.

West End Visiting Directory. Philadelphia: Collins, 1878.

Whelchel, Harriet, ed. *John Ruskin and the Victorian Eye.* New York: Harry N. Abrams, 1933.

Whiteside, James. *Colorado: A Sports History.* Niwot: University Press of Colorado, 1999.

Wilcox, Rhoda Davis. *The Man on the Iron Horse.* Manitou Springs: Martin Associates, 1959.

Wilkins, Tivis E. *Shortline to Cripple Creek.* Golden: Colorado Railroad Museum, 1983. (Rail Annual No. 16.)

———. *Colorado Railroads.* Boulder: Pruett, 1974.

Wilson, George. *Yesterday's Philadelphia.* Miami: E. A. Seemann, 1975.

Young, Otis, E. *Western Mining: An Informal Account of Precious Metals Prospecting, Placering, Lode Mining, and Milling on the American Frontier From Spanish Times to 1893.* Norman: University of Oklahoma Press, 1970.

PERIODICALS

Broadmoor Magazine
Colorado Springs Free Press
Colorado Springs Gazette
Colorado Springs Gazette-Telegraph
Colorado Springs Sun
Cripple Creek Crusher
Cripple Creek Gold Rush
Cripple Creek Mail (1895–1896)
Cripple Creek Prospector (1892–1893)
Cripple Creek Sunday Herald (1895)
Cripple Creek Times (1895–1918)
Cripple Creek Weekly Journal (1893–1894)
Denver Post
Engineering and Mining Journal
Miner's Magazine (April 1903)
Mining and Scientific Press (1904)
Mining Magazine
New York Telegram
Philadelphia Bulletin
Philadelphia Inquirer
Philadelphia Morning Time
Philadelphia Sunday Times
Rocky Mountain News
Salt Lake City Herald-Republican
Salt Lake City Tribune
Salt Lake Mining Review
San Francisco Chronicle
Saturday Evening Post
Sun (Colorado Springs)

ARTICLES

Aldrige, Dorothy. "Retired Nuns Share Glimpses of Spencer and Julie Penrose." *Pikes Peak Journal*. Undated article from Julie Penrose file at Penrose Public Library, Colorado Springs.

Boutwell, J. M. "Ore Deposits of Bingham, Utah." *Engineering and Mining Journal*. June 22, 1905.

Brinsmade, Robert B. "Mining at Bingham, Utah. History and Geology of the Region—Methods of Stripping and Mining Copper Ores With Steam Shovels." *Mines and Minerals*. September 1907.

DeGette, Cara. "The House the Lord Built." *Colorado Springs Independent*. February 1, 1994.

"Doctor Penrose Dead—Emeritus Professor at the University Since 1888." *Old Penn—Weekly Review of the University of Pennsylvania*. Philadelphia: University of Pennsylvania. Vol. 7, No. 13, January 9, 1909.

Guilbert, John M. "The Penrose Legacy, GSA's Benefactor, R.A.F. Penrose Jr." *GSA News and Information*. September 1983.

Hansen, Ralph W. "Anatomy of Acquisition." *Manuscripts*. Chicago: Manuscript Society. Vol. 17, Winter 1965.

Hines, Al. "The Broadmoor." *Holiday*. September 1953.

Ingalls, Walter Renton. "Mining the Porphyry Ore of Bingham." *Engineering and Mining Journal*. September 7, 1907.

Jackling, D. C. "Work of the Utah Copper Company." *Mining and Scientific Press*. May 11, 1912.

Luckas, John. "Big Grizzley." *American Heritage*. New York: American Heritage. October/November 1978.

McCullough, John, and Art Rothstein. "Colorado." *Look*. August 25, 1953.

McFerren, H. W. "The Story of Bingham Canyon." *Mining and Scientific Press*. July 24, 1909.

Noel, Thomas J. "William D. Haywood." *Colorado Heritage*. Issue 2, 1984.

Parkhill, Forbes. "The Last of the Penroses." *Saturday Evening Post*. July 24, 1937.

Peterson, Jon A. "The Nation's First Comprehensive City Plan—A Political Analysis of the McMillan Plan for Washington, D.C., 1900–1902." *American Planning Association Journal*. Spring 1985.

"Presentation and Unveiling of the Statue of Daniel Cowan Jackling." Salt Lake City: National Society of the Sons of Utah Pioneers, 1954.

Sprague, Marshall. "A Touch of History." *Around Pikes Peak*. Colorado Springs: Junior League, 1967.

Thurlow, George. "The Foundation Upon Which Colorado Springs Is Built." Colorado Springs *Independent*. June 22–29, 1997.

PAMPHLETS

The American Philosophical Society Year Book. Philadelphia: American Philosophical Society, 1937, 1938, 1958, 1961.

The Broadmoor Art Academy. Colorado Springs: Dentan, 1924, 1927, 1928, 1929.

Chance, Myrtle. *The Story of Pauline Chapel.* Colorado Springs: Colorado Springs Printing, ca. 1950.

Churchman, Michael. *The Armit Family.* Colorado Springs: self-published, 1978.

Colorado Springs and Cripple Creek District Railway. The Short Line Blue Book.

Colorado Springs Salutes Fort Carson on the Occasion of Their 25th Anniversary, 1942–1967. Colorado Springs: Colorado Springs Chamber of Commerce, 1967.

El Pomar Art Collection. Colorado Springs: El Pomar Center, ca. 1997.

El Pomar Center. Colorado Springs: El Pomar Center, ca. 1997.

El Pomar Foundation—Annual Report. Colorado Springs: El Pomar Foundation, 1996.

El Pomar Foundation—Awards for Excellence. Colorado Springs: El Pomar Foundation, 1996.

The El Pomar Nonprofit Resource Library. Colorado Springs: El Pomar Foundation, 1996.

EPCYS—El Pomar Fellowship in Community Service. Colorado Springs: El Pomar Foundation, 1996.

EPCYS—El Pomar Youth in Community Service. Colorado Springs: El Pomar Foundation, 1996.

Helping Hands—A Directory of Nonprofit Organizations in the Pikes Peak Region. Colorado Springs Gazette-Telegraph. December 1, 1996.

Hunter, Jay F. *The Genealogy of Marie Muir Lewis and William Howe Muir of Detroit, Michigan.* Detroit: Muir Family, 1991.

Inside the U.S. Olympic Movement—A to Z. Colorado Springs: Public Information and Media Relations Division of the United States Olympic Committee, 1997.

Mrs. Spencer Penrose, Contributions to Central City Opera. Central City Opera Association Fact Sheet, 1997.

1996–1997 United States Figure Skating Association Media Guide. Colorado Springs: United States Figure Skating Association, 1996.

The Penrose Cancer Center. Colorado Springs: Penrose Hospital, 1997.

Pikes Peak Center—Catch the Magic! Colorado Springs: City of Colorado Springs, ca. 1997.

Program for the 1994 World Junior Figure Skating Championships. Colorado Springs: United States Figure Skating Association, 1994.

A Record of Service for Pennsylvania and the Nation. Philadelphia: Pennsylvania Protective Union, ca. 1921.

Sacred Land: Indian and Hispanic Cultures of the Southwest. Colorado Springs: Colorado Springs Fine Arts Center, ca. 1996.

Towne, Dorothy J. *The Treasures of Pauline Chapel—The Story of a Journey in Faith,* 4th ed. Colorado Springs: Myron J. Tassin, 1984.

The Tutt Family of Virginia, Philadelphia, and Colorado Springs. Colorado Springs: Russell T. Tutt, 1975 (rev. 1978, 1979, 1982, 1983, and 1984).

Tutt, William Thayer. "The Broadmoor Story." Address delivered at 1969 Colorado Dinner, May 23, 1969, in Colorado Springs. New York: Newcomen Society in North America, 1969.

United States Olympic Committee 97/98 Fact Book. Colorado Springs: USOC, 1997.

United States Olympic Complex. Colorado Springs: USOC, 1997.

Unveiling of the Bust of Richard Alexander Fullerton Penrose Jr. Proceedings of the Geological Society of America, 1935.

Will Rogers Shrine of the Sun on Cheyenne Mountain. Colorado Springs: End of the Trail Association, 1994.

Wilson, George. *Yesterday's Philadelphia.* Miami: E. A. Seemann, 1975.

Wilson, Robert H. *Philadelphia USA.* Radnor, Pa: Chilton, 1976.

The World Figure Skating Museum and Hall of Fame. Colorado Springs: United States Figure Skating Association, ca. 1995.

Wren, Spencer W., Jr. *Rack, Rock, and Rail: The Manitou and Pike's Peak Railway.* Colorado Springs: n.p., ca. 1992.

GOVERNMENT DOCUMENTS

Cross, Whitman, and R.A.F. Penrose. *Geology and Mining Industries of the Cripple Creek District,* Vol. 2. *Colorado.* Sixteenth Annual Report of the United States Geological Survey, Part 2. Washington, D.C.: Government Printing Office, 1895.

Lyons, Nancy. *National Register Nomination for El Pomar Mansion.* Denver: Colorado Historical Society, Office of Archeology and Historic Preservation, 1994.

Roberts, Karin M., and James Schneck. *Turkey Creek Ranch Site Report.* Lincoln: National Park Service, Midwest Archeological Center, 1997.

United States Census, Philadelphia. Washington, D.C.: Government Printing Office, 1860, 1870.

VIDEOTAPES

Antonuccio, Steve, producer. "A Witness to Colorado Springs History—A Video Portrait of Ben Wendelken." Colorado Springs: Pikes Peak Library District, 1989.

"Kennecott Copper's Bingham Canyon Mine." Salt Lake City: Kennecott Copper, 1994.

"Pike's Peak by Rail: The Manitou and Pike's Peak Railway." Colorado Springs: Mountain Automation, 1997.

"The Tutt Legacy." Colorado Springs: Pikes Peak Library District, 1994.

SITE VISITS/TOURS

Bingham Canyon, Utah
    Kennecott Utah Copper Mine, April 4, 1997
Cambridge, Massachusetts
    Harvard Yard, October 12, 1996
Colorado Springs, Colorado
    Air Force Academy, July 3, 1997
    Broadmoor Hotel with Nancy Steward, February 12, 1997

Cheyenne Mountain Country Club with Steve Wahlborg and R. Thayer Tutt Jr., March 10, 1997

Cheyenne Mountain Zoo, March 21 and June 18, 1997

Colorado College, El Pomar Athletic Center, Charles L. Tutt Library, Lloyd Woerner Campus Center with Elaine Freed, September 3, 1997

Colorado Springs Fine Arts Center, June 24, 1997

Cooking Club with Joe Spiers and R. Thayer Tutt Jr., March 10, 1997

El Paso Club, 30 East Platte, March 10, 1997

Glen Eyrie, February 9, 1997

Pauline Chapel, June 18, 1997

Penrose Cancer Center at Penrose Hospital, September 8, 1997

Pikes Peak Center with Bee Vradenburg, September 3, 1997

Pikes Peak Cog Railway, June 18, 1997

Pikes Peak Hill Climb Museum, June 7, 1997

Turkey Creek Ranch with David Thompson and Dennis Kotke, March 10, 1997

United States Figure Skating Museum, April 1, 1997

United States Olympic Complex, July 25, 1997

University of Colorado—Colorado Springs/Cragmoor—Main Hall, September 9, 1997

Will Rogers Shrine of the Sun with George Guerrero, February 12, 1997

Glenwood Springs, Colorado

Hotel Colorado, February 22, 1997

Philadelphia, Pennsylvania

912 Spruce Street, Judge Thayer family residence

1331 Spruce Street, site Penrose family residence

Ritz-Carlton Hotel site

University of Pennsylvania

INTERVIEWS BY THOMAS J. NOEL AND/OR CATHLEEN NORMAN

Bartolin, Steve J. Colorado Springs, September 8, 1997.

Baschleben, Paul. Colorado Springs, June 3, 1997.

Bell, Dr. J. Whitfield, Jr., retired executive of the American Philosophical Society. Philadelphia, July 16, 1997.

Brittain, Nancy. Denver, June 10 and July 17, 1997.

Brown, Peter A.G. Williamsburg, Virginia, April 17, 1997.

Cameron, Patricia. Colorado Springs, March 15, 1996.

Clark, Sherry. Broadmoor Golf Club, Colorado Springs, April 2, 1997.

Croke, Patricia Bates. Colorado Springs, April 9, 1997.

Davis, Beth, curator, World Figure Skating Museum and Hall of Fame. Colorado Springs, April 1, 1997.

Eitel, Karl E. Colorado Springs, August 15, 1997.

Fleming, Kathy, Hotel Colorado historian. Glenwood Springs, April 2, 1997.

Freed, Elaine. Colorado College, Colorado Springs, September 3, 1997.

Freymuth, G. Russell. Colorado Springs, April 18, 1997.

Fuller, Dr. Timothy. Colorado Springs, July 2, 1997.

Guerrero, George. Colorado Springs, February 12 and July 17, 1997.

Hilbert, Robert. Colorado Springs, September 5 and 8, 1997.

Hybl, William. Colorado Springs, June 26 and July 11, 1997; April 21, 1999.

Knowlton, Stephen A. Denver, September 13, 1998.

Kruse, Caroline. Colorado Springs, April 16, 1997.

Littrell, Harold U. Colorado Springs, July 24, 1997.

Love, John A. Denver, January 24, 1999.

McColl, Ellie. Colorado Springs, July 8, 1997.

McGregor, Dougald. Santa Monica, California, March 19, 1997.

McIntyre, Robert. Colorado Springs, July 11, 1997.

McCleary, Eugene. Colorado Springs, March 15, 1996.

Miller, David. Denver, January 10, 1999.

Olin, Kent. Colorado Springs, October 12, 1997.

Palmer, Dorothy. Boulder, May 10, 1997.

Penrose, Charles. Sandwich, New Hampshire, June 2 and July 20, 1997.

Penrose, Francis Haythe. Greenwich, Connecticut, July 19 and 20, 1997.

Peterson, Dr. Pete. Colorado Springs, July 8, 1997.

Roub, William. Colorado Springs, July 7, 1997.

Susemihl, Peter. Colorado Springs, July 2, 1997.

Sweeney, Robert. Denver, April 10, 1997; September 17, 1999.

Tutt, Charles, IV. Colorado Springs, August 28, 1997.

Tutt, John Wood. Telluride, November 10, 1996.

Tutt, R. Thayer, Jr. Colorado Springs, June 5 and 10, 1997.

Tutt, William B. Colorado Springs, July 22, 1997.

Vanderhoof, Richard. Colorado Springs, July 22, 1997.

Vradenberg, Bea (Mrs. George). Colorado Springs, July 8 and September 3, 1997.

Ward, William R. Denver, August 22, 1997.

Index

Pages in italics indicate illustrations.